I0809854

CARL F. SCHALK

A Life in Song

CARL F. SCHALK

A Life in Song

NANCY M. RAABE

CONCORDIA PUBLISHING HOUSE · SAINT LOUIS

3558 S. Jefferson Avenue, St. Louis, MO 63118-3968
1-800-325-3040 • www.cph.org

ISBN 978-0-7586-4154-0

Manufactured in the United States of America

1 2 3 4 5 6 7 8 9 10 22 21 20 19 18 17 16 15 14 13

God is love, forgiveness free,
undeserving though we be.
Three in One, for thee we long:
Be our poem, prayer, and song!

NMR, 2009

This book is dedicated to church musicians everywhere as they strive to proclaim the Gospel through song.

CONTENTS

All books, articles, and quotations throughout this book not otherwise attributed are by Carl Schalk.

FOREWORD

The world of a college student at Concordia College, River Forest, Illinois, back in the 1970s was filled with all of life's pressing questions. Did I really wish to eat in the cafeteria on Sunday night when they served "mystery meat"? Should I ask the cute blonde girl out on a date? Should I play on our floor's intramural basketball team? Was Earth Science at 7:30 on Tuesday and Thursday mornings really the only way to get my science requirement? At that stage in life, those were the important, life-changing questions.

Even the war in Vietnam and one's draft status were almost secondary to the daily decisions of college life. Let's face it, we were students, finally out on our own—away from daily parental oversight. We were, after all, beginning to stretch our wings and fly.

At Concordia, my first encounter with the Schalk family was not with Professor Schalk but with his wife, Noël. She was a part of the academic advising team of Schalk and Hannemann, who guided and cajoled us college students into taking the appropriate courses for our majors. They were also the "moms" on campus who helped us with our daily struggles and priorities and did all of it with smiles on their faces and warmth in their hearts.

I was a Director of Parish Music (DPM) student, preparing to be both a teacher and a musician. All DPM majors were encouraged to practice our instruments, study for our classes, and be on time for our ensembles. The gathering place was the drinking fountain just outside the practice rooms in Kretzmann Hall. That's where all the action was.

With our lives so filled with daily happenings and pressing questions, none of us fully realized that we were in a rare time. It was a time when The Lutheran Church—Missouri Synod had one hymn book and one order of service that nearly everyone used. It was also a time when the music professors at Concordia, River Forest, were all "legends" in their fields.

In our naïve youth, we didn't realize what legends our instructors were. But as freshman year gave way to sophomore year and sophomore to junior and so on, we found ourselves singing or playing their music from their manuscripts, or using textbooks that they had written, or playing or singing the liturgy and hymns of whose creation they were partly responsible. You could not help but come to the realization that our instructors were indeed legends.

My first encounter with Professor Schalk was as a senior student in his Musical Heritage of the Church class. I can honestly say that I was a bit intimidated by him and his reputation. He was extremely prepared for the class, as he had written the textbook we used. He had researched the topic so completely that he had assembled his own book. How could any student not be a bit intimidated by that?

Before I graduated, Professor Schalk asked me to stop by his office. I said "okay" and then proceed to think, "What did I do?" What I discovered was that he just wanted to share words of encouragement with me about being a Lutheran church musician, something he probably did for most DPM majors.

So why is a book on Carl Schalk needed? Well, Carl Schalk is one of the top, if not *the* top, authorities on the theology and practice of Lutheran church music. His works in the field of church music, especially his books *Key Words in Church Music* and *A Handbook of Church Music*, often serve as textbooks for college courses. In regard to music composition, Carl has a unique gift in composing transcendent hymn tunes that have been chosen for numerous new hymnals. And his choral compositions have been widely sung by all of God's creatures, from the youngest children, to teens, to church choirs small and large, and even by university and professional choral groups.

Carl Schalk believes that the Church's song should tell the story of salvation, proclaim Law and Gospel, and be sung by all of God's people. This he has demonstrated by his life's work.

He has been and continues to be a professor/teacher/mentor/friend who has had a vast influence on his students and many other church musicians, who also proclaim the Church's song. It is with fondness and love that these friends of Carl Schalk recall the stories, retell the jokes, and transmit that important philosophy of church music to others.

And why should Nancy Raabe author a book about Carl Schalk? It's because Nancy has a unique skill set. She possesses years of training and experience as a music critic, having worked for the *Milwaukee Sentinel* and *The Birmingham News*. Her articles have appeared in the *New York Times*, the *Boston Globe*, *American Music Guide*, *Opera News*, the *Columbus Dispatch*, and *Playbill*. She combines that expertise with a deep-seated passion for church music and liturgical Lutheran practices. Nancy has served as a musician in several churches; she has numerous published texts and music compositions for organ, choir, voice, and piano. This is indeed a unique and potent combination for the task of writing a book on the work of Carl Schalk.

I hope you will enjoy reading Nancy's book, for it examines the life and work of the legend Carl Schalk and the philosophy of how the Church's song should tell the story of salvation and proclaim the Gospel of our Lord Jesus Christ.

To God be the glory!

John A. Behnke, D. Mus.
Professor of Music
Concordia University, Mequon, Wisconsin

Nancy Raabe, Carl Schalk, and Noël Schalk at *Thine the Amen, Thine the Praise: Celebrating the Music of Carl F. Schalk*, hymn festival, ALCM Columbus: Cantor Connection, Bexley, Ohio, 2010.

Photo credit: Viki Rogers

PREFACE

Someday the complete and true story of the life and works of Carl F. Schalk will need to be written.[1]

Many years ago, as music critic for *The Birmingham News*, I brainstormed as Christmas neared about new ways to approach the subject of Christmas carols in a feature article that would be of interest to general readers. It occurred to me that many of the most meaningful carols were not those that sang of comfort and joy, but rather those that addressed the reality that this child was *born to die*—and then to be raised to eternal life, demonstrating for all time that death no longer has power over us and that we are free to live fully as baptized children of God. In other words, they were carols that told not one piece of the story of salvation but at least hinted at the entire story. I thought particularly of this stanza from the carol "What Child Is This":

Why lies He in such mean estate
Where ox and ass are feeding?
Good Christian, fear; for sinners here
The silent Word is pleading.
Nails, spear shall pierce Him through,
The cross be borne for me, for you;
Hail, hail the Word made flesh,
The babe, the son of Mary!

And even in an otherwise quiet lullaby:

Sing lullaby!
Lullaby baby, now a-dozing,
Sing lullaby!
Hush, do not wake the infant King!
Soon comes the cross, the nails, the piercing,

---

[1] Richard Hillert, "Composers for the Church: Carl F. Schalk," *CrossAccent* 10, no. 1 (Spring 2002): 17.

Then in the grave at last reposing;
Sing lullaby!

Sing lullaby!
Lullaby, is the babe a-waking?
Sing lullaby!
Hush, do not stir the infant King!
Dreaming of Easter, gladsome morning,
Conquering death, its bondage breaking;
Sing lullaby![2]

A good idea, I thought. But every news story needs sources. To whom could I go to elaborate on the "dark side" of Christmas carols?

Carl Schalk suddenly sprang to mind. I knew many of Carl's writings, and from those I suspected that with his lively wit, his frank, engaging manner, and his vast knowledge of hymns and carols, he would be good at least for a few quotes.

He was happy to talk with me, and I was richly rewarded. The article itself has been lost in the sands of time, but I vividly remember my lively phone conversation with Carl for that story and how delighted he was that I would be writing on the subject. For years, I heard from others that he would occasionally drop a pointed quip about the piece as the kind of thing one would not normally expect to find in the pages of a daily newspaper around Christmas.

Since then, as I moved into my vocation as church musician, I gradually came to know and admire Carl through his music, his writings, and his keynote addresses at conferences. What has struck me at every encounter is that he always speaks the truth—the truth about the Church, the truth about its worship life, the truth about the way in which music was or was not received into that life—and that his compositions likewise bear the truth about what music in worship should be. Blazing at the heart of everything Carl undertakes is the conviction that the music of the Church proclaims the Gospel, which means that it tells the story of salvation. He is fond of emphasizing that this does not mean that we sing *about* the story but actually tell *how* God accomplished our salvation. He has little patience for texts that do not do this, such as the old chestnut in which "we sing about

---

[2] Sabine Baring-Gould, 1834–1924.

how we 'love to tell the story.' Unfortunately, this 'Gospel song' never gets around to telling it."[3]

Carl is a person of high spirits and great wit. Perpetrators of this or that rarely escape unscathed. And he relishes colorful words, always uttered in the highest good humor, to demonstrate his fine disdain for choice subjects of critique. Yet, to borrow from his arsenal of adjectives, neither in music nor in words does he ever descend to the maudlin or the sentimental. Every aspect of his life and work is dedicated to the mandate—articulated in Ronald Klug's "Rise, Shine, You People!"—to "Tell how the Father sent His Son to save us. Tell of the Son, who life and freedom gave us. Tell how the Spirit calls from ev'ry nation His new creation."[4] Likewise, he urges us to proclaim that story in our own contexts and in our own voices, drawing on the riches of music and liturgy that are the great legacy of Lutheranism.

It is my fervent hope that those who become better acquainted with Carl through this book may be strengthened and encouraged to receive gladly, as he himself has done, Martin Luther's bold invitation to new and vigorous life in Christ:

Dear Christians, one and all, rejoice,
With exultation springing,
And with united heart and voice
And holy rapture singing,
Proclaim the wonders God has done,
How His right arm the vict'ry won.
What price our ransom cost Him!

Nancy M. Raabe
Milton, Wisconsin
January 2013

---

[3] "The Church and the Composer," *CrossAccent* 8, no. 1 (Spring 2000): 4.
[4] Ibid., 5.

ACKNOWLEDGMENTS

This book represents the culmination of the efforts of a number of sources. Most important to acknowledge is Carl Schalk himself, whom I have known and admired for many years, and with whom I spent many hours in interviews and lively conversations. He and his wife, Noël, graciously welcomed me into their home on several occasions and were always gracious and supremely accommodating hosts.

I appreciate the efforts of my editor, David Johnson, in supporting and shaping this project and in providing music and other important resources. I conducted significant research as well at the Hamma Library of Trinity Lutheran Seminary, Columbus, Ohio.

I gained many insights from my interviews with the following friends and colleagues of Carl Schalk: Barry Bobb, Tom Leeseberg-Lange, Carlos Messerli, Evangeline Rimbach, Rodney Schrank, and Steven Wente. I thank Lisa Dahill, Jonathan Kohrs, and Katherine Brewer for their insights and suggestions.

Additional assistance came from Michael Costello, cantor, Grace Lutheran Church, River Forest, Illinois; consultant Luke Bouman; Richard E. Mueller, pastor of Lutheran Church of the Atonement in St. Louis; Eric Benoy, music librarian at New Orleans Baptist Theological Seminary; and Carla Birkhimer and Ray Olson, librarians at Hamma Library, Trinity Lutheran Seminary. Leonard Flachman, publisher, Lutheran University Press, kindly gave permission to use the list of Carl Schalk's works dated through 2004.

I am most deeply grateful to my husband, William A. Raabe, for creative and editorial ideas and for countless forms of support and encouragement.

Nancy M. Raabe
Milton, Wisconsin
May 2013

CHAPTER ONE

The Nature and Purpose of the Song of the Church

> Luther's primary view of the relation between music and Christian life and worship is the understanding that it is the good and gracious gift of God the Creator, given to humanity that we might in turn use it in God's praise and in the proclamation of the Gospel.[1]

> The Church must continue to offer the substance of its message in music—simple or complex—which stands as a witness to the integrity of its faith as well as a witness to the Church's love for those to whom it speaks.[2]

More comprehensively than any musician of our age, Carl Flentge Schalk has given voice in our time to Martin Luther's deepest convictions of the nature and purpose of the song of the Church. In his composing and his teaching, in his conducting and his writing, in his work as a parish musician and in his tireless advocacy both in person and in print of the deepest truths of what it means to be the people of God in worship, Schalk has lived out the conviction that music has the capacity to proclaim the Gospel in a way that words alone cannot.

Schalk has never been one to engage in self-promotion, nor is his name widely recognized outside of the circles of Lutheran church musicians, pastors, and theologians. But in the annals of modern-day church music, he stands alone. Prolific composer and author, tireless educator, beloved mentor and colleague, Schalk has cheerfully

---

[1] *Luther on Music: Paradigms of Praise* (St. Louis: Concordia Publishing House, 1988), 34.
[2] *Lutheran Hour Music News* 4, no. 2 (February, 1963).

dedicated his life to the understanding and realization of church music as proclamation, always with the trademark twinkle in his eye. Because the Gospel is always his overriding concern, he continues to transcend denominational and political divisions and—defying conventional wisdom—remains a friend to all, enemy to none.

Christians sing their faith. We sing because in the act of singing, faith is cultivated and deepened. We sing in order to recall the nature and story of God's saving acts throughout history. We sing as a response to these acts. "As redeemed Christians it is also what we *want* to do, what we cannot help but do," Schalk affirms. "It is the 'cantus firmus' of our lives, that great central melody which extols God's glory and praise, especially for the great central act of God in Jesus Christ."[3]

In the act of singing we respond in gratitude to the proclamation of what God in Christ has done for us. In its liturgy and song, the Church bears witness to the truth of the Gospel. "The history of the Christian worshiping community is the history of a singing and music-making community," Schalk writes. "We cannot imagine it otherwise."[4]

In the act of singing, we respond as the body of Christ, transcending time and space and joining together with the song of the redeemed across the ages. "The song of the Church," Schalk writes, "is a response of faith to what God has done in Jesus Christ. It is a song from the heart of the Church to the heart of God, from the heart of the Church to the heart of each believer, and from the heart of the Church to the world."[5] We are also more closely bound in community. "Christian song was the vehicle by which young and old, educated and uneducated, could join together in the prayer life of the church. As Christians join in that song, they are doing no more than that which they are enjoined to do by the psalmist, 'Let all who take refuge in you be glad; let them ever sing for joy' (Ps. 5:11a)."[6]

---

[3] *Praising God in Song: An Introduction to Christian Hymnody for Congregational Study* (St. Louis: Concordia Publishing House, 1993), 7.

[4] *God's Song in a New Land: Lutheran Hymnals in America* (St. Louis: Concordia Publishing House, 1995), 13.

[5] "The Church's Song: Proclamation, Pedagogy, and Praise," *Lutheran Service Book: Hymnal Companion* (St. Louis: Concordia Publishing House, forthcoming).

[6] "Music and Liturgy: The Lutheran Tradition," *Lutheran Worship: History and Practice* (St. Louis: Concordia Publishing House, 1993), 244.

Schalk is fond of saying that this is not *our* song but one "in which we, in our short life, are permitted to join with angels and archangels and the whole host of heaven. It is a song which has gone on long before we arrived," one that is not ours to shape but that shapes and molds us. It is a song of unparalleled richness and dimension "in which proclamation, teaching, and praise interweave in a tapestry of music unique to the Church."[7]

Song as Proclamation

At the heart of the Church's song lies the proclamation of the Gospel of Jesus Christ. In its liturgy and hymnody the music of the Church recounts the narrative of this good news of salvation through Christ. This is how generations are taught and how faith is deepened.

"It is in the Church's liturgy and hymns that the Christian narrative is kept alive," Schalk affirms. "There we tell the story that makes us a Christian community. The formation of Christians young and old is carried out by the handing over of the words of faith as contained in the liturgy and hymnody. We *must* teach the faith of the church and not our own ideas."[8]

Schalk calls to mind a line from the encomium to music written by Luther's friend and adviser Johann Walter, *Lob und Preis der löblichen Kunst Musica* ("Glory and Praise of the Laudable Art of Music"), translated by Samuel Janzow at Schalk's request, which emphasizes that the role of music is to help keep "fresh in human memory" the story of salvation. Starting from the fall of humankind in the Garden of Eden it reads,

But God's love from eternity
Had pity on their misery.
He promised them the Woman's Seed
To save them and their human breed
From sin, from Satan's wicked hands,
From mighty death's dark fiery bands.
That Seed would their Redeemer be

And for God's service set them free.
That such unmerited free grace

[7] "The Church's Song."

[8] "Basic Lutheran Understandings of Music in Worship" (preconference address at the biennial conference of the Association of Lutheran Church Musicians, San Diego, California, June 28, 2003).

(Which God from love for all our race
Had promised in His Word) might be
Kept fresh in human memory
And move the heart to high delight
In praising God both day and night—

This is the weightiest reason why
God music did at once supply . . . .[9]

"Music *has* to be telling that story in some way or other," Schalk emphasizes. "So, from my point view, is it sinful to sing 'the Lord is in his holy temple, let all the earth keep silent'? Probably not. But it doesn't project the story of salvation."[10]

The 'good news' for people of the Old Testament "was not simply who God was, but how God acted on their behalf to rescue them from their sin," Schalk says. "That was the content of their song." This is particularly true in the Biblical canticles, which rehearse the story of how God acted to save His people and praise Him for what He has done. The songs of the New Testament continue this narrative but add to it the news of the revelation of God's Son in the person of Jesus Christ. In this way, the story of Christ and the hope He brings for the future lies at the heart of the Church's song.

"It is a specific story that is both history and promise," Schalk writes. "It became the basic content of the songs of the New Testament and the early Church. It became the essential content of the Church's liturgy and song in succeeding centuries." However, Schalk cautions, for those who would take the music of the Church into their own hands, whenever it becomes separated from that story of Jesus' death and resurrection, "the Church's song ceases to be the *Church's* song."[11]

What *is* the good news of the Gospel? It is not, Schalk stresses, the "golden rule" of doing unto others as we would have them do to us. It is not a general moral principle or a religious philosophy.

---

[9] *Music in Early Lutheranism: Shaping the Tradition* (1524–1672) (St. Louis: Concordia Publishing House, 2001), 188.
[10] Conversation with the author, July 26, 2012.
[11] "The Church's Song."

Neither is it a form of spirituality—a mindset that he considers is often "a way of *not* talking about God."[12]

Rather, Schalk never tires of saying, the good news is *that God was sent to us and that Christ suffered, died, was buried and rose again*. We experience this news of salvation and the way it came about in all the Church's great hymns. Schalk points especially to John of Damascus's "Come, You Faithful, Raise the Strain," which boldly recounts the entire span of salvation history; to "Sing, My Tongue, the Glorious Battle" (given new life in our celebration of Easter through Schalk's bold tune FORTUNATUS NEW), in which Christians are enjoined to "sound the loud triumphant lay" by which we "tell how Christ, the world's redeemer, as a victim won the day";[13] and to "Rise, Shine, You People," which recounts how "Christ the Lord has entered our human story" and exhorts worshipers to "Tell how the Father sent his Son to save us."

For the same reason, Schalk notes, in Martin Luther's first collection of hymns in 1524, pride of place was given to "Dear Christians, One and All, Rejoice" with its imperative to "Proclaim the wonders God has done." And in Paul Gerhardt's "Awake, My Heart, with Gladness," Schalk adds, Gerhardt implores us in his text to "see what today is done."[14]

"It is hardly a coincidence," Schalk writes, "that Luther's only known polyphonic musical composition, the motet 'Non moriar sed vivam', was based on a verse from Psalm 118 that states simply: 'I shall not die, but live, and *declare the works of the Lord*.'"[15]

Quoting treasured words of the liturgy, Schalk emphasizes that we sing "because it is our duty and our delight." We sing because God made us in God's own image, and "because it is our *obligation* as creatures of the Creator: 'O come, let us sing to the Lord, for he is our Maker.'" But as redeemed Christians, he says, "it is also what we *want* to do, what we cannot help but do. It is the cantus firmus of our

---

[12] "Proclamation, Pedagogy and Praise" (keynote address to the Region 3 conference of the Association of Lutheran Church Musicians, River Forest, Illinois, July 27, 2012).

[13] Conversation with the author, July 26, 2012. This hymn may be used on Good Friday, Schalk notes, "because *we know* how it turns out—so it's okay for us to sing it!"

[14] Ibid.

[15] "The Church's Song."

lives, that great central melody which extols God's glory and praise, especially for the great central act of God in Jesus Christ."[16]

The Centrality of the Liturgy

A counterpoint to this conviction is Schalk's grasp of the centrality of liturgical worship to Lutheran identity and heritage. "It is a Lutheran conviction," he writes, "that the needs of the people at worship are most effectively met by forms and structures of prayer which draw on the collective experience of the whole church at worship."[17]

This has to do with the essential understanding that Lutherans are part of the one, holy, catholic, and apostolic Church. Therefore, Schalk stresses, "Lutheranism looks to the experience of the church at worship throughout its history as an important source of its way of worship. Its use of forms and practices with which the church has prayed and praised for centuries . . . affirms Lutheranism's continuity with the whole church. In its life of worship, Lutheranism gives such forms and practices a central place."[18]

What are the content of these forms and practices? Simply said, they rehearse the story of salvation, week after week, year after year, in ways that are both specific and varied. In so doing, the liturgy and its story takes a central place in the hearts and lives of all faithful Christians.

As an illustration, Schalk calls attention to the closing canticle that first appeared in all three services of Holy Communion in *Lutheran Book of Worship*, where worshipers sing "Thank the Lord and sing his praise; tell everyone what he has done." Or consider Martin Luther's great baptism prayer,[19] he suggests, which recalls how God condemned the wicked through the flood and saved Noah and his family, led Israel by a pillar of cloud and fire through the sea, and how Jesus was baptized by John and filled with the Holy Spirit. That, Schalk stresses, is the purpose of the liturgy—not (for example), "here is this person standing here waiting to be baptized." If the

---

[16] *Praising God in Song*, 7.
[17] *A Handbook of Church Music*, edited with Carl Halter (St. Louis: Concordia Publishing House, 1978), 17.
[18] Ibid., 16.
[19] *Liturgy and Hymns*, ed. Ulrich S. Leupold, vol. 53 of *Luther's Works* (Philadelphia: Fortress Press, 1965), 107. Adapted in the *Lutheran Book of Worship* for the service of Holy Baptism, 122, and in *Lutheran Service Book*, 268–69.

narrative is omitted in the service of Baptism or in the eucharistic liturgy, "we lose the whole context: how God *always* acts to save His people, and how He is now acting to save you."[20]

Schalk acknowledges that newcomers to liturgical worship may be unfamiliar with its forms. Once these forms "become a normal part of the life of worship, however, their richness, strength, diversity, power to nourish faith and life, and their ability to help Christians praise God and enjoy Him forever soon become apparent."[21] In familiarity, Schalk implies, we find freedom—freedom to embrace the truth of the narrative and the freedom to allow it to change us and deepen our faith. In this way, the liturgy shapes us to God's way rather than being a device we use to shape God to our own needs and understandings.[22]

Echoing Luther, Schalk emphasizes that when we proclaim the good news of the Gospel, that is the way in which God is rightly praised. This leads him to an important question. To whom are we directing our praise and our proclamation?

Schalk's answer is threefold.

First, it is directed to God—not that God doesn't know the story, of course, but in the sense that we are remembering and confessing all of God's promises and His covenant.

Second, it is directed to each other in the building up of faith. "How do we do that?" he asks. "Through the Word of the Gospel." There are many interesting and provocative words we can use, he continues, "but there is ultimately only one nourishing Word as we worship, and that's the good news of the Gospel."

And third, our praise through proclamation is directed to the world. "We say, 'as often as we eat this bread and drink this cup, we proclaim the Lord's death until He comes.'"[23]

Schalk finds similar significance in the melodic climax of the Offertory song of the Service of Word and Prayer in *With One Voice*: "Ours be the telling of deeds greatly done." Pondering this moves him deeply. "*That's* what it's all about!" he exclaims. "The telling of God's deeds! *That's* what we are to do—to remind people of the story

---

[20] "Proclamation, Pedagogy and Praise."

[21] *A Handbook of Church Music*, 17.

[22] "Basic Lutheran Understandings of Music in Worship."

[23] Conversation with the author, July 26, 2012.

of salvation. The liturgy is infused with it—the Magnificat, the Nunc Dimittis, the Canticles."[24]

Under the Discipline of the Liturgy

If the song of the Church is the cantus firmus of the Christian life, then the understanding that the music of the Church finds its most appropriate place in the context of the liturgy is the overarching theme of Schalk's life and work.

The Church Year and its cycle of readings provide a discipline for the community, he writes, "in which it is exposed to the full counsel of God. It is, therefore, the living tradition of communal praise, proclamation, prayer, and mutual edification—the liturgy—that best determines how music is to be used, what its spirit and mood should be, and the appropriateness of specific selections for particular occasions."[25]

It is the duty and delight of the church musician, Schalk affirms, to allow all one's decisions, large and small, to be guided by the opportunities presented by the forms and cycles of liturgical worship. "It is the liturgy that must discipline our choices (of music) and ultimately determine use and suitability."[26]

The musician is thus called "to give primary attention to those texts that are of particular *liturgical* significance for a specific celebration."[27] For many, this "will mean a realignment in the priorities given to various segments of present musical repertories. It will surely mean a more serious searching of the church's song for music that underscores the specificity of particular celebrations."[28] And it will mean a major realignment of congregational expectations. "Congregations that have come to view music as 'additions to the service,' however beautiful, must be carefully, gradually, and winsomely led to see the organic relation between liturgy and the church's song."[29]

Schalk calls the process of this realignment "placing oneself under the discipline of the liturgy."

---

[24] Conversation with the author, July 26, 2012.

[25] *Luther on Music: Paradigms of Praise*, 52.

[26] "The Church Musician as Steward of the Mysteries," *Grace Upon Grace: Institute of Liturgical Studies Occasional Papers 9* (1996), 59–66, 64.

[27] *Luther on Music: Paradigms of Praise*, 52.

[28] Ibid., 52–53.

[29] Ibid.

"To place oneself under the discipline of the liturgy is to make available to the worshiping community the wealth and experience of the church at worship throughout the centuries," he writes, "rather than placing it at the mercy of the more limited and less satisfying experience of the individual or at the mercy of a passing faddishness disguised as relevance." This will be a new experience for some in their music or preaching ministry, and perhaps an unsettling one at that. "But as one grows under such a discipline—and as one helps congregations to grow under it—the result will be to bring a richness and depth to worship not possible in any other way."[30]

Radical Simplicity

Here we arrive at the characteristic that Schalk considers indispensable for the church musician and that also stands as the defining element throughout Schalk's career as musician, composer, choir director, teacher, author, advocate, and consummate churchman. This is the quality of *radical simplicity.*

To place oneself and one's art under the discipline of the liturgy, Schalk asserts, "Church music will have to find its way back to a more radical simplicity."[31] Used here, the word *radical* implies not the common usage of "extreme" or "drastic," but instead refers to that which goes to the root or origin—that which is fundamental. And *simplicity* does not imply a deficiency or lack of depth, but instead signifies that which is unaffected, unassuming, and unpretentious.

In this quality of radical simplicity lies the integrity of all music for the Church in worship. Once the musician fully grasps the nature and indispensability of liturgy in the Church's worship life, the practice of radical simplicity emerges as a natural consequence. Music therefore comes to assume the role of that which underscores and affirms the particular liturgical action at hand, in contrast to music that effectively denies the liturgy by virtue of its primary purpose as entertainment.

This entails "a movement away from music that is pretentious, that strives for the 'big effect' with musical materials that do not justify it, and that places a premium on winning acceptance from the hearer with a superficial attractiveness," Schalk writes. Radical simplicity as a response to the discipline of the liturgy thus implies in

[30] Ibid., 53.
[31] Ibid.

the practice of church music "a greater understanding of what worship is really all about, its musical priorities, the flow of the liturgical action, and the use of music as doxological proclamation."[32]

Under the discipline of the liturgy, composers write in response to the need at hand. The musician produces a new tune for a worthy text that underscores and enhances the theme of a given Sunday's cycle of readings, a new setting of a liturgical movement that draws the worshiper more fully into the story of salvation, a motet that proclaims the Gospel reading in a way that excites the imagination and stirs the soul, or a psalm setting that opens new windows into the anguish and yearning of the psalmist.

It follows, therefore, that the genesis of virtually every piece of music Schalk has created was located in the needs of the Church in worship. Often, these came as the result of requests or commissions, but they always fulfilled a liturgical purpose. In the introduction to *The Carl Schalk Hymnary*, a collection of twenty-five hymns and twenty-two carols first published in 1989, he affirms, "In almost every instance, these hymn tunes were attempts to serve the needs of particular circumstances, prompted by requests or commissions from a wide variety of sources" including "individuals, congregations, church bodies, hymnal committees, and the needs of the college community" in which he served for more than two decades.[33]

All told, Schalk has penned to date some 110 hymn tunes, comprising eighty that are published and thirty that remain unpublished, with new ones always in the works. The sole purpose of his efforts in hymnody has been to support the worship life of the Church. "My goal is not to carve out a whole new musical language for congregational song," he says. "It is just to provide hopefully substantial or good melodies for new texts. I'm completely aware of the fact that maybe one, two or three, or maybe none at all will be in hymnals a hundred years from now. I'm not worried about that. But they are 'signposts along the way' of one person who is attempting to provide song for the people."[34]

---

[32] *Luther on Music: Paradigms of Praise*, 53.

[33] *The Carl Schalk Hymnary: Forty-seven New Hymntunes and Carols with Various Texts* (Chicago: GIA Publications, Inc., 1989). Reprinted in *Thine the Praise: The Hymntunes and Carols of Carl Schalk* (Chicago: GIA Publications, Inc., 1996).

[34] Conversation with the author, July 26, 2012.

Music in Lutheran Worship

A central conviction of Lutheran worship is that God calls musicians into service through the Church to receive the Gospel as a living treasure and invites them to offer it back to God in community, using the "fair and glorious"[35] gift of music that God has given humankind.

This liaison of music and Christian worship is not born of chance. Rather, Schalk asserts, it was "the deliberate result of the church's concern for the faith joined together with an understanding of the power of music to move our minds and hearts. In theory the wedding of music and words may appear to be a wedding of convenience; in practice it is the unavoidable result of the new life in Christ."[36]

For Schalk, as for Luther, music is not first and foremost the means for a mystical encounter with God but instead constitutes "a practical art, closely tied to theology and its goal of praise of the Creator and the proclamation of the Word."[37] Indeed, what Schalk writes about Luther in the way the many strands of his life and work are interwoven through music may be applied to Schalk himself:

> Luther's concept was truly reformative in that it shifted the emphasis from music as a science about which one might speculate to *musica practica*, music as a performed art. That music occupied just such a place in Luther's own life is clearly evident from his immersion in the various aspects of music as they touched his personal and family life, as well as the high prominence he gave to music in the church.
>
> His personal participation in music making, his acquaintance with the music and musicians of his day, his concern that pastors and teachers were thoroughly trained in music, his interest in seeing that church music received adequate financial support, his encouragement of the musical education of children, his ventures into musical composition in connection with both hymnody and polyphony, together with his direct collaboration with musicians in the preparation of

---

[35] Martin Luther, "Of the Power of Music," *The Table Talk of Doctor Martin Luther, 4th Centenary Edition* (London: T. Fisher Unwin, 1883), 116.
[36] *God's Song in a New Land*, 13.
[37] *Luther on Music: Paradigms of Praise*, 19.

> music for the liturgy all suggest an emphasis on music as a practical and performing art that has a direct and crucially important role in the life and worship of the church.[38]

Schalk's life illustrates this well-integrated focus on music in the life of the Church. He has authored many books and articles constituting original research on the history of Lutheran music, hymnody, and hymnbooks that are indispensable to all who treasure the music of the Church. His vast catalog of hymns and other congregational and choral compositions and settings continues to grow. For decades, he brought his creative gifts to bear on his work as parish music director and university choral conductor. He schooled a generation or more of students in the great heritage of Lutheran choral music; well equipped, they have become today's leaders and are now training the next generation. He introduced millions to that great heritage through his work as founding director of the Lutheran Hour Choir and encouraged for that context the creation of new music by other composers.

On the faculty of Concordia University, River Forest, for nearly three decades, Schalk inaugurated the Master of Church Music program and launched the highly influential *Lectures in Church Music*. He helped start the Bach Cantata Vespers series at Grace Lutheran Church, where he served for many years as Paul Bouman's assistant and exercised the fullness of his passion for liturgical worship. He helped guide the scope and shape the music publications at Concordia Publishing House through years of service on its Music Editorial Advisory Committee. In founding the journal *Church Music* and in editing it for the entirety of its fifteen-year run, he helped create a lively medium for the sharing of important research, ideas, practical advice, reviews, and trends.

Schalk contributed to the dramatic reconfiguration of the content, shape, and scope of Lutheran worship in his service on the group that prepared the 1969 *Worship Supplement* for Concordia Publishing House[39] and in his participation on the Hymn Music Committee of the

---

[38] *Luther on Music: Paradigms of Praise*, 19.

[39] Comprising ninety-three hymns and musical settings of liturgies for Holy Communion, Matins, and Vespers, this modest volume laid the groundwork for many of the innovations pioneered in *Lutheran Book of Worship*. Others serving with Schalk on the Music Committee of the LCMS Commission on Worship were Theodore Beck, Jan Bender, Paul Bunjes, Richard Hillert, Edward Klammer, and Herbert Nuechterlein. For an appreciation of the legacy of this hymnal, see Nancy

Inter-Lutheran Commission on Worship, which produced *Lutheran Book of Worship*, a landmark in the history of Lutheranism in America. Through his involvement in the *Association of Lutheran Church Musicians*, the *Lutheran Music Program*, and *Lutheran Summer Music*, he has inspired, delighted, and enriched countless people of all ages who love and care about the song of the Church in all its aspects. He continues his active involvement in currents of the day through the Center for Church Music at Concordia University Chicago, where his vast repository of more than five hundred hymnals is now stored and many of his manuscripts reside, along with those of Richard Hillert and others.

For Schalk, as for Luther, music in worship functions as *viva vox evangelii*, "the 'living voice of the Gospel,' praising God and proclaiming His Word to the world."[40] Lutherans everywhere embrace this proclamation through music as a distinctive mark of the Church. This understanding emerges out of a number of essential principles about worship in the Lutheran tradition that Schalk articulates in his writing, which reverberate through the entirety of his work for the life of the Church:

- Worship is "the indispensable and central work of the gathered Christian community from which all other facets of the church's life and mission . . . derive their strength, purpose and direction."
- The Lutheran Church "is a liturgical church." It shares a concern for ordered worship in forms and practices that place Lutherans "in the long line of worshipers from the New Testament to the Parousia." As part of the one holy catholic and apostolic Church, "Lutheranism looks to the experience of the church at worship throughout its history as an important source of its way of worship. Its use of forms and practices with which the church has prayed and praised for centuries . . . affirms Lutheranism's continuity with the whole church."
- Lutherans worship using the recurring cycles of the Church Year. They hear the Word proclaimed through ordered

Raabe, "*Worship Supplement* 1969: The Vatican II of Lutheran Worship?" *CrossAccent* 21, no. 2 (July, 2013): 22–27.

[40] *Luther on Music: Paradigms of Praise*, 51.

readings, preaching, and celebration of the Sacraments. In so doing, they "are united with Christians of other times and places."

- The music of Lutheran worship represents a living tradition. "For Lutherans, the word tradition—in the sense of the gathered experience of the church at worship throughout its history—is an important working concept. For Lutherans, their worship tradition is always a living tradition, continuously developing and living in a vital parish practice."[41]

Music in Lutheran worship builds on these understandings and, in so doing, nourishes faith. Indeed, Schalk emphasizes, it can do no other. "Where it has fallen short of these understandings, where it has substituted other goals,[42] where it has become man-centered rather than God-centered, to that extent it has ceased to be Lutheran in motivation, realization, and result."[43]

Hymnody at the Heart

For Schalk, as for Luther, hymnody lies at the heart of the Church's song—not simply as a diversion from the liturgy but as "the very vehicle by which the congregation could *sing the liturgy*."[44] The uniqueness of Lutheran hymnody, he writes, "lies in the fact that from the very beginning it has been an important part of the liturgy, not—as in most other traditions—a general Christian song loosely attached to worship."[45]

One need only examine the body of Luther's vast output to grasp how much of it serves this purpose. Well-known examples include psalm paraphrases ("A Mighty Fortress Is Our God," "From Depths of Woe I Cry to Thee," "May God Bestow on Us His Grace"); paraphrases of components of the Ordinary of the Mass and the Medieval Offices ("All Glory Be to God on High," "We All Believe in One True God," "Isaiah, Mighty Seer in Days of Old," "Come,

---

[41] All quoted material in the above from *A Handbook of Church Music*, 14–17.

[42] Schalk is most troubled by the goal of music as entertainer, which is "perhaps the most pervasive view of the relation between music and worship practically operative in American Protestantism today" (*Luther on Music: Paradigms of Praise*, 50).

[43] *A Handbook of Church Music*, 14–15.

[44] *Praising God in Song*, 27.

[45] *A Handbook of Church Music*, 18.

Holy Ghost, God and Lord"); and hymns that serve the Church Year ("Savior of the Nations, Come" for Advent, "We Praise You, Jesus, at Your Birth"[46] for Christmas, "In Peace and Joy I Now Depart" for the Presentation of our Lord, "Christ Jesus Lay in Death's Strong Bands" for Easter, and "To God the Holy Spirit Let Us Pray" for Pentecost).

The same holds true of Schalk. The body of his music best known to congregations, however, consists not so much of settings of specific liturgical movements but more of hymns, hymn arrangements, concertatos, psalm settings, and motets that offer a fuller experience of liturgical parts of the service, including the entrance hymn, the Hymn of the Day, psalmody, music for Holy Communion, and motets that frame the reading of the Gospel.

Hymns Teach and Strengthen Faith

A central tenet of hymnody that Schalk energetically supports is the capacity of hymns to teach and strengthen faith. "Liturgy and hymnody are ways the faith is inculcated into hearts and minds," he emphasizes. "We must lead each new generation into the treasures of the church's song."[47]

The rise of hymnody, Schalk stresses, coincided with the rise against heretical teaching. In the West, the most dangerous heresy was that of Arianism, the charge that Christ is not truly divine. We therefore sing to better grasp and take to heart Christ's true nature and all that God has done in the person of Christ through the story of salvation. In a like manner, "the Doxology doesn't just round out a hymn. It reminds us of a specific theological statement, that all the persons of the Trinity are equal."[48]

Schalk takes vigorous exception to the statement made by the editors of *Service Book and Hymnal* that "hymns should be devotional rather than didactic or homiletical."[49] Martin Luther, he points out, wrote many didactic hymns, including those on Baptism, Communion, the Lord's Prayer, and the Ten Commandments. "Too

---

46 Included originally in *Worship Supplement* as "We Praise, O Christ, Your Holy Name," Concordia Publishing House, 1969.
47 "Basic Lutheran Understandings of Music in Worship."
48 "Proclamation, Pedagogy and Praise."
49 "Introduction to the Common Hymnal," *Service Book and Hymnal*. (Minneapolis: Augsburg Publishing House, 1958), 286.

many hymns wash over us in a cooling breeze of theological slush," Schalk cautions with a characteristic twinkle in his eye.[50]

In similar fashion, Schalk asserts that the best Christmas carols are not those that meditate on "sweet baby Jesus" but instead the ones that "remind us that Christ came to die."[51] In addition to the second stanza of "What Child Is This" ("Nails, spear shall pierce Him through, The cross be borne for me, for you."), he cites as a favorite example the traditional sixteenth-century German Advent carol "Maria durch ein'n Dornwald ging" ("Mary Walks among the Thorns"), which reads in Henry S. Drinker's translation:

Maria walks amid the thorn,
Kyrie eleison.
Maria walks amid the thorn,
Which seven years no leaf has born.
Jesus and Maria.

What 'neath her heart doth Mary bear?
Kyrie eleison.
A little child doth Mary bear,
Beneath her heart He nestles there.
Jesus and Maria.

And as the two are passing near,
Kyrie eleison,
Lo! roses on the thorns appear,
Lo! roses on the thorns appear.
Jesus and Maria.

Schalk never tires of pointing out that every good hymn must contain some aspect of the story of salvation.

"Someone asked me, 'Does every hymn have to have the entire story in it?' I answered, 'Not exactly.' But the problem is this: Because many churches are abandoning the liturgy, there is no other place for the story of salvation to be told than in the hymnody. The richness and fullness of the liturgy is not there—you just have hymn, prayer, sermon, go home. Therefore, the burden is greater on the hymnody to tell a significant part of the story. So every hymn should

[50] Conversation with the author, July 26, 2012.
[51] Ibid.

tell some part of the story or the particular part which is being celebrated by that season or festival."[52]

The Chorale as a Unique Vehicle of Proclamation

For Schalk, as for Luther, the chorale stands alone as the central vehicle for congregational song. Flowering as a new form in the early years of the Reformation, "its texts spoke clearly of sin and salvation, of death and resurrection; they recounted the story of man's fall into sin and his redemption won by Christ's victory over death and the devil. Its melodies—sung by the congregation in unison and without accompaniment—were vigorous, rhythmic and truly popular."[53] For Luther and his followers, it was a vehicle for doxological proclamation, to "proclaim the wonders God has done."[54] Writes Schalk, "The chorale was a confession of faith, not a vehicle for personal feelings or emotion. It was designed neither to be listened to, nor as a vehicle for entertainment. It was meant to be sung by a congregation as a vehicle through which they professed their common faith, rehearsed the story of salvation, and proclaimed God's Word to the world."[55]

But it is more than just texts joined to tunes. Testifying to the unique proclamatory power of music, Schalk affirms with Luther that the chorale *is* the Word of God, not simply a representation of it. It is "the biblical word itself, not its substitute,"[56] just as it was "an essential part of the liturgy, not its appendage."[57] Luther's genius was to admit to worship both accessible song and the more sophisticated music of his day. The Lutheran chorale held these two traditions together.[58]

Even today, the words and tunes of the chorales continue to provide strength and comfort to worshipers wherever they are used. Schalk is delighted that some that lay dormant for centuries have been restored to common practice. Two chorales introduced for the first time in the modern era, "Lord, Thee I Love with All My Heart" in

---

[52] Conversation with the author, September 3, 2012.
[53] *A Handbook of Church Music*, 18.
[54] "Dear Christians, One and All, Rejoice," *LSB* 556:1.
[55] *God's Song in a New Land*, 22.
[56] Friedrich Blume, *Protestant Church Music* (New York: W. W. Norton & Company, Inc., 1974), 48. Quoted in *God's Song in a New Land*, 22.
[57] Ibid.
[58] "Basic Lutheran Understandings of Music in Worship."

The Lutheran Hymnal and "In Thee Is Gladness" in *Worship Supplement*, both of which were included in *Lutheran Book of Worship*, have gone on to win an enduring place in the hearts of worshipers wherever they are sung.

Schalk considers the popularity of these two chorales to be particularly remarkable in that planners of *LBW* considered them "the least likely to succeed and the hardest to sell" because both occupied two full pages in the book.[59] He credits the success of "Lord, Thee I Love" in part to its tireless advocacy by Paul Bouman at Grace Lutheran Church. "You can scarcely go to a funeral at Grace Church where you don't hear that hymn," Schalk says, "and that is due almost solely to Paul Bouman's dogged determination that people were going to learn and learn to love it. He did just that, and it bore fruit."[60]

The Hymn of the Day

A central concern of Schalk's throughout his career is the importance of the Hymn of the Day, originally a sixteenth-century liturgical practice that Schalk has tirelessly worked to revive in modern-day Lutheran worship. The *de tempore* principle emerged out of the understanding of hymnody as a vehicle for helping worshipers sing the liturgy. To this constellation of liturgical pieces, the *de tempore* hymn was added as one that embraced the major themes of the readings for a given Sunday and of the season as well. "These hymns are a special treasure of Lutheran hymnody and are an example of how hymnody should be employed liturgically," Schalk explains.[61]

As the chief hymn of the service, it should be well known to the congregation and calls for special musical treatment such as the singing of stanzas in alternation and the addition of choir and instruments. "The particular genius of the Hymn of the Day is that it enables all parts of the congregation—people, choir, organ, instrumentalists—to participate together in the great liturgical hymn of the service," Schalk writes.[62] It was a hymn that "had the practical significance of an additional proper" and served as "a vehicle for the congregation's unique proclamation and response to the Word first

---

[59] Conversation with the author, September 3, 2012.
[60] Ibid.
[61] "Music and Liturgy: The Lutheran Tradition," 248.
[62] *The Hymn of the Day and Its Use in Lutheran Worship*, Church Music Pamphlet Series (St. Louis: Concordia Publishing House, 1983), 25.

heard in the readings, proclaimed in the sermon and confessed in the Creed."[63]

The concept corrects the tradition of the "sermon hymn" that grew up in American Lutheranism in the nineteenth and early-twentieth centuries as pietism came to dominate the aesthetic of worship. This was a hymn preceding the sermon that was intended to prepare the hearts and minds for the content of the sermon. The Hymn of the Day serves as a reminder that both preaching and hymnody are components of the liturgy and proclaim the central theme of the service as articulated in the appointed readings and the position of the day in the Church Year. Schalk emphasizes that this concept brings the congregation closer to Bach's ideal of "a well-ordered church music."[64] With the publication of *LBW*, the Hymn of the Day attained official recognition.[65]

Schalk's commitment to the *de tempore* principle continues in full force. He is working on an expansion of his 1983 pamphlet, in which he intends to offer more historical background and a list of around thirty-five *de tempore* hymns that would be suitable for the appointed Sundays in the three-year lectionary cycles. (Some will work for more than one Sunday, he notes.)

The impetus for the project came from Schalk's scrutiny of lists of Hymn of the Day suggestions in print and online[66] that offer a wide variety of choices. "When you do that, you effectively *don't* have a Hymn of the Day," he explains. "So here's my thesis: If you have ten choices for any given Sunday, you've lost the idea of the effect of repetition and growing into that. One of the things that has contributed to this larger number of choices is the lectionary, and there's no way you're going to dislodge the three-year lectionary. But you can have one single hymn of the day, such as 'Christ lag in

---

[63] Ibid., 7.

[64] Ibid., 6.

[65] *Lutheran Book of Worship* specifies that the Hymn of the Day is to be sung after the sermon, but offers a secondary option to have it precede the sermon. In *Lutheran Worship* and *Lutheran Service Book* as well as in *Christian Worship*, the Hymn of the Day is to be sung before the sermon, while in *Evangelical Lutheran Worship*, it is to follow a brief period of silence after the conclusion of the sermon. It should be noted that the concept was pioneered in *Worship Supplement*, where it was referred to as the "Hymn of the Week."

[66] These include Augsburg Fortress' *Sundays and Seasons* and *Indexes to Evangelical Lutheran Worship*, in which there are as many as six choices for the Hymn of the Day on some Sundays and rarely fewer than three.

Todesbanden' ('Christ Jesus Lay in Death's Strong Bands'), for Easter across the three years for a particular Sunday even though the Gospel readings are different. I don't want to sever the tie between the Hymn of the Day and the Gospel reading; I want to expand the concept of what the Gospel proclaims, connecting the readings for the day and ultimately offering one hymn which encapsulates this day and works for all three years."[67]

His concept addresses the heart of what the *de tempore* hymn is intended to be.

"The Hymn of the Day shouldn't be irrelevant to the lessons," Schalk says. "But if you narrowly make it simply a restatement of the specific lessons, it becomes a sermon hymn all over again. That's what the practice has become in many churches."[68]

Principles of Lutheran Worship

Nearly four decades ago, writing in the spirit of cooperation among Lutheran church bodies as the joint hymnal project approached completion, Schalk formulated a series of essential principles concerning Lutheran worship. For all who value the heritage of the Lutheran church, they are as central to our lives today as they were then.

- Lutherans claim a rich tradition of worship and music.
- The way Lutherans worship is part of how they confess who they are and what they believe.
- The tradition is kept alive in congregational worship.
- The continuity of a dynamic tradition of worship and church music provides an invaluable anchor for Lutherans in a constantly changing culture.[69]

To bring these principles to fruition, Schalk offered a number of "basic, simple, unspectacular suggestions"[70] for the nature and shape of worship that went on to become central tenets of *Lutheran Book of Worship*. These include

[67] Conversation with the author, July 26, 2012.
[68] Ibid.
[69] "The Search for a Usable Tradition of Church Music," *Church Music* 75.1, 2–5.
[70] Ibid.

- a return to the full and vital observance of the Church Year, including celebration not just of festival days but also of seasons.
- a return to weekly celebration of the Eucharist.
- use of full non-Eucharistic rites in non-Communion services, such as Matins and Vespers.
- a return to the use of more than one congregational setting of the liturgy as the norm. The purpose here is not variety but to "reflect the changing moods and emphases of the Church Year."
- a return to the regular use of the *de tempore* hymn.[71]

It is important for the Church and its people to revisit these principles on occasion because congregations that depart from them may better understand that they are also choosing to step away from those qualities that define them as distinctively Lutheran.

"However one chooses to accept Carl Schalk's choral writing and hymn tune compositions in their stylistic and practical parameters," Richard Hillert writes near the end of a substantial analysis of his style and works,

> "there is no question that the composer has been immovable in defense of his concepts of what constitutes the Lutheran musical heritage. For him this is not a vague, all-embracing, unfocused heritage. It is still as focused as it has been since its beginnings in the sixteenth century when it grew from many roots, including Gregorian chant, spiritual folk song, and the contrapuntal proprieties of Renaissance choral polyphony. It is focused in that it is basically designed to serve a fundamental role in liturgical worship. And in that focus it needs constantly to move into the future without abandoning the central tenets of that heritage."[72]

---

[71] Ibid., 5.

[72] Richard Hillert, "Composers for the Church: Carl F. Schalk," *CrossAccent* 10, no. 1 (Spring 2002): 17.

CHAPTER TWO

An Integrated Life

> For Luther music was an art that one practiced and performed, that delighted the soul and brought life to the Word of the gospel. For Luther, music was always the *viva vox evangelii*, the living voice of the Gospel, a gift of God to be used in all its fullness in Christian praise and prayer.[73]

Writing about the hymn for which Carl Schalk is best known, "Now the Silence," Schalk's longtime colleague Richard Hillert stresses that "it is important to know that NOW is emblematic of something more than innovation. It is rather representative of a significant *continuity* that is so evident in his life's work. That continuity defines the singular career of Carl Schalk, dedicated from its beginning to the musical heritage of the church, and to preserving both the vitality and validity of that heritage in our time."[74]

The Church as the fellowship of the faithful, which is called, gathered, and enlightened knows Carl Schalk primarily as a composer. Interestingly, that is not how Schalk sees himself.

"One of the problems in church music publishing, if you think about it, is all the people who think they are composers," Schalk says, referring to the steady stream of non-liturgical anthems being released by many of the major publishing houses. "I don't think of myself as a composer." Then he admits, perhaps in reference to some of his more ambitious recent projects, "Well, I am *beginning* to think of myself as a composer."[75]

---

[73] *Luther on Music: Paradigms of Praise*, 30.

[74] Richard Hillert, "Composers for the Church: Carl F. Schalk," 3.

[75] Conversation with the author, July 26, 2012. These projects include two sets of Gospel motets, thirty-five for Grace Lutheran Church in River Forest that remain unpublished and twelve for Augsburg Fortress, published in 2009 as *Scenes from the New Testament*; six motets also for Augsburg published in 2011, *Simeon's Song: The*

Eastman and Wausau

What Schalk is implying is that for the duration of his call, in all its various forms, he has simply created music to serve the needs at hand. Schalk did not begin his vocation with any idea that he would become a well-known composer. Profoundly influenced by choral director Victor Hildner while a student at Concordia Lutheran High School in River Forest, Illinois, where he served as Hildner's assistant in his last years there, Schalk went on to study organ with Hildner and Carl Halter at Concordia Teachers College (now Concordia University Chicago) and graduated in 1952 with a major in music and a B.S. in education. Upon graduation, Schalk accepted a call to serve as parish musician at Zion Lutheran Church in Wausau, Wisconsin, a thriving parish of around fifteen hundred members, and to teach in the elementary school there. He succeeded Paul Bunjes, who had left Zion a year earlier after a decade and a half there to join the faculty at Concordia Teachers College. Consequently, Schalk inherited at Zion a robust music program and a worship life steeped in faithful Lutheran liturgical practices. He taught fifth and sixth grades, led the school's music program, played organ for three services each Sunday (including one in German), and directed several choirs.

The summer after Schalk's first year in Wausau, he entered the master's degree program in music theory at the Eastman School of Music in Rochester, New York. Studies at Eastman occupied him the next four summers as he continued to serve and teach at Zion during the school year.[76]

At Eastman, Schalk had no desire to concentrate in organ. "This is my hubris coming to the fore," Schalk admits. "I thought, I can play the organ better than any congregation will need to have me play. So, what else can I do? The thing I knew least about was theory. So I majored in theory." As a result, Schalk acquired expert grounding in the subject and studied a wide variety of styles in depth. "I focused on music theory," he elaborates, "because I knew that as a church musician, I will need to be able to write a descant, to push the notes around, to work out something for two-part children's choir."[77]

Nunc Dimittis; and *Four Choruses from the Song of Solomon* (unpublished, 2011). See chapter 9 for details and analysis.

[76] Conversation with the author, July 26, 2012.

[77] Ibid.

Schalk completed the degree in 1958 with a master's thesis that offered a stylistic analysis of Peter Mennin's *The Christmas Story*.[78] The great contrapuntal energy and influences of Renaissance polyphony that define Mennin's style were to become central hallmarks as well of Schalk's compositional voice—realized, of course, in a different way.

During his first year in Wausau, Schalk lived in the church parsonage where Bunjes had resided. This came about, Schalk recounts, because movers were unable to get his baby grand piano into the apartment he had been planning to occupy. On short notice, he therefore took up residence in the parsonage. There he found himself under close scrutiny of the pastor and his wife, to whom Bunjes had been like a son. "Now I am living in the place of their beloved son," Schalk recalls. "So I had to prove myself."[79]

It was a tall assignment. Bunjes had built a major music program in his fifteen years in Wausau and, in so doing, expanded the horizons of the congregation's hymnody and revitalized their liturgical worship. Schalk points to Vaughan Williams' "Hail Thee, Festival Day" as one of the hymns Bunjes introduced to the congregation, which came to be a central part of their worship life.

Bunjes also made significant adaptations to the liturgy as printed in *The Lutheran Hymnal*. "When *TLH* comes out," Schalk explains, "he looked at the music for the liturgy and said to himself, 'I can do better.' So he set out to write another liturgy in which he maintained the melodies of the Anglican chant but in new harmonizations and Gregorian-style accompaniments, and he rebarred it all. It was very nice. The congregation never even knew what was in *TLH*. Right from the beginning they sang his liturgy—the Bunjes liturgy. And they sang it very well."

Then, along came Carl Schalk. "I'm the young kid trying to follow this legend up there. But he had only redone page five because they didn't celebrate Communion that often. Then you'd jump to page 24 in the hymnal." Schalk decided that it would therefore be useful if

---

[78] Peter Mennin (1923–83) earned degrees from the Oberlin Conservatory and the Eastman School of Music before going on to teach composition at the Juilliard School in New York and later directing both the Peabody Conservatory and the Juilliard School. He is remembered for an appealing style grounded in diatonic harmony that was energetic and individualistic. His many works include nine symphonies.

[79] Conversation with the author, July 26, 2012.

he completed the rewriting of the service. "So I wrote the communion part in a similar vein. This became known as the Bunjes-Schalk liturgy. That's all they sang, nothing else except for Matins and Vespers, which they sang right out of the book. That's the only communion music they knew."[80]

Decades later on a car trip through Wisconsin, Carl and Noël Schalk stopped in at Zion, a soaring Gothic structure with superb acoustics.

"It had been a wonderful place to work," Schalk remembers. "We went into the sanctuary, and there was somebody puttering around. 'Can I help you?' he asked. 'No, I used to teach here, probably before you were born,' I said, and told him who I was. He replied, 'Carl Schalk . . . oh! The Bunjes-Schalk liturgy! We still use that once in a while—the old-timers like it.'" Schalk asked what they were currently using. "He told me, 'We kind of like the Marty Haugen liturgy.'"[81]

As a newcomer to the well-established music program in Wausau, Schalk recalls making one misstep common to many conductors who are eager to please. "As a choir director, you want to ingratiate yourself with the singers. Sometimes in doing that, you give them this piece or that one only because you know they're going to love it even though it might be against your better judgment."

Schalk explains that he succumbed to this tendency shortly after starting at Zion.

"I'm right out of college, and I'm following Paul Bunjes. His image was huge. And I was living with the pastor, where Paul had lived for fifteen years. So I thought, I have to do something to get these people to love me. I thought: I have the perfect hymn. It's a simple little hymn, and they're going to love me forever ever after. So I ran off a copy of 'Children of the Heavenly Father.' They sang it and it seemed all right. Then we got home later that night and pastor's wife said, 'You know, we don't sing that kind of music in this church.' She was very nice and gracious. But she was essentially saying, 'You don't have to pander to us.' Bunjes never pandered to them at all, even though every choir director in some way or other wants to do that."[82]

---

[80] Ibid.

[81] Ibid. "Now the Feast and Celebration," originally in *Hymnal Supplement 1991* (Chicago: GIA Publications, Inc., 1991). Available in a variety of editions from Augsburg Fortress.

[82] Conversation with the author, October 24, 2012.

The summer after his first year in Wausau, Schalk was joined by his new wife, Noël, who was also a graduate of Concordia Teachers College. Across town, yet another graduate was at work: Richard Hillert, with whom Schalk forged a close collegial relationship that would endure to Hillert's death in 2010, had just begun serving his call to Wausau's Trinity Lutheran Church.

The following year, Schalk and Hillert decided to start up an informal enterprise that would prepare and distribute copies of music they had recently written for use in worship. "At the time, I thought we were getting some good things together which ought to be made available more widely," Schalk recalls. "So I said, why not print these up?"

Funding to pay for the offset process had to be secured, however. Another teacher at Zion recommended that Schalk and Hillert approach a local radiologist. "A radiologist—this meant big bucks," Schalk laughs. "So we went to him and explained how we wanted to make these available, and how we would have a lending library. He listened to all this patiently and then said, 'How much are you asking for?' This was in 1954, and I had never asked anybody for money before. So I screwed up my courage and said, 'How about $25?' He said, 'Well, I think I can do that.'" A delightful postscript to this story is that upon his death years later, this same donor left a major bequest to Zion Lutheran Church, which supported the installation of the new Charles Kegg organ in 2010.

Schalk's years at Eastman yielded what was to become his first published work: the set of four choruses from *Lamentations of Jeremiah* (SATB; first published by Concordia Publishing House in 1961 and reprinted in 2000), written as a student exercise.

"There I am at Eastman with a B.S. in education," he says. "There were sixteen people in the class. It was divided into two sections, those who were Ph.D. candidates and those who weren't. The first summer we studied Wagner, Debussy, and Scriabin. I can tell you more about the music of those composers than you'd ever want to know."

The second summer, the class focused on American composers. Each student selected one to study in depth. "We each had a class period to lecture on the one we had chosen, and then we wrote a piece in the style of that composer and talked about it from a theory perspective," Schalk recounts. "I picked Randall Thompson, who was

'Mr. Bland' in that company. So I wrote those four choruses for that class, and they were published in 1961 in a slightly altered form."[83]

While his choice of Thompson might not have impressed his classmates, it shows Schalk's concern for music of good craftsmanship that is also accessible to the average choir.

"He demonstrated the finest in terms of voice leading and easily singable music," Schalk notes. "And of course everyone was singing his *Alleluia*."[84] Schalk also found himself strongly influenced by Healey Willan, a British-Canadian composer who was later to submit to the Inter-Lutheran Commission on Worship a setting of the Holy Communion liturgy for consideration in what became *Lutheran Book of Worship*. "Again, very singable lines," he says.[85]

During his Wausau years, Schalk composed only what was needed. "I wrote a few little descants, things you do for necessity," he says. "I was not writing big pieces. That's one thing I don't often see today. If there is somebody who has any talent for writing at all, immediately they think, 'I'm going to write some big splashy piece.' And then they think, 'Who will publish this?' I would say, don't worry about that. If it's worthwhile, if it's worth publishing, if it's worth a wider distribution, you will find somebody. But you don't start by looking at a publisher's catalog and say 'What are they weak in? I'll write something to fit that.'"[86]

---

[83] Conversation with the author, October 24, 2012.

[84] Written in 1940 for the opening of the Berkshire Music Center at Tanglewood, Thompson's *Alleluia* remains the most widely known work of the American choral repertoire. Serge Koussevitzky, director of the Tanglewood Music Festival, had asked for a "fanfare" for voices for the opening of the new Berkshire Music Center but instead received this somber, introspective work, the product of Thompson's ruminations on the war in Europe and the recent fall of France.

[85] A few years later, Schalk helped promote a hymn by Willan, "O Gracious Father, God of Love," written for the twenty-fifth broadcasting season of *The Lutheran Hour*. Copies were made available to congregations for use on Lutheran Hour Sunday, Feb. 28, 1960. When the LCMS Commission on Worship, Liturgics, and Hymnology asked for suggestions for the next edition of *The Lutheran Hymnal*, Schalk submitted the hymn for consideration. Although it was published by CPH, it never made it into any Lutheran hymnal.

[86] Conversation with the author, July 26, 2012.

St. Louis Years

In 1958, Schalk was called from Wausau to St. Louis to serve as the first music director for *The Lutheran Hour*.[87] During his seven years in that post, Schalk expanded his vigorous advocacy of the heritage of Lutheran church music. He also completed a Master of Arts in Religion at Concordia Seminary while several others who were to become the next generation's most influential leaders were students there. His former student Barry Bobb, who served for years as vice president of Concordia Publishing House, credits this degree with giving Schalk the theological expertise that has served him so well.

"The MAR was important," Bobb says. "Because of it, he knows how to talk to pastors, to say things in theological terms."[88]

Schalk's first charge from *The Lutheran Hour* was to organize a mixed choir to record music for the program. Until then, all the music sung on the show had been performed by a male chorus, conducted by William B. Heyne, director of the Concordia Seminary chorus and the St. Louis Bach Chorus. "At some point, they decided to expand the repertoire, and they thought a mixed chorus would be good," Schalk remembers. "The main part of my job was to organize that mixed choir in St. Louis, to decide what music they should learn, and to rehearse it and record it for the library. You didn't record the program in one shot; it was all pieced together later. So my job was to build a library of mixed choir music that would be useful."

The Lutheran Hour Choir was convened with thirty-two singers, a size that he felt "came close to balancing the two poles of good choral sound and intelligibility of words." (Schalk notes it also happened to be the size of the Robert Shaw Chorale.) "I knew we needed to pay these people something, so we decided on five dollars per rehearsal to cover babysitting expenses."[89]

The installation of a pipe organ in the chapel of The Lutheran Hour was another major accomplishment of Schalk's during those

---

[87] Launched in the 1930s by the Lutheran Laymen's League with the goal of "bringing Christ to the nation." At its height in 1948, this weekly radio broadcast reached a worldwide audience estimated at 20 million with 450,000 pieces of mail received that year, 17,000 in a single day. In the 1930s, the program was launched to the "nation"; it was changed to the "nations" in 1940 when they began the Spanish broadcast.

[88] Barry Bobb, conversation with the author, November 9, 2012.

[89] Conversation with the author, July 26, 2012.

years. At the time he arrived in St. Louis, the organization's offices were located at Concordia Publishing House. The following year, the operation moved into its own quarters.

"There, they had a chapel which seated maybe 150," Schalk recalls. "They had chapel a couple of times a week. One of the first questions I was asked when I was being interviewed, by someone with the unlikely name of Harry Smith, said, 'You know, in our chapel we need to get an electronic organ. So what kind of electronic organ do you think we should get?' I said, 'Well, I don't think you should get an electronic organ.'"

Schalk made his case for a pipe organ in the pages of a newsletter he developed, which was to have a major impact on his career. He called it the *Lutheran Hour Music News*. His clarion calls for an instrument were rewarded with the installation of a ten-rank Schlicker, christened the Gloria Dei Organ.

Writes Schalk in the newsletter, "The Gloria Dei Organ in the Christ of the Nations Chapel may well become one of the most widely heard organs of our day. While not always being acknowledged as such, its voice will literally go forth into all the world. . . . In the firmness of its construction and in the flexibility of its design, the Gloria Dei Organ stands as a witness to the faith in Jesus Christ which has made it possible—a faith which is at the same time sturdy, vigorous, yet flexible, and capable of infinite variety. Consistent with that faith, the Gloria Dei Organ stands as evidence of a high concern. A concern not only for the use of music in the church, but concern for the faithfulness of the Church's witness and for the integrity of those to whom its witness is given."[90]

The *Lutheran Hour Music News*, typically six typewritten pages that were mimeographed and stapled, may have struck the average reader as a modest effort. But because of what Schalk was able to say in those pages and the people to whom it was sent, its impact was enormous. It fact, it was a carefully calculated strategy on Schalk's part to convey to people in positions of influence the values that Schalk considered indispensable to Lutheran church music.

"It wasn't for listeners of the show," Schalk explains. "It was really directed to church musicians. I was trying to tell them: This is a radio program and you can still do good things, things related to the heritage. And if I can do it here on this program, then you can do it in

---

[90] *Lutheran Hour Music News* 3, no. 4 (April, 1962): 6.

your parish. I was talking to fellow church musicians, encouraging them, broadening them."

Another audience he was trying to reach included members of the Lutheran Hour Operating Committee, which was a lay committee of the Lutheran Laymen's League, the parent company of *The Lutheran Hour*. "I was trying to educate them," Schalk says, "or at least open them up to some possibilities."[91]

In planning music for the radio broadcasts, Schalk dug deep into his knowledge of the historic Lutheran repertoire. But program directors sometimes felt that some of what Schalk chose was too complex for the average listener. "One of the things the announcer [Dr. Oswald C. J. Hoffmann, speaker from 1955–88] was concerned about was that the person listening on the radio should be able to understand everything that was being sung," Schalk recalls. "That was a laudable goal but it's not always possible. He didn't particularly want anything polyphonic, which he felt muddies the waters in terms of what you can hear."

Schalk responded in the resourceful manner that would serve him so well in the years to come: He created what was needed.

"I wrote a lot of stuff for them—sort of polyphonic but not really," he says. Out of these efforts came the first two *Crown Choir Books*.[92] Designed as "easy anthems for the small parish," the volumes offer straightforward yet substantial settings for unison and two-part choirs (with a good deal of canonic writing) of the great chorales and hymns of the Lutheran church of the sixteenth and seventeenth centuries along with some original works by Schalk in that same vein. The two volumes remain staples in church music libraries wherever choral music is valued.

Schalk needed to be cunning at times in his advocacy of great music from the Lutheran heritage. The aforementioned Harry Smith, fan of electronic organs, apparently did not appreciate the music of Bach.

"He made sure that I knew what the rules were around there," Schalk remembers with a smile. "He said, 'We're not too wild about Bach here, so don't be singing a lot of Bach.' So I'd take some of the

---

91 Conversation with the author, September 2, 2012.

92 Organized primarily according to the liturgical calendar, *The Crown Choir Book* and *A Second Crown Choir Book* were published by CPH respectively in 1964 and 1969. Schalk added a third volume to the series in 1988. For a closer look at these books, see chapter 9.

simpler Bach chorales and copy them out with whatever words we were going to use. But I'd never put 'J. S. Bach' on there, so he wouldn't see it and get all upset. The result was that we were singing Bach but he didn't know that—although of course the singers knew."[93]

Schalk not only wrote music himself for the broadcasts, he also commissioned others to write for the program as well. He remembers in particular a series of commissions from Thomas Canning, then on the faculty of the Eastman School of Music. One is featured on The Lutheran Hour Choir's album *A Mighty Fortress* (Word Records WST-9003), a setting for strings, brass, organ, and choir of the great Reformation hymn "O God, Our Lord, Thy Holy Word" (*TLH* 266). A subsequent album, *Praise the Almighty* (Word Records WST-9006), concluded with Canning's "Alleluia, Sing to Jesus" and also featured his instrumental "Meditation on Hyfrydol."[94] Both albums feature stirring, confident singing, a clear sense of purpose, and a finely blended choral sound.

The Meditation came about, Schalk said, because he was always looking for pieces the producers could use as theme music, which would then fade into the sermon delivered by the announcer. "It was set for strings and oboe, and we knew what oboist was going to be the principal oboist of the St. Louis Symphony, George Hussey," Schalk recalls. "So Thomas Canning sends me the score, and the opening time signature is *four and a half quarters*. I thought, 'Oh no, how do you do this?' Well, I quickly learned how to do it. That was a big learning experience."

At that time, the producers would compile various elements into a master tape of the program that was sent to a company in St. Louis downtown. "They'd make LPs, and it was the LP that they'd send to radio stations. There was a program on each side, so there was two weeks' worth on one album."

Part of Schalk's job, after the program director learned to trust him, was to make it all fit. "You'd put all these pieces together and it's a minute and twenty seconds too long or short. So someone had to go down there, often I would, with a couple of options. You could add a stanza, or delete one; or you could trim something from the

---

[93] Conversation with the author, September 2, 2012.

[94] The later album included settings by Richard Hillert, Paul Bunjes, and Healey Willan in addition to several by Schalk.

sermon. Ozzie Hoffmann guarded his words, but sometimes I would trim a sentence out to get it to the right length. I did that for seven years and had a great time."

Schalk isn't sure, however, whether Noël would say the same. "Well, don't ask her if it was great!" Schalk says with a twinkle in his eye. "We had three kids all under four, and the last one, Tim, was born two months after we arrived there. We had three in three years." Born in 1955, daughter Jan (now Jan Westrick) is a fine flautist and currently chairs the education department at Valparaiso University. Rebecca (now Rebecca Nagel), born in 1957, is a professional oboist and professor of music at the University of South Carolina. Timothy was born in 1958 and works as a scientist specializing in environmental engineering.

The remoteness of their home, its spare surroundings, and their no-frills automobile also now cause Schalk to wonder if Noël would call their time in St. Louis "great." The young family led a simple life, for which the sparse landscape surrounding their newly constructed home and newly acquired car served as metaphors.

"We were living in this subdivision, brand new—no trees, no shrubs, because they had to clear the land," Schalk recalls. "I was gone all day and a lot in the evenings. So Noël was in this house in St. Louis County. She didn't drive, so she was stuck there. Pretty soon I taught her to drive, but we had just one car, the one we bought to drive to St. Louis." It did not weather the trip to St. Louis well and so had to be replaced.

"Someone said, 'Go to Koenig Chevrolet in Kirkwood. He's Lutheran.'" Schalk recalled. "So we did, and we decided on one of those Chevrolets with the fins in the back. It was really classy. But I said, 'We want nothing on it.' A heater, but no air conditioning—which was a mistake. It didn't even have a radio, so we ended up putting a little transistor radio on the dashboard." The Lutheran sense of economy was not lost on the salesman. "He says, 'You know, I've only sold two of these [with no frills] all year—the other guy, he's the principal of a Lutheran high school.' It turns out he lived right across the street from us and went on to become Executive Director of Higher Education for The Lutheran Church—Missouri Synod."[95]

[95] Conversation with the author, September 2, 2012. The neighbor in question was Michael Stelmachowicz.

Schalk credits his success at *The Lutheran Hour* to supportive leadership. "I must say, I had a good boss. The person who hired me, Paul Friedrich, wasn't looking over my shoulder. He gave me pretty much a free hand—so if you hang yourself, you hang yourself—and I appreciated that."[96] After Schalk left St. Louis, the choir continued for a year or two and was then disbanded. *The Lutheran Hour* never called another person to what had been Schalk's position.

Work for Concordia Publishing House

In the mid-1960s, Schalk was invited to join the Music Editorial Advisory Committee of Concordia Publishing House. The publishing house had started its music department in 1950 and hired Edward Klammer to administer it. Together with the existing music advisory group, Klammer managed an effective collaboration to formulate recommendations for what should be published. In those years, the group included Theodore Hoelty-Nickel, Paul Bunjes, and Walter Buszin.

"They would meet three or four times a year and bounce ideas around," Schalk says. "The unspoken rule was that they would publish nothing that was not approved by this committee." In 1964, Buszin decided to retire from the committee. Klammer called Schalk to ask whether he would take Buszin's place; Schalk was happy to oblige. Then there was a surprising twist.

Klammer had invited Schalk to attend the last meeting with Buszin so that a smooth transition could be made. "This was on a Saturday," Schalk recalls. "Then Monday morning, Walter Buszin called to say he decided he wanted to stay on the committee after all. So he came back, and there were four of us."

Occasionally, Schalk says, composers might complain that their rejected submissions were subject to the whims and ideas of the editorial advisory board. "But at least there was a point of view which was not based in merchandising," Schalk points out.[97]

Schalk remembers the review procedure as "a good working arrangement. The music department was usually left alone by the rest of the company as long as the department was carrying a profit and not doing something dishonorable." Projects were carefully balanced so that those that were more likely to sell would support those that

---

[96] Conversation with the author, July 26, 2012.
[97] Ibid.

were more innovative. "You knew you were going to make money off of Drummond Wolff,"[98] Schalk says, "but then those profits could go to support projects which were less profitable."

Call to Concordia Teachers College

In 1964, Schalk received a call to serve as assistant professor of music at Concordia Teachers College in River Forest and began work there in mid-1965. The school had celebrated its 100th anniversary the year before and decided to expand its advocacy of church music. Two major components of Schalk's call included starting a new journal devoted to church music and establishing an annual lecture series also devoted to church music.

Why did Concordia's academic dean Carl Waldschmidt (a fine musician in his own right) and music department chair Paul Bunjes consider Schalk to be ideal? He was well known to both, as well as to other top administrators who also held church music in high esteem. But Schalk himself agrees with the suggestion that a leading impetus might have been the modest *Lutheran Hour Music News*.

"Exactly right!" Schalk says with a smile. "I saw to it that they received it. Nowadays, if you're trying to climb the corporate ladder, you do all kinds of things to let your superiors know how good you are. That really wasn't in the front of my mind, but I did let them see these things that I was doing." To the suggestion that today such a publication would take the shape of a blog, Schalk laughs. "That is probably what I would do if I were forty years younger."[99]

The two projects became the highly respected periodical *Church Music*, produced jointly from 1966–80 by Concordia Teachers College (now Concordia University Chicago) and Concordia Publishing House, and the annual series, Lectures in Church Music, which continues in full force today.

Church Music

At the time of his call, Schalk had relatively few publications to his credit and even fewer in mainstream journals. He wrote occasional columns for *Spirit* magazine, a St. Louis tabloid publication directed

---

[98] Stanley Drummond Wolff, English composer and organist (1916–2004), was widely published by Concordia Publishing House and MorningStar Music Publishers. He reportedly disliked his first name, so for professional purposes, he used only the initial.

[99] Conversation with the author, October 24, 2012.

at teenagers, and had published two articles in *Lutheran Education*, "A Second Look at the Lutheran Heritage" (1956) and "Music and the Word" (1959).

In the latter article, Schalk was ahead of his time. "I had to argue with the editor who screened the music," he remembers. "Of course I talked about how words were closely associated with music. But then you get to the subject, what about music without words? At the time, I was enamored with Susanne K. Langer, especially her *Philosophy in a New Key* and *Feeling and Form*, in which she was exploring the idea of whether it is possible for something to be communicated through form or other abstract means. I was making some of those points, and the editor thought it sounded a little suspect. No one knew what I was talking about."

The invitation to launch a new journal was entirely open-ended. "The idea was that I was to start a magazine of some kind; they didn't know what. It was to be determined by me with whoever I chose," Schalk said.[100] The college would support expenses needed in preparation of the copy. The publishing house would then handle all the layout, production and design, and assumed all costs for printing and distribution.

Seizing the opportunity with gusto, Schalk first determined what kind of publication would be of the greatest value. The only thing like it at the time was the *Journal of Church Music*, published by Fortress Press. As he describes it, that small octavo-sized periodical was basically "a how-to-do-it magazine: ten tips to get more people in your choir, here are some nice warm-ups." Consequently, he decided first of all that the new journal would be distinguished by a full-size format. Another feature Schalk considered vital was that it represent a pan-Lutheran perspective. This emphasis was warmly supported by Concordia president Martin L. Koehneke. "The president thought that was just the way to go," Schalk recalls.[101]

Schalk also determined that the new journal should draw on theologically minded musicians and musicologists across all of Lutheran higher education. At the time, most had recently received or were pursuing doctorates.

"I thought, 'We've got these music departments in all these colleges, and they're all going and getting doctorates by the bushel-

---

[100] Ibid.
[101] Ibid.

basket.' So I said we had to capitalize on some of these things they were doing musicologically."[102]

With these criteria in place, Schalk set to work building an editorial board that would serve mainly in an advisory capacity. He reached out to recognized authorities in the field in Lutheran church music and beyond, assembling a board of uncommon strength and depth that included Ed Brown, Ulrich Leupold, Walter Buszin, Herb Lindemann, A. R. Kretzmann, Leonard Ellinwood, Carlton Young, and William Reynolds. Schalk met with them and explained that the responsibilities for each issue would fall to the group of contributing editors—a pool of writers Schalk would call on for articles—and the editorial staff, consisting of himself as editor and Richard Hillert as assistant editor.

The title of the new publication was a point of lively discussion by the editorial board, Schalk recalls. The group came up with various arcane and exotic titles, including some in Latin. At last, Schalk interceded with his trademark common-sense approach. "I said, 'Why don't we just call it *Church Music*? Because that's what we're talking about: music made for the Church, in the Church.' So that's what we settled on."[103]

Schalk's main responsibility as editor was to secure contributors and prepare the copy for Concordia Publishing House. He determined that the first issue, published in 1966, would focus on congregational song; he engaged Reuben G. Pirner of Wartburg Theological Seminary to write the lead article. Each issue of the journal featured three or four substantial musicological or theological articles on whatever the main topic was. "I never asked anyone for a how-to-do-it article," he notes. "We had book reviews, choral reviews, and organ reviews."

Occasionally, things got spicy. "The person who was in charge of the choral reviews, Richard Heschke, had a sharp tongue, and he got a few people mad in his reviews," Schalk notes. "But it was always lively reading. You'd turn to it to see who he's going to embarrass this time—of course, within reason." Other early contributors included Herb Gotsch of Concordia Teachers College, who drew on his doctoral dissertation to discuss the very different role the organ

---

[102] Ibid.

[103] Ibid.

played in early Lutheranism. "All this was new to a lot of people," Schalk remembers. "So you had all this ferment going on."[104]

With the exception of the first year and the last two, which each saw just one issue, *Church Music* was published twice annually through the end of the next decade, setting a new standard as a periodical that made significant scholarly contributions yet at the same time engaged the average church musician. Its first issue laid out its mission: "It is to the renewal of the musical life of the church at the parish level that this journal is dedicated."[105]

In every issue except that during which he was on sabbatical, Schalk wrote a lengthy editorial much in the style of those in the *Lutheran Hour Music News*. These essays addressed in frank terms many of the most pressing issues of the day. Other regular features included periodic updates by Eugene Brand, project director of the Inter-Lutheran Commission on Worship, on the progress being made on the new common hymnal project by The Lutheran Church—Missouri Synod, the American Lutheran Church, the Lutheran Church in America, and the Evangelical Lutheran Church of Canada.

The mid-1970s saw a shift in leadership both at the Synod and at the college. Resulting theological controversies ultimately affected the viability of *Church Music*. "It wasn't so much the change in synodical leadership as the retirement of our president, Martin Koehneke," Schalk says. Paul Zimmerman, who served as president of Concordia Teachers College from 1973 to 1984, was called in his stead and was less sympathetic to the concept and mission of the journal. "This pan-Lutheran thing stuck in his craw," Schalk says of Zimmerman, although the new president couched his reservations in economic terms. "He would say, 'How many new students have we gotten as a result of this magazine?' We'd say, 'That's not the purpose of the journal, to enhance the reputation of the music department.'"[106] At the same time, however, a diminishing subscriber base meant that it was no longer viable from a financial point of view for Concordia Publishing House. *Church Music* published its last issue in 1980.

The legacy of the journal is enormous. "Carl's contribution as editor of *Church Music* was formative for the careers of at least two

---

[104] Ibid.

[105] *Church Music* 66.1: 37.

[106] Conversation with the author, October 24, 2012.

or three generations of church musicians," Schalk's good friend Carlos Messerli affirms.[107] Not only does the publication remain a font of scholarly wisdom that at the same time had its finger securely on the pulse of currents in music and worship, but it is also written in a practical and accessible style. At the time, readers knew to go there to learn about both historical subjects that would inform their ministry as well as important contemporary topics and trends, and it remains a vital resource still today for those who have access to back issues or to university libraries. The journal also served as a vehicle by which Lutheran voices and those drawn from the wider Church were able to mingle.

Historically, Schalk considers *Church Music* to be the successor to *Response*, the journal of the Lutheran Society for Worship, Music, and the Arts, which published its first issue in 1959, a year after the society was founded. That predecessor publication emerged as a response to the public call issued by Walter Buszin in 1955: "In the entire United States we do not have a single first-class inter- or supradenominational periodical on church music, hymnody, liturgics, and church art which, in its own field, might, for example, be put aside *The Musical Quarterly*. We in America need a good quarterly. We have several publications, but they are largely newsy in character and restrict themselves chiefly to the organ and to choral music. Christian hymnody should be included in said periodical; likewise, church art and architecture."[108]

Schalk's involvement with *Church Music* gained him access in 1966 to a gathering of distinguished Roman Catholic musicians and liturgists wrestling with the musical needs of the Church at worship. The event in question was a joint conference held in Kansas City in late 1966 by The Liturgical Conference and the Church Music Society of America.[109] "At some point, there was a movement to

---

[107] Carlos Messerli, conversation with the author, November 13, 2012.

[108] "The Publication of Good Church Music in Our Day" (essay read at the convention of the Music Teachers National Association, St. Louis, Missouri, February 14, 1955). Referenced in *Concordia Theological Quarterly* 43, no. 1 (January, 1979): 6.

[109] A decade later, The Liturgical Conference merged with the Lutheran Society for Worship, Music, and the Arts to create an ecumenical organization dedicated to liturgical renewal in the local assembly. For background on The Liturgical Conference, see liturgicalconference.org/Liturgical_Conference/About_the_Liturgical_Conference.html; on the Church Music Association of America, see musicasacra.com.

merge those two," Schalk remembers. "That was the intent of the conference. So I called the Liturgical Conference office and said I would like to cover the meeting for *Church Music*. They said, 'Of course.'"

A few days later, Schalk was surprised by a call from the same office to invite him to give one of the major presentations.

"They wanted me to talk on the Lutheran tradition in worship," Schalk says. "The conference was attended mostly by priests and nuns. So there I was, talking about congregational song and the importance of singing the liturgy. At some point, I emphasized that the idea of segmenting the congregation—having a "golden age" mass, a teenage mass, a family mass, with different music for each of those—is counterproductive, because when does the whole people of God in that place ever get together and do one thing? Suddenly there was an eruption of applause, mostly from the more conservative people who were not too wild about all the hootenanny stuff [in the Catholic Church] that was going on. I realized I was getting into the middle of a hornet's nest."[110]

Schalk's essay, "Music in Lutheran Worship," was published with the conference proceedings in a volume titled *Crisis in Church Music?*[111] The book includes articles by Rembert Weakland, at the time chairman of the Music Advisory Board of the Bishops' Commission on the Liturgical Apostolate and later Archbishop of Milwaukee; Godfrey Diekmann, editor of *Worship* magazine and faculty member at St. John's University, Collegeville, Minnesota; and Francis P. Schmitt, the beloved director of music at Boys Town, Nebraska, and chair of the Commission on Church Music for the Archdiocese of Omaha.

Lectures in Church Music

The annual conference spearheaded by Schalk that became Lectures in Church Music, and ultimately the Vi Messerli Memorial Lectures in Church Music, was closely intertwined with *Church Music* for the duration of the journal's publication. Major contributors to the journal were regularly invited to speak at Lectures, and this

---

[110] Conversation with the author, October 24, 2012.

[111] *Crisis in Church Music?* (proceedings of a meeting on church music conducted by The Liturgical Conference and The Church Music Association of America. Washington, D.C., 1967), 40–51.

symbiotic relationship infused energy into both endeavors. "I think that is what built the Lectures up," Schalk reflects, noting that at its peak, the conference typically hosted about two hundred registrants. Contributing as well to good attendance was department chair Thomas Gieschen's idea of sending two promotional brochures to each person on the mailing list with the request that they pass one on to a friend.[112] Like the journal, the conference featured a pan-Lutheran emphasis. As a result, Schalk says, "it was attractive to all Lutherans."[113]

When Schalk arrived at Concordia in 1965, Paul Bunjes had already secured Hans T. David to deliver an address to the student body on George Frideric Handel.

"You have a thousand students there and probably the last thing they want to hear is an address on Handel," Schalk admits. "It took the place of the chapel period that day. Then he met with the music faculty and did another presentation. I had nothing to do with that; it was all set up when I got there, but we called it the first Lectures."

The next year, the school brought in scholar Jaroslav Pelikan, who made similar presentations to the music faculty and the theology faculty as a kind of continuing education enterprise. At that point, Schalk was still only peripherally involved.

"The third year, I took over and we were in the swing of it," he says. "We had more or less a full schedule like we've had since."[114]

Planning ahead was the key to success. "You're always thinking two, three, four years down the line," Schalk says. "When I retired, I made a list for my own amazement of all the people who presented at Lectures. It really reads like a 'Who's Who.' In asking them, I had more gall than sense, because we paid them not very much." The conference continues to combine substantial musical and theological presentations with workshops of a more practical nature. It consistently attracts around two hundred attendees each year.

To Schalk, the remarkable cross-fertilization that he encouraged through *Church Music*, the Lectures in Church Music, and his ongoing work on *Lutheran Book of Worship* seemed to be the natural thing to do. "I thought, why not?" he says. "I was going out and doing

---

[112] Barry Bobb, conversation with the author, November 9, 2012.
[113] Conversation with the author, October 24, 2012.
[114] Ibid.

workshops for *LBW*. You get around, you talk to people, and they are attracted by the idea of coming to Lectures."[115]

By the 1980s, however, the winds had shifted away from pan-Lutheranism. "Things were tightening up theologically in the Synod," Schalk says, referring to the increased emphasis on doctrinal adherence. "I refer to those times as 'the troubles.' Most people hunkered down, but I kept doing things. By that time, *LBW* was out, and Dick Hillert and I were both pretty prominent. So I think I was fairly secure. There was nothing Paul Zimmerman could do to me, as long as I was not guilty of theological error or moral turpitude. So even though I realized which way the wind was blowing, we just pretty much kept doing what we were doing. I was the one who hunkered down the least; Dick Hillert hunkered down more because that was his personality. And Paul Bunjes was mad because they didn't buy his dream of the hymnal, so he just went into hibernation as if nothing was happening around him."[116]

Typical of the fine line Schalk trod was his involvement with MorningStar Music Publishers, which was launched by Rodney Schrank, formerly head of the music department at Concordia Publishing House, when Paul Manz withdrew his catalog from Concordia. "Carl had to kind of walk a tightrope," Schrank recalls, "in that he was a synodical employee at River Forest. So he had to be careful. He would send things to me, but he also felt an obligation to support Synod with some of his manuscripts."[117]

Master of Church Music

Another initiative Schalk spearheaded at Concordia that was to have enormous impact on the Church was the development of the Master of Church Music program. "Working together with other members of the music department and the graduate school, Carl planned a unique masters program, one that incorporated broad studies in theology, music theory and history, church music, and applied study," writes Steven Wente, who has served on the music faculty at Concordia since 1984; he currently chairs the music

---

[115] Conversation with the author, October 24, 2012.

[116] Ibid. See chapter 3 for a discussion of the split that eventually produced *Lutheran Worship*, for which Paul Bunjes served as primary editor.

[117] Rodney Schrank, conversation with the author, January 9, 2013.

department and supervises the graduate music programs.[118] Courses Schalk developed include Lutheran Hymnody in America, Traditions of Christian Hymnody, and Musical Monuments of the Reformation, which examined music of the masters between Luther and Bach, including Walter, Rhau, Praetorius, Hassler, Schein, Scheidt, and Schütz. (His 2001 book *Music in Early Lutheranism* for Concordia Publishing House emerged out of his years of immersion in this subject.) Graduates of the program have gone on to assume many of the most influential positions in church music across denominations. "Perhaps Carl's most important contribution to Concordia was developing the Master of Church Music program," affirms Evangeline Rimbach, a longtime Schalk colleague at River Forest. "This was a rare and unique program which has produced many fine Church musicians over the past forty-some years."[119]

Most students attended in the summer because of teaching obligations during the school year. "In those summer classes, you'd have fifteen to twenty in a class, which would make for a decent choir," Schalk remembers. "We always gave a concert every summer." He adds with a laugh, "I was always doing music by dead white guys."

Chapel Choir

As director of Concordia's Chapel Choir during his entire tenure at Concordia, Schalk regularly crafted new settings and original works that addressed the liturgical needs of the weekly worship services. "I was writing stuff we needed to do and have," he explains. Typically, he did not concern himself with trying to get it published. "Some of it turned out well, and some," he adds with a chuckle, "well, it is best left 'to posterior.'"[120]

Schalk fondly categorizes the Chapel Choir as "essentially leftovers" from the more polished senior choir. It varied in size, from as few as fifteen some years to thirty or more in others.

---

118 Steven Wente, "A Focused Life," *Thine the Amen: Essays on Lutheran Church Music in Honor of Carl Schalk*, ed. Carlos Messerli (Minneapolis: Lutheran University Press, 2005), 273–74.

119 Evangeline Rimbach, "Carl Schalk: An Appreciation" (essay written for "Thine the Amen, Thine the Praise: Celebrating Carl Schalk, a Hymn Festival from Advent to Pentecost," produced by ALCM Columbus: Cantor Connection, a local chapter of the Association of Lutheran Church Musicians, Columbus, Ohio, May, 2010).

120 Conversation with the author, October 24, 2012.

"At first, there was a junior college choir and a senior college choir, which eventually became the Kapelle," he says. "When Thomas Gieschen finally took over from Victor Hildner, there was a touring choir, which was the Kapelle, and a Chapel Choir, which was mine. For the most part, that consisted of singers who didn't quite make it into the touring choir."

The College Chorus formed a third group on the musically active campus. This was a large body of around 120 that performed major works with orchestra. Schalk also directed that for a few years. "We did things that had never been done there before—the Schubert Mass in G, big pieces by Dick Hillert, and Stravinsky's Symphony of Psalms."[121]

The advantage of the Chapel Choir, however, was that it provided singers with valuable church choir experience. "All my years there, they sang in chapel twice a week, Wednesday and Friday. Wednesday was the longer service, with communion. We did other things as well: In Holy Week, we always did a St. John Passion. We premiered Dick Hillert's St. John Passion and the Victoria Passion, and we usually did an O Antiphon service in Advent."[122] Schalk kept a record of what the choir sang each year and would hand that out at the end of the year with full publication information so the singers could obtain the music for their own church choirs.

Schalk fondly harkens back to the early years of his time at Concordia, when the faculty had the solid backing of the administration and enrollments were burgeoning. Today, the student body totals around five thousand, but many of those are part-time and commuter students. Since the primary focus is no longer to prepare teachers for Lutheran classrooms, the emphasis on music in the school's mission has been lessened to some extent.

"When I came in 1965, every student in the school—not just every music student, but every student—had to take keyboard, piano until you were able to get on organ. Or if you couldn't get on the organ, you just kept taking piano," Schalk recalls. "You had to be able to at least play the keyboard well enough to play hymns or simple songs in the classroom. So you had a lot of piano teachers and organ teachers. Every member of the music faculty taught some organ: Bunjes, Gotsch, Waldschmidt, me, Hillert, Harlan

[121] Ibid.
[122] Ibid.

McConnell—there were at least six organ teachers. Plus, there were lots and lots of women teaching piano lessons, from 8 to 4:30, five days a week."

As Concordia moved away from a single-purpose institution to a more general liberal-arts curriculum, those programs stayed, Schalk says, but they shrank in size because the demand for music in the schools has diminished. "And now in the schools, it's hard to find a classroom with a piano," Schalk notes ruefully. "You typically have a music teacher who comes in to teach music" in place of one on the staff.[123]

Grace Lutheran Church

During his time in River Forest, Schalk served Grace Lutheran Church, next to the Concordia campus, as assistant director of music under Paul Bouman from 1968 to 1997. Bouman had been director of music at Grace Church since 1953, and the two shared many of the same convictions about Lutheran worship. It proved to be a mutually enriching partnership.

"Paul was always more comfortable at the organ," Schalk says. "So at first he would say, 'Carl, why don't you direct this on Sunday?' It wasn't a big deal. I'd just get up from the choir and come down and direct. Then after about a year, he hired me to be his assistant for the princely sum of twenty-five dollars a month. So we had this relationship at the time when the ILCW (Inter-Lutheran Commission on Worship, the body that eventually produced *Lutheran Book of Worship*) was starting."[124] The two were also on an equal footing in their involvement in worship planning with Pastor Dean Lueking.

In its continuing commitment to the best liturgical worship practices of the Lutheran tradition, Grace Lutheran Church constitutes Schalk's only exception to his "Rule Number One": That, no matter how hard one works to build a program, its survival cannot be guaranteed in the hands of one's successors.

"You're influential in a place while you're there," Schalk reflects. "Maybe it will last a while, more in some cases than others. But in general, this is Rule Number One for me: You can't count on your contribution continuing into eternity."

---

[123] Ibid.

[124] Conversation with the author, July 26, 2012.

Schalk is not being critical, just realistic.

"When I went to Wausau, I followed Paul Bunjes, who had built up this really wonderful practice. You say, 'Well, I wouldn't have done it that way,' but he did a lot of wonderful stuff. My job was to build on what he had done and carry it further in whatever direction I thought it was supposed to go. So when I left, I thought, the next guy will continue to build on that. *It never happens*. It doesn't happen in the congregation; it doesn't happen with pastors. Because the next guy has ideas that are all different from yours, and they want to 'move in a different direction.'"[125]

His case in point is that Zion in Wausau now uses the Marty Haugen liturgy from the GIA *Hymnal Supplement 1991*[126] instead of one that is more traditionally Lutheran.

"You always wish it was not that way. The one exception, I think, is Grace Church. When Dean Lueking was retiring (in 1998), they would have conversations about people they were interviewing. At one point, somebody said, 'Well, what are we going to do about such and such?' Someone else said, 'Maybe we should defer action on this until the new pastor gets here, and we'll see what the new pastor wants.' Then someone else said, 'If the pastor doesn't like that, then we don't want that pastor!' So they *knew* where the congregation should be going and what it should be doing." Among churches today, Schalk asserts, that is a rarity. "With many parishes, either they don't know their tradition or the tradition is whatever the pastor says. And if you have a new pastor, often you have new traditions."[127]

Schalk credits Bouman with developing strong liturgical worship based in the Lutheran heritage and crafting enduring musical traditions at Grace grounded in the Lutheran heritage. Before Bouman, under Otto A. Geiseman, pastor there from 1922 until his death in 1963, worship approximated what Schalk calls "a generic Protestant service." The congregation used the hymnal but sang a truncated form of the liturgy. They sang the first page of Matins, he explains, "and then the rest of it was invented."[128]

As an example of Bouman's ability to create enduring new traditions while respecting treasured practices, Schalk points to the

---

[125] Conversation with the author, July 26, 2012.
[126] "Now the Feast and Celebration," *Hymnal Supplement 1991* (Chicago: GIA Publications, Inc., 1991). An "alternate Eucharistic setting."
[127] Conversation with the author, September 2, 2012.
[128] Conversation with the author, October 24, 2012.

beloved tradition at Grace of singing "O Holy Night" at the children's Lessons and Carols Christmas Eve service. Bouman inherited the practice of using the popular French carol, too sweet for some Lutheran tastes, at that service. Respecting the congregation, he was reluctant to dispense with it. So instead, Schalk notes, he devised a medley of familiar carols that the children would sing as they moved forward up into the chancel to create the cross formation in which "O Holy Night" would be sung.

"Finally, they're all up where they should be, and he seamlessly moves into 'O Holy Night' in the darkness," Schalk relates, marveling at the power of the repetition, year after year, of cherished traditions. "Our kids went through that and they couldn't wait to get into the 'big' choir (the fifth through eighth grade choir, which forms the cross), which gives them things which are worthwhile carrying into their memory the rest of their lives."[129] Writes former pastor Dean Lueking, "The candle cross formed by the children each Christmas Eve has become a deeply loved tradition at Grace Church. For the children who participate, it's a defining moment. Fourth-graders watching it from the pews think 'Next year I'll be up there!' and eighth-graders realize 'Next year I won't.'"[130]

Schalk recounts another much-loved tradition at Grace. While Bouman was director, the children's choir sang his "Behold the Lamb of God" every year since it was composed in 1955.[131] "On the one hand, people say, 'We don't want to sing the same things every year.' But for the children who are coming up, when you have a tradition like that, they think, 'Now it's our turn to learn that!'" That element of excitement and anticipation is often missing when musicians are always introducing new repertoire, Schalk adds.[132]

When Bouman arrived at Grace in 1953 to succeed Carl Halter, he advocated for following the hymnal faithfully and introduced other music important to the heritage of the Lutheran church. As an example of a faithful pastor-musician relationship, he was always supported by Otto Geiseman and then by Dean Lueking.

---

[129] Ibid.

[130] "The Candle Cross Tradition at Grace," reprinted at graceriverforest.org/pages/Grace_ChurchLife_Worship_ChristmasEveTraditions.

[131] It is contained in *The Morning Star Choir Book* (St. Louis: Concordia Publishing House, 1957).

[132] Conversation with the author, October 24, 2012.

"Paul always gives the example that when he first came to Grace, Carl Halter had done a few Bach cantatas there over the years for special occasions," Schalk notes. "But when he arrived, he was told by the elders in no uncertain terms, 'Nobody at Grace Church will ever thank you for singing Bach here.' That was not exactly uncommon, but they let you know that they were not going to be highfalutin, whatever that meant to them. But Geiseman trusted Paul. He said, 'You're the musician,' and didn't second-guess him." The same was true under Dean Lueking, Geiseman's former assistant. "We were introducing all these things, and Dean trusted Paul. He was very deferential to Paul."[133]

With this vote of confidence in hand, in 1971, Bouman and Schalk initiated the Bach Cantata Vespers series at Grace, which is still going strong under Cantor Michael D. Costello. The series presents one cantata each month from September through May. In 2013, it included a performance on Passion Sunday of Bach's *St. Matthew Passion*.

Typically for Schalk and Bouman, their concept for the Vespers service was not confined to the performance of a single work. Instead, it presented a comprehensive vision for an immersion in great music of the Lutheran heritage, a vision that continues today. Schalk has detailed the prescriptions:

- Each service is to include a homily, based on the lessons for the day or the texts of the cantata, which is to be "Gospel proclamation," not a musicological treatise.
- The cantatas are to be sung in German.
- The motets chosen are to be from the rich choral repertoire from the early centuries of Lutheran music.
- The hymns are to be selected from the great German chorales from Luther to Bach, and the preservice music is to be by Bach or others from that period.
- Preparation for the cantata should not eclipse the church choir's primary responsibility for the Sunday morning service. "The Bach cantata series would be above and beyond

[133] Conversation with the author, September 2, 2012.

their regular continued involvement in the regular worship of the congregation."[134]

The series was conceived by Bouman and Schalk as a joint venture with Grace Church and Concordia Teachers College, with the choirs from each institution splitting the duties. Four cantatas were to be performed by one group and four by the other. After that first year, it settled into a pattern by which the choirs from Grace and Concordia Teachers College shared each service: One would sing the cantata and the other a motet. When Grace Church withdrew from the Missouri Synod later in the 1970s, "the edict came down that the college was no longer to participate," Schalk recalls. "So the Grace choir said, 'We'll just do them all.'"[135] In recent years, Concordia University Chicago's Kapelle has appeared as a guest ensemble.

The manner in which the *Lutheran Book of Worship* was introduced at Grace spoke as well of a collegial working relationship between pastor and musicians.

"The congregation decided to get *LBW*," Schalk recalls. "This was in the late 1970s and they'd been using *TLH* since 1941, so they were ready for something new. So the books were shipped and arrived in June. Paul and I decided on the procedure: We'll have the congregation start using it in Advent. Between now and Advent, really starting in September once things got going, every Sunday Paul and I would lead one of the adult education offerings in which we would introduce the liturgies and talk about the hymns. The goal was that, by Advent, you'd have a core of people who knew what this was and at least weren't overtly hostile to it." (It helped that they already loved Hillert's "This Is the Feast," the Hymn of Praise in *LBW*'s Holy Communion Setting One, which they had been singing during the Easter season for several years by that time.)

But their plan to introduce the hymnal worked even better than Bouman and Schalk had expected. "By October, people were asking to start using *LBW* right away," Schalk says. "We said, no, we are going to start in Advent. So when we did get to Advent, by that time, they were really looking forward to it."[136]

---

[134] "Bach Cantatas at Grace Lutheran Church, River Forest, Illinois" (prepared as part of a large history Schalk is compiling on the series, found at bachvespers.org/pdf/SchalkArticle.pdf.

[135] Conversation with the author, September 2, 2012.

[136] Ibid.

Using a process that was friendly and inviting, Bouman and Schalk introduced to Grace the new style of chantlike-sung psalmody that was a major contribution of *Lutheran Book of Worship*.

"The other thing we did, which I think was good, contrary to the general practice in other churches, was the introduction of the psalm tones," he says. "We had rehearsed them with the choir and had sung them that way. But now, the congregation was going to sing them. So, ten minutes before church, I'd go up in front and we'd have a little rehearsal with the congregation: 'Here's the tone we're going to sing,' and we'd practice it. I would josh them into it, so they felt a little more comfortable."

Other Activities

In the early 1980s, Schalk participated in the formation of the *Lutheran Music Program*, for which Schalk's good friend Carlos Messerli served as founding director. *Lutheran Music Program* is the parent organization of *Lutheran Summer Music*, a four-week residential training and performance program that unites high-school musicians from across the country in intentional community. Schalk went on to serve on the organization's governing board. In 2007, he was commissioned by the program to set to music Martin Luther's Morning Prayer, which employs a metrical paraphrase by Schalk of the familiar prayer from Luther's Small Catechism. In publishing the work, he paired it with a similar setting of Luther's Evening Prayer. (For a closer look at this music, see chapter 8.)

During the 1980s, Schalk edited Concordia Publishing House's popular Church Music Pamphlet series. Titles that became indispensable to musicians far and wide include *An Introduction to Organ Registration*, *Acoustics in the Worship Space*, *Music in Lutheran Worship*, and *The Hymn of the Day and Its Use in Lutheran Worship*, the latter two authored by Schalk himself.

Schalk also served as lead consultant for *Celebrating the Musical Heritage of the Lutheran Church*, an interactive CD-ROM with five audio CDs covering the sixteenth through twentieth centuries and including a fifty-page booklet. The beautifully produced set was produced in 2002 by Thrivent Financial for Lutherans and was distributed free of charge to all Lutheran churches and schools. (Unfortunately, it is no longer available.) The CD-ROM includes "key remarks" for each century by two leading scholars. Those for the sixteenth century feature Schalk in the company of Walter Bouman, a theologian with a great heart for music just as Schalk is a musician with a great heart for theology.[137]

To honor Schalk's long involvement with the Association of Lutheran Church Musicians, the organization presented him in 1995 with its Faithful Servant Award. Richard Hillert received the award that year as well. Also for ALCM, Schalk later headed a working group, comprising Paul Westermeyer, Paul Weber, Grace Wessell, and Greg Peterson, which formulated the organization's definitive Statement on Worship. With Schalk as the statement's principal architect, it was adopted without dissent at the 2003 biennial conference in San Diego and remains an expression of ALCM's guiding principles.[138] Schalk has also been a frequent contributor to ALCM's journal, *CrossAccent*.

Schalk continues to create new avenues for a wider appreciation of the heritage of Lutheran church music. In 2010, he made a gift to Concordia University Chicago of his vast library of hymnals to help create the Center for Church Music. The family of Richard Hillert made a similar gift of a permanent loan of Hillert's manuscripts and published compositions. The Center is housed in the rare book room of Concordia's Klinck Memorial Library.[139] The Carl Schalk Hymnody Collection comprises more than 530 volumes, including Lutheran hymnals in English, German, Norwegian, and Swedish published in the United States and Pennsylvania colony as early as 1786, in Germany between 1726 and 1787, and in Australia since 1936. It also includes first editions from the presses of important early American printers and publishers such as Christopher Sauer, Peter Leibert, and Michael Billmeyer.

Under the auspices of the Center, Schalk recently launched a series of new monographs devoted to important figures in the history of Lutheran hymnody to be published by Lutheran University Press. The first, *Prelude and Fugue on the Life of Harriet Reynolds Krauth Spaeth* by Robert D. Hawkins, recounts the accomplishments of the only woman up to that time to serve as a hymnal editor (*Church Book with Music*, 1872). A study of August Crull by Jon Vieker is

---

[137] Information about the set is found at www.lutheransonline.com/lutheransonline/music.

[138] The statement can be found at alcm.org/about/worship_statement and is available in downloadable leaflet form.

[139] Readers may learn more at cuchicago.edu/about-concordia/center-for-church-music.

forthcoming. Several more are planned, and Schalk is seeking ideas for additional titles.

Schalk has other projects in mind for the Center. One would foster a deeper appreciation of the Church's hymnody by posting on the Center's Web site, each week for a year, a simple four-part setting of a hymn from the Lutheran tradition in tandem with a short devotion focusing on the hymn. The second year would offer a similar format but substitute for the hymn a simple four-part setting for choir from our Lutheran heritage.

On alternate weeks, Schalk continues, the site could feature an opinion piece devoted to some aspect of Church music. Some of these would be unobjectionable, he suggests, while others could "get some hackles to rise." Schalk has already written three of these as samples. "For the one on the extreme end, I described a contemporary service I went to," he recounts. "All the things happened that you'd expect to happen: You have a little combo all miked up, and the congregation isn't singing worth a darn, and the solution of the musicians is to sing louder into the mike. I described all this dispassionately. The result was that nobody sang. The title of the piece is 'The Day the Music Died'—which tells you where my roots are."[140]

Recent efforts by Schalk's former student Barry Bobb to augment the scope and reach of the Center for Church Music are beginning to bear fruit. Under a business plan developed by Bobb and endorsed by Schalk, the family of Richard Hillert, and the university, the Center for Church Music will be a place of research for Church music scholars from around the country and the world. It will also serve as a place of education for practicing church musicians from the LCMS and other denominations, for music leaders from the Chicago area and the Midwest, for young musicians, and for Lutheran pastors and members of the laity who have an interest in Lutheran worship and church music. Those connections will happen through on-site visits, at events, online, and through social media.

Taken in broad perspective, the career of Carl Schalk is singular. He continues to be a vigorous, outspoken, and enthusiastic advocate of worship that is confessional, sacramental, and imbued with principles deeply rooted in the practices and heritage of the Lutheran

[140] Conversation with the author, October 24, 2012. Schalk refers to the lyrics drawn from Don McLean's "American Pie," which is the result of McLean contemplating the death of Buddy Holly.

tradition while remaining one of the most highly respected and well-liked personalities in the wider Lutheran Church. Schalk has a rare ability to articulate positions that may differ significantly from those of others while keeping all parties engaged in conversation. Together with his artistic gifts and his theological insight, this ultimate respect for the intrinsic worth of every individual—born of his abiding concern for humanity in all its delightful dimensions—has created for him an enduring place in the panorama of those throughout history for whom service, the Church, and life are inextricably intertwined.

CHAPTER THREE

One Church, One Book

> Bibles may go unread and catechisms set aside as a regular part of Christian education, but it is the hymnal, it can be argued with some justification, that, encountered on a regular basis Sunday after Sunday, has had the most significant effect on the piety of American Lutherans.[141]

The voice of visionary witness embraces past, present, and future. It testifies to the truths of the present in the awareness of what has come before and in the anticipation of what can be. Schalk the composer cannot be separated from Schalk the historian or Schalk the educator or Schalk the guardian and advocate of that which most deeply defines what it means to be Lutheran.

At the center burns the desire for unity within the Church. As Kirby L. Koriath points out in his book on Schalk's mentor at Concordia Seminary, Walter Buszin, "the hymnal is one of the most visible symbols of the Church and its unity."[142]

It therefore follows that the history of Lutheran hymnals, particularly those in America, has long been a passion of Schalk's. He has written no fewer than six books on the history of hymns and hymnals. Foremost among these is *God's Song in a New Land: Lutheran Hymnals in America*, published in 1995, exemplary in all of church music scholarship in its wealth of original research presented in a readable and engaging style.

---

[141] "Some Thoughts on the Hymnody of *Lutheran Book of Worship*: Context, Issues, Legacy," *Currents in Theology and Mission* (*Essays in Honor of Eugene L. Brand and the Twenty-Fifth Anniversary of the* Lutheran Book of Worship) 30, no. 5 (October, 2003), 366.

[142] Kirby L. Koriath, *Music for the Church: The Life of Walter E. Buszin*. (Fort Wayne, Indiana: Concordia Theological Seminary Press, 2003), 70.

In the preface, Schalk articulates the reason he considers the subject of hymnals to be of indispensable value. Of the three books central to shaping Lutheran piety, Schalk writes—"the Bible, the catechism, and the hymnbook—one might reasonably argue that it is the hymnbook, certainly the most regularly and frequently encountered, that has had the most enduring and lasting influence. It is unquestionably the regular and recurrent use of hymns in worship that has shaped so much of our basic vocabulary of words, phrases, and images that have become part of our individual and collective memory as a Church. Hymns implanted deep in our memory and recalled to mind in the varied situations of the Christian life, are more powerful and influential in our spiritual nurture than we might imagine."[143]

Schalk contends that as a catholic and comprehensive collection of the Church's song, the hymnal is the most cross-cultural *and* countercultural book the Church uses. "It unites us with all Christians," he writes, "and reminds us we are part of a communion of saints long before we were born. In a very real sense, the Church is always countercultural—against culture—and supracultural—in the midst of the world yet above all time and culture."[144]

Schalk shares a long-held dream with Henry Melchior Muhlenberg (1711–87) for a hymnbook that would be shared in common by all American Lutherans. For this reason, it is worth quoting in detail from the preface to the landmark 1786 hymnal Muhlenberg compiled in the effort to unite Lutheran congregations throughout the region.

> We should note what until now has hindered complete unity in connection with singing in our public worship, namely the many kinds of hymnbooks, since in almost every one various little alterations have been made, and in some there are few hymns, in others many. If only there were one hymnbook for all American congregations which would contain the best of the old and new spiritual songs, how much more convenient and harmonious it would be.[145]

---

[143] *God's Song in a New Land*, 14.

[144] "Basic Lutheran Understandings of Music in Worship."

[145] Preface to the *Erbauliche Liedersammlung zum Gottesdienstlichen Gebrauch in den Vereinigten Evangelisch Lutherischen Gemeinen in Nord-America* (Leibert and Billmeyer, 1786). Quoted in *God's Song in a New Land*, 48.

A Proliferation of Hymnals

The tides of history did not usher in Muhlenberg's great hope. Schalk, in his book, tells the stories of thirty hymnals in circulation in America from 1741 and beyond. At the same time, he explains that the succession of hymnbooks represented neither arbitrary initiatives nor aimless innovation. Instead, the changing shape of Lutheran hymnody in America "has been rather the result of the intellectual and religious ferment of each particular age which gave it birth." Each hymnal was accepted "precisely because it was in harmony with its time."[146]

Carl Schalk was entering the mainstream of church music scholarship at precisely the moment that Lutherans in America were attempting to consolidate their hymnody and worship practices into a common book. Schalk was, in fact, a man completely in harmony with his time.

Schalk's longstanding participation on the Hymn Music Committee of the Inter-Lutheran Commission on Worship (ILCW), which produced the *Lutheran Book of Worship*—the hymnal that was conceived in the hope of finally uniting all the major strands of Lutheranism in America—stands as a defining element of his professional career. This holds true both for what he did on its behalf, and for two remarkable examples of what he respectfully declined to do. Of these, one occurred before the *LBW* project got underway and the other took place after it was concluded.

By the early 1960s, the majority of Lutherans in the United States used one of two hymnbooks. The Lutheran Church—Missouri Synod continued to sing from *The Lutheran Hymnal*, published in 1941 and centered on the heritage of Lutheran Reformation hymnody. *Service Book and Hymnal* was published in 1958 by eight bodies, including the American Evangelical Lutheran Church and the American Lutheran Church, and was grounded in the conviction that "hymns should be devotional rather than didactic or homiletical."[147]

In its emphasis on hymns as primarily devotional, Schalk suggests, the planning commission for *Service Book and Hymnal* "departed quite radically from a distinctly Lutheran view of the place of hymnody in the life of the Church."[148] He argues, "If the

---

[146] *God's Song in a New Land*, 18.
[147] *Service Book and Hymnal* (Minneapolis: Augsburg Publishing House, 1958), 286.
[148] *God's Song in a New Land*, 171.

Reformation chorales were anything, they were didactic and homiletical. Moreover, it was precisely the emphasis on literary excellence that had been used by earlier committees to disqualify many of the translations from German, Norwegian, Danish, and Finnish heritages in the late nineteenth and early twentieth-century American Lutheran hymnals."[149]

Movement toward Revision

In the mid-1950s, The Lutheran Church—Missouri Synod began contemplating a unilateral revision of *The Lutheran Hymnal.* However, as a product of the openness toward other Lutherans that blossomed during the ensuing years, resolutions were offered at the 1965 LCMS convention in Dallas to immediately pursue a cooperative venture with other Lutheran bodies that would result in a shared worship book, although work on the revision of *TLH* continued and ultimately culminated in the 1969 publication of *Worship Supplement.*

"I came to River Forest in the summer of 1965," Schalk recalls. "Concordia Publishing House had just published my little monograph *The Roots of Hymnody in the Missouri Synod,*[150] which I had done as an independent study project at the seminary with Carlos Meier. I was literally unpacking boxes in my office when Paul Bunjes, chairman of the music department, came in and said he wanted me to go to the synodical convention to study all the resolutions about the new hymnal."

Paul Bunjes was selected to serve on the CPH Music Committee in 1942 to help "set direction or standards for the department. Manuscripts would be sent to the committee members, who would review them and make a decision as to which should be published."[151]

---

[149] "Some Thoughts on the Hymnody of *Lutheran Book of Worship,*" 368. Schalk estimates that *Common Service Book and Hymnal* (1917) contained only seven highly literate German and Scandinavian hymns and the *Service Book and Hymnal* (1958) only nine, while *The Lutheran Hymnary* (1913) contained twenty-one, the *American Lutheran Hymnal* (1930) had seventeen, and *The Lutheran Hymnal* (1941) had thirty. See *God's Song in a New Land,* Appendix E.

[150] *The Roots of Hymnody in The Lutheran Church–Missouri Synod: The Story of Congregational Song—the Hymnals and the Chorale Books from the Saxon Immigration to the Present.* Church Music Pamphlet Series, Hymnology, Number Two (St. Louis: Concordia Publishing House, 1965).

[151] Clayton A. Peak, *Edward W. Klammer and the Concordia Publishing House Music Department* (M.A. thesis, Northeast Missouri State University, 1993), 28.

During his lengthy tenure on the committee, Bunjes pushed for a revision of *The Lutheran Hymnal.* "I had just had the monograph published," Schalk recounts, "which simply detailed that the hymnody should be true to the doctrine of the Church. But that was interpreted by Paul Bunjes, as I view it—although he never told me—that I would be on the side of the unilateral revision of the hymnal. There were rumblings of doing hymnals with other Lutheran groups, and he probably thought I would be in favor of not doing that.

"So he said, 'We want you to go to the synodical convention and look over all the resolutions, and say whether this is a great idea or not.' It was clear he wanted me to come to the convention to speak *against* working with the other bodies. I said, 'Paul, we just moved. This is just not going to work out.' Anyway, I wouldn't have said what he wanted me to say."[152]

The report from the 1965 LCMS convention titled "Report of the Commission on Worship, Liturgics, and Hymnology" spells out Bunjes' vision: "The members of the commission hope that the revised edition of *The Lutheran Hymnal* as it is presently envisioned will become a major contribution of our church toward the eventual production of one major hymnal for all American Lutheran churches, very possibly within the present century."[153] Bunjes served on the ILCW's Liturgical Music Committee for its first couple of years but then left, Schalk says, largely because of the group's rejection of his elaborate, multivolume proposal for the new hymnal that was essentially the unilateral LCMS plan Bunjes had put together years before.[154]

The resolution was approved, and President Oliver Harms subsequently invited representatives from the other church bodies to a meeting in Chicago in February, 1966. This consultation gathering was attended by twenty-nine delegates representing the ALC, LCA, and LCMS, along with six observers for Wisconsin Evangelical Lutheran Synod (WELS) and the Evangelical Lutheran Synod—Norwegian (ELSN). Out of this consultation emerged the recommendation to organize the Inter-Lutheran Commission on

---

[152] Conversation with the author, September 3, 2012.

[153] "Worship, Liturgics, and Hymnology" (convention proceedings, report of the Commission on Worship, Liturgics, and Hymnology, Detroit, Michigan, 1965), 389.

[154] Document 36, as reproduced in *Heritage in Motion: Readings in the History of The Lutheran Church—Missouri Synod, 1962–1995* (St. Louis: Concordia Publishing House, 1998), 225.

Worship (ILCW), which held its first meeting in Chicago later that year. The structure of the commission provided for three representatives of each body (ALC, LCA, and LCMS) in each of four areas—Liturgical Texts, Hymn Texts, Liturgical Music, and Music for the Hymns.[155] Representing the Missouri Synod in the latter two categories respectively were Paul Bunjes, Richard Hillert, and Carlos Messerli and Jan Bender, Walter Buszin, and Edward Klammer.[156]

Schalk and the Hymn Music Committee

Schalk's call to service on the Hymn Music Committee came in its second year. At the end of 1966, Fred Precht, then executive director of the LCMS Commission on Worship, found himself unable to attend the first joint meeting of the ILCW's Hymn Text Committee and the Hymn Music Committee in Columbus, Ohio. Schalk took his place and the next year was appointed to the Hymn Music Committee, on which he served until the ILCW was disbanded in 1978.

The work of the ILCW proceeded calmly and in focused fashion over the years. It was largely unaffected by the theological tempests buffeting the Missouri Synod, which resulted in the firing of forty-five of the fifty faculty members of Concordia Seminary, St. Louis, in 1974 and the subsequent formation of Concordia Seminary in Exile, known as Seminex. Indeed, the level of cooperation among members of the ILCW remained very high throughout the entire effort.[157]

The Hymn Text Committee and the Hymn Music Committee worked side by side. "In addition to their expertise in language, several of the members of the Hymn Texts Committee were also familiar enough in the area of music to be alert to musical concerns that might be raised in connection with the choice of particular texts," Schalk writes. "Even more important, and certainly new in American Lutheran hymnal-making experience, was that a significant number of the members of the Hymn Music Committee were theologically trained."[158]

---

[155] John Groth, *A Historical Study of the Inter-Lutheran Commission on Worship* (thesis submitted for the Master of Sacred Theology, Trinity Lutheran Seminary, Columbus, Ohio, 1992), 13–14.
[156] Ibid., 17.
[157] Ibid., 267.
[158] "Some Thoughts on the Hymnody of *Lutheran Book of Worship*," 369.

This new experience made for lively give-and-take between the members of the two committees. "What was not anticipated was the genuine collegiality that quickly developed within and between the two groups," Schalk continues. "Decisions regarding various issues before the committee and regarding specific hymns were almost never taken along what might be assumed to be the 'party lines' of the church bodies. Members could and did, often vehemently, disagree. The strengths and weaknesses of conflicting views were frankly and honestly debated, the final result the better for it. It was an example of collegiality at its best."[159]

There was a good deal of broadening of horizons that ensued as different traditions were shared and discussed. "In many instances, treasures of one group were unknown to the others," Schalk notes. "I recall one meeting where heated conversation occurred regarding a particular hymn ("On Our Way Rejoicing"), a hymn unknown to me at that time, though one obviously highly treasured by many others. I am certain that the situation was the same in the case of many of the sixteenth-century chorales. This, then, was part of the context in which the hymn committees were to do their work."[160]

Topics of Discussion

The proper melodic form of the Reformation chorales was a subject of lively discussion. Members of the hymn committee from the LCA and ALC were accustomed to singing chorales in their modernized isometric form, while the chorales in their original rhythmic forms remained a central feature of hymnody in the LCMS. It was ultimately agreed that *LBW* would include twenty-six Reformation-era chorales, most in their historic form. Regardless of the committee members' backgrounds, Schalk points out, "The support for use of the original rhythmic forms of the chorale melodies actually cut across synodical lines and was the overwhelming, although not always the unanimous, choice of the music committee. In some cases (for example, 'A Mighty Fortress Is Our God' or 'Wake, Awake, for Night Is Flying'), the melodies appear in both rhythmic and isometric forms." Indeed, Schalk adds, "The recovery in *LBW* of a significant number of early Reformation chorales together with their original rhythmic melodies, and the official use of the

---

[159] Ibid.

[160] Ibid.

Hymn of the Day, constituted probably the most significant hymnic contributions of *LBW*."[161]

The other signature accomplishment of the Hymn Music Committee was the establishment in *LBW* of the Hymn of the Day as a standard feature of the liturgy of Holy Communion. The complete list, originally compiled by committee chair Ed Klammer of Concordia Publishing House, specifies one hymn to serve in this position each Sunday for all three lectionary cycles during most of the year. Once during Epiphany, once in Lent, and several times during Pentecost, a different hymn is indicated depending on whether the year is A, B, or C.[162]

A topic of considerable discussion among committee members, Schalk recalls, had to do with time signatures. Inclusion of time signatures in pew editions tended to be customary in Lutheran usage until the publication of *Service Book and Hymnal* in 1958. They were not included in the 1969 *Worship Supplement* or in the ILCW's Contemporary Worship series that served as test ground for *LBW*.[163]

"One thing we argued over was that some hymns under consideration were in odd meters. The suggestion was, people won't know how to handle hymns that shift between 5/4 and 4/4, so we should include time signatures. That did not happen." The argument Schalk supported was that "if those changes in meter are designed, as they usually are, to try to match the flow of the text, then the music should be obvious and you don't have to say, 'Watch out for this measure of 5/4!' If the music is written well enough, it will just flow naturally. You don't have to point out how modern this is, with all these changing key signatures. I'm not holding myself up as the perfect example, but I'm at least conscious of that."[164]

The growing instance at the time of hymns that presented this problem, Schalk adds, was due to the trend among hymn writers of taking an existing prose text from Scripture and turning it into strophic form. "That meant you had a lot of lines of unequal lengths,

---

[161] Ibid., 371.

[162] The list appears as Appendix I in *LBW's Manual on the Liturgy* by Carlos R. Messerli and Philip H. Pfatteicher (Minneapolis: Augsburg Fortress, 1979), 109–112.

[163] Neither are time signatures found in pew editions of *With One Voice*, *Lutheran Service Book*, or *Evangelical Lutheran Worship*, but they are used in Augsburg Fortress' *Libro de Liturgia y Cántico* (1998) and *Worship and Praise Songbook* (1999).

[164] Conversation with the author, September 3, 2012.

and you had to change the meter to accommodate those," Schalk explains. "But in doing so, with all the changing meters, it ends up looking complicated." Constantly changing time signatures then amounts to "throwing up barriers for the very people who are going to have to execute this."[165]

Another point of discussion concerned the abundance of standard four-part writing.

"People asked, 'Why does the texture of the hymn accompaniments all have to be four-part?'" Schalk recalls. *Worship Supplement* provided for two different accompaniments in the organist's edition, one of which was often in three parts. And Concordia's old Parish Organist series featured a three-part harmonization at the end of each prelude. "The idea there was, 'You've already got the four-part harmonization in the hymnal, so here it is in three parts.'"

But three-part harmonizations never worked, Schalk says.

"Most churches don't have an organ that could support the congregation singing in three parts. For the most part, it wasn't successful." In *LBW*, there are a few three-part settings, Schalk added, the fourth part of which would be instinctively filled in by the organist.[166] But concerning the three-part settings in *Worship Supplement*, Schalk continued, "it was one of those experiments: 'Let's have a real variety of accompaniments.' I'm not in favor of having them all the same in cookie-cutter fashion. But you learn some things, and one of them is that generally three-part accompaniments don't work. The effect is weaker in three parts."[167]

Completion of *LBW*

By early 1976, the hymn list was complete. In April, *Lutheran Standard* published a list of more than 510 hymns planned for inclusion.[168] ILCW Project Director Eugene Brand has testified to the ecumenical breadth with which the hymn committee approached its task. "Not only did they determine which hymns of the predecessor books had actually been used in the churches," he wrote, "but they

---

[165] Conversation with the author, July 26, 2012.

[166] Examples of three-part harmonizations include *LBW* 66, "Come Rejoicing, Praises Voicing," and *LBW* 217, "We Place upon Your Table, Lord."

[167] Conversation with the author, July 26, 2012.

[168] "Addition of 14 popular hymns to ILCW list recommended," *Lutheran Standard*, April 6, 1976, 20. Referenced in Groth, *A Historical Study*, 209.

gave full weight to a list of hymns compiled by The Consultation on Ecumenical Hymnody. Where new tunes were needed, special preference was given to the American heritage of hymnody. It should go without saying that great care was taken to pass on the classic heritage of Reformation hymnody."[169]

At the final meeting of the entire Inter-Lutheran Commission on Worship in May, 1977, reports from all participating church bodies including LCMS were favorable.[170] Correspondence between ILCW project director Eugene Brand and LCMS president J. A. O. Preus in March and April, however, alludes to Brand's frustration over the apparent lack of forward movement in the review process by the LCMS. In response to a letter from Brand on March 30, Preus addresses Brand's question of "why should it take the LCMS more time than the ALC and LCA to review the Hymnal" and explains that "the Missouri Synod got a late start" because, he said, funds for the testing had not been allocated in a timely manner. Preus adds that "probably the most positive word I can give you is that it would be best to delay action on the hymnal."[171] A letter to Preus in mid-April from the LCMS Commission on Worship refutes his apparent accusation that the *LBW* decision needed to be delayed because congregations hadn't seen the materials. "To say at this late date that the congregations of the Synod have not been exposed to these materials is simply not true."[172]

Indeed, the Commission on Worship had been wholly supportive of the *LBW*. Its report, included in the 1977 LCMS Convention Workbook, praises the long effort and states that "the commission . . . believes that the *LBW* is wholly faithful to Scripture and the Lutheran Confessions. . . . The commission recommends the *Lutheran Book of Worship* to the use of congregations in the Synod with enthusiasm and conviction." That same report directly addressed the accusations that the materials were not widely disseminated ahead of time. "The attackers consistently, openly, and by insinuation have charged the ILCW—and the Synod's own Commission on Worship—with attempting to hide something since they did not publish study documents, position papers, and provisional texts." The Commission

[169] Eugene L. Brand, "The *Lutheran Book of Worship*: Quarter-Century Reckoning." *Currents in Theology and Mission* 30, no. 5 (October, 2003), 330.
[170] Groth, *A Historical Study*, 220.
[171] Ibid., 217–18.
[172] Groth, *A Historical Study*, 219. From April 19, 1977.

on Worship, the document continues, "repeatedly has attempted to provide for at least information output, only to have this portion of its program eliminated year after year for lack of budget funding. . . . The first two ILCW provisional booklets were purchased by the commission and mailed to all pastors of the Synod."[173]

In June, Concordia Publishing House solicited reports from individual LCMS doctrinal reviewers. Two of the reports found several objectionable items. These helped fuel the resolution that was submitted for consideration at the Dallas LCMS convention a few months later to delay consideration of the hymnal "to permit adequate theological review."[174]

Shortly thereafter, Brand reminded all ILCW members that "the recommendation going to the [1977] Dallas Convention of the LCMS calls for delay until the 1979 convention to permit adequate theological review of the materials. This resolution marks the victory of the CTCR [Commission on Theology and Church Relations] recommendation over that of the Commission on Worship. If passed by the convention it would, of course, complicate matters greatly."[175] In July, Brand reported that the new hymnal had been approved by the LCA, ALC, and ELCC.

LCMS Approval Delayed

At its convention that month, the Missouri Synod voted to delay approval.[176] Confusion grew about what this implied. The Minneapolis Tribune published a report in October stating that Concordia Publishing House still planned to publish the new *LBW* despite the LCMS vote. Concordia Publishing House president Ralph Reinke was quoted as saying "I feel we must keep our hand in. It's unclear at this time what the committee is going to do, and what our response should be."[177]

In November, the entire LCMS Commission on Worship resigned in protest. Members who resigned were chairman Paul Foelber, Paul

---

173 Document 37, as reproduced in *Heritage in Motion: Readings in the History of The Lutheran Church—Missouri Synod, 1962–1995* (St. Louis: Concordia Publishing House, 1998), 227–28.

174 Groth, *A Historical Study*, 223.

175 Ibid., 223.

176 Ibid., 224.

177 Lori Sturdevant, "Missouri Synod Publisher Keeps Plans for Hymnal" *Minneapolis Tribune*, October 11, 1977. Quoted in Groth, 226.

Peterson, Henry Abram, Jaroslav Vajda, Carlos Messerli, and Rodney Schrank.[178] A statement attached to the letter of resignation expressed their belief that the repeated delays in the LCMS review process were deliberate and noted that there had been no objection throughout the entire process until a few months before the Dallas convention.[179] According to the *Lutheran Witness*, their statement articulated the belief that "the question of fellowship rather than alleged doctrinal error is the real reason for delaying approval of the book."[180]

An LCMS special hymn review committee, which had been formed in September, 1977, responded that objections to the book were indeed doctrinal in nature. These involved word and phrase changes in the three creeds, including a dozen in the Nicene Creed alone which "are not merely new translations," committee chair Robert Sauer wrote, "but changes which actually remove, add, or substitute words from the centuries-old text of the creeds." Objections were voiced as well to language in the rites of marriage, burial, and baptism "which have no support in Scripture," and to hymns including "At the Cross, Her Station Keeping" (*LBW* 110), in which the committee "found the Virgin Mary described as sharing Christ's suffering in a manner not compatible with Lutheran theology."[181]

In *God's Song in a New Land*, Schalk suggests that politics and other factors "may have influenced the discussion of the two hymnals, but the Missouri Synod was more concerned about a 'doctrinal reorientation' that seemed to pervade the *LBW*, often the result of omissions, for example, removing well-known hymns—especially deleting specific stanzas or changing phrases—that emphasized the redemption." He adds that details may be found in the LCMS convention workbooks for the 52nd and 53rd Regular Convention.[182]

LBW was published on schedule in 1978, but without The Lutheran Church—Missouri Synod represented on the title page, although the carefully worded note was included that the book was "prepared by the churches participating in the Inter-Lutheran Commission on Worship," including the LCMS. A report released in May, 1978, by the special hymnal review committee convened by the

---

[178] Groth, *A Historical Study*, 226–27.
[179] Ibid., 227.
[180] "Committee Completing Study of New Hymnal" *Lutheran Witness* 22 (December 18, 1977): 518. Quoted in Groth, 228.
[181] From the same article in *Lutheran Witness*, quoted in Groth, 228–229.
[182] *God's Song in a New Land*, note 81.

LCMS recommended that the LCMS make its own edition of *LBW*, including alterations to the liturgical section and changing or omitting some fifty hymns. In a resolution approved by the 1979 convention in St. Louis, the revised book was to be called *Lutheran Worship* and was eventually published in 1982 with Fred Precht (who was serving as secretary for the Commission on Worship) as general editor and Paul Bunjes as music editor.

All this led Carl Schalk to the brink of an unexpected call from the church.

"All through that decade [during the work of the ILCW], there was almost no negative news about *LBW* from within Missouri," Schalk remembers. "It wasn't until the last two or three years before the 1979 convention they started building up the argument (against *LBW*). You started to see articles in *Christian News*[183] and elsewhere."[184] Similarly, the LCMS blue-ribbon committee convened after the 1977 convention to study the proposed book served mainly to stir up uncertainty, Schalk suggests. "They raised questions mostly in the hymn section. But the questions were all like, 'In hymn number 27, there is a phrase that reads: . . . What does that really mean?' And they wouldn't answer, but the implication was that there was something wrong. So they were raising doubt. They did that repeatedly and ended up with a whole bill of particulars: 'There are serious questions about lots of things, so we need our own revision.' That became *Lutheran Worship*, and the only real difference is that the cover is blue."[185]

To try to soothe the wounds over Missouri's rejection of *LBW*, students in the master of church music program at Concordia held a surprise banquet for Schalk and Hillert. "They knew we had been up to our necks in *LBW*," Schalk remembers. "Gloria Hillert called and said, 'The four of us are going out for dinner.' So we go to this restaurant; she was in on this and Noël was too. It turned out to be a big banquet honoring us with a lot of students in the master's program and recent graduates. They were basically saying, 'We're sorry this happened, and we're behind you.' It was very nice."[186]

---

[183] *Christian News* is a newsletter self-published and widely distributed by Herman Otten.
[184] Conversation with the author, September 3, 2012.
[185] Ibid.
[186] Ibid.

Unwilling to Preside Over the Demise of *LBW*

But for Schalk, that was not the end of the story.

"So all this is happening, *LBW* is published in 1978, and the Missouri Synod Commission on Worship, which was a really qualified commission, they were just furious about the whole thing," he relates. "All but maybe one or two resigned. At the same time, Fred Precht was leaving the position of Executive Director of Worship of The Lutheran Church—Missouri Synod.

"So the commission resigns and they call a new executive director. And the new person they called was . . . *me*! This was during the interim; Synod hadn't yet passed their resolution to adopt or not. That was going to happen the following summer. So I get this call. They had to know I wasn't about to accept. But it was sort of their protest. So I did all the things you were supposed to do with a call: The first thing, if you are on the faculty, is that you meet with the college president and tell him you have a call. So I went in to meet with Paul Zimmerman, and of course he knew about it by then. I told him I had this call, and with any call, you always want to prayerfully consider it."

Among other things, Schalk asked Zimmerman was what his duties would be as executive director of the Commission on Worship.

"One of the things the handbook says is that the executive director generally oversees worship in Synod colleges and seminaries. It doesn't really mean anything; you're not going to go into colleges and tell them what to do, other than in a general, grandfatherly way. So because that's one of the duties listed in the handbook, and because you always have to go according to the handbook since it's a legalistic document, I said, 'How would you feel about that, if I were to have general supervision over the spiritual life of the community?' I know that the role of the college president is to guide the spiritual life of the college, and I knew full well he wouldn't want *me* doing that. Well, we were all kind of just playing games."

Schalk wrote to the Synod to acknowledge that he had received the call and requested a meeting with President Preus as well as with what remained of the Commission on Worship.

"I was immediately informed this wasn't going to happen, but I was told I could meet with one of the vice presidents. So I met at Concordia Seminary with Robert Sauer. We sat down in the dining hall there; as I was talking, it was clear to me that he couldn't have cared less about this interview. He was completely uninvolved.

"So I wrote back my answer after a 'decent interval,' as they say, and thanked them for extending this call to me and said I was very sorry that for whatever reason I was unable to meet with the president of the Synod."

Schalk carefully crafted one particular sentence in that letter. "The line that I wrote was, 'I am returning this call because I am unwilling to preside over the demise of the *Lutheran Book of Worship* in the Missouri Synod.' Because that would have been my job."[187]

Indeed, soon after Schalk submitted the letter, it was sent to *Missouri in Perspective*, a newsletter published by ELIM (Evangelical Lutherans in Mission, a liberal caucus within the Missouri Synod). "It was a big story: 'Schalk Won't Preside Over Hymnal Demise.'[188] I knew full well that it would somehow get out, and I wrote that line with that in mind," he says with a smile. "So I was *persona non grata* with the president after that."

The Development of *Lutheran Worship*

As a colleague of Paul Bunjes at Concordia Teachers College, Schalk was able to witness at close range the musical decisions that went into creating what became the blue hymnal, *Lutheran Worship*.

Following passage of the resolution not to accept *LBW*, Schalk recalls, the pressure was on for the Missouri Synod to get its revision out. The LCMS part-ownership of the *LBW* copyright allowed the Synod to include materials from that volume.

"So who does the Missouri Synod turn to, to get this thing out, and fast? They turn to the guy who had the plan in 1965 to do this (a major hymnal revision) in the first place, Paul Bunjes, whose ideas were rejected by the ILCW.[189] He had been lying low, and now his chance has come. He was all too ready and willing to pop back in there and correct all the musical things which he thought should have been better, or different."

---

[187] Conversation with the author, September 3, 2012.

[188] *Missouri in Perspective* (January 16, 1978): 3.

[189] Conversation with the author, July 8, 2013. Bunjes eventually resigned from the ILCW when it was clear his elaborate plan for a multivolume revision of *TLH*, including separate editions for organist and choir, was not going to be adopted by the pan-Lutheran group.

Bunjes secured a half-year sabbatical from Concordia to focus on the hymnal. The tension in the department was palpable. "His office and Dick Hillert's office were either next to each other or one door away," Schalk says. "They had been close personal friends: Bunjes had hired Dick Hillert; they were colleagues; they were godparents to each other's children. Now, Bunjes has agreed to be the musical editor of this, which is basically saying, 'The musical job of *LBW* was deficient in significant ways, and I'm going to fix that.' So this didn't help the atmosphere. There was a 'deep gulf fixed,' as the King James would say."[190]

Bunjes drew on the "Bunjes–Schalk" liturgy from Wausau for what became Divine Service I, but editing the hymns was a formidable assignment.

"Now there was the problem of harmonizing the hymns," Schalk explains. "He decides he had to redo many of the harmonizations (from *LBW*). This is a huge undertaking. Because this is a big job, he wants to enlist his friends. He asked me; he asked Dick Hillert. He couldn't see the disconnect. He asked Jan Bender, who wrote back and said, 'No, thank you, I could not betray my friends.'"

Bunjes was therefore faced with doing the bulk of it himself. An excellent theory teacher with many outstanding students, he tried enlisting some of those who had recently graduated from the master's program. But the arrangement broke down, Schalk says, because Bunjes corrected their submissions without consulting them; one of the former students, Richard Gieseke, even began copyrighting his harmonizations. As a result, Bunjes still had more than 150 hymns to account for. Thus were born the two *noms de plume*, George Leonard and Wilhelm Quampen, who are dutifully indexed in *LW* as having arranged a number of hymn settings.

"It would look unseemly to have 166 numbers behind your name in the index," Schalk says with a laugh. "So that's why he invented those two names. The joke of it was, when they were preparing the handbook for *Lutheran Worship* in the early 1990s, one of the fact checkers spent a day and a half trying to find information about this

---

[190] Conversation with the author, September 3, 2012. "And beside all this, between us and you there is a great gulf fixed," Abraham says to the rich man (Luke 16:26).

Wilhelm Quampen. When he found out it was made up, he was furious."[191]

Criticism of *Lutheran Worship*

Ironically, it was Bunjes' harmonizations that were the focus of much of the criticism of *Lutheran Worship* when it was published in 1982. "There was a lot of turmoil when *Lutheran Worship* came out," Schalk recalls. "On the one hand, many people were just mad because Missouri didn't accept *LBW*, so they weren't prepared to like anything else that came out. Then was another group that simply couldn't stand Bunjes' harmonizations. They were all quirky."

Bunjes' approach, Schalk explains, dates back to the Missouri Synod's landmark 1969 *Worship Supplement*. "The pew edition had only melody words, but the organ book had the accompaniments. One was a straightforward harmonization, and the second was a 'different' harmonization that was useful if you had six stanzas and wanted to use something different for one. What Bunjes did in *LW* is make the second kind of harmonization the main one." As a result, many hymns begin on a chord other than the tonic in root position. "You can do this if it's stanza 4 and the congregation is in the swing of it," Schalk says. "But for the whole hymn, that just irked people."[192]

Lutheran Worship was never widely accepted, and by 1999 was used by only slightly more than half of LCMS congregations.[193] "I haven't seen the numbers," Schalk says, "but every time you got together with anyone who had it, they were grumbling about it. So some congregations bought *LW*, some bought *LBW*, and many kept

---

[191] Dr. Mark Bangert of the Lutheran Theological Seminary at Chicago and his brother, the late Rev. Martin Bangert, collaborated to create detailed tongue-in-cheek biographies of Leonard and Quampen, which are still making the rounds in some circles.

[192] An example is "All People That on Earth Do Dwell," *LW* 435, harmonized by "George Leonard," which begins on a first-inversion chord. This may be compared to the root-position harmonization of the opening of the hymn in *LBW* 245. Another example is found at the beginning of "What God Ordains Is Always Good," *LW* 422, harmonized by Paul Bunjes. Instead of an upbeat and first-measure downbeat both using the tonic in root position as in *The Lutheran Hymnal* 521, the upbeat in *LW* uses a first-inversion dominant which moves to the relative minor on the downbeat.

[193] Concordia Publishing House and Commission on Worship; The *1999 Worship Survey* indicates only 58.2 percent of LCMS congregation used *LW* on a regular basis.

The Lutheran Hymnal, in essence saying, 'A plague on both your houses!'"

Trends Since *Lutheran Book of Worship*

The concept of the Hymn of the Day was integral to the publication of *Lutheran Book of Worship*. However, Schalk has noted the tendency to provide an increasing number of choices for the Hymn of the Day. (See chapter 1.) The *Indexes for Worship Planning* (1996), geared to *LBW*, and the 1995 supplement *With One Voice* provide two or three choices for each Sunday in all three-year cycles. *Indexes to Evangelical Lutheran Worship* (Augsburg Fortress, 2007) provides between three and six suggested Hymns of the Day. This dilutes Schalk's thesis of "the Hymn of the Day as the Word sung, in close juxtaposition to the Word heard in the lessons, preached in the sermon, and confessed in the Creed" and makes more difficult an "appreciation of the true significance of this important musical component in the liturgy."[194]

From Schalk's perspective, signs emerging from the twentieth century's midpoint were full of hope. "By the middle of the twentieth century, American Lutheranism was coming close to realizing Muhlenberg's dream as the great majority of Lutherans worked together on one hymnal that could be used by all Lutherans in America," he writes. Political and theological currents were to prove otherwise, however. As the century drew to a close, "the achievement of that vision seemed to elude them."[195]

Christians, however, are people of hope. Schalk remains convinced that Muhlenberg's vision of "one Church, one book" is alive and well while acknowledging that "the particular shape it may take in the years ahead is no longer quite as clear as it was once thought to be."[196]

One Hope, but Two Books

It is unlikely that the publication of two major denominational hymnals in 2006, *Lutheran Service Book* (*LSB*) for The Lutheran Church—Missouri Synod and *Evangelical Lutheran Worship* (*ELW*) for the Evangelical Lutheran Church in America, has brought this

---

[194] *The Hymn of the Day* (St. Louis: Concordia Publishing House, 1983), 16.
[195] *God's Song in a New Land*, 18.
[196] Ibid.

vision any closer to fruition. The chasm between the two denominations widened as well when the LCMS made significant changes to the Revised Common Lectionary used by many Protestant denominations, including the ELCA.[197]

For its part, *Evangelical Lutheran Worship* draws heavily on global hymnody and contemporary song. "A growing awareness of the interrelatedness of the world, coupled with new understandings of the world's diverse cultures, has had implications . . . for the Church as the one body of Christ throughout the world," its editors state.[198] In contrast, *Lutheran Service Book* represents "a careful blending of *The Lutheran Hymnal* and *Lutheran Worship*"[199] and focuses more sharply on the Lutheran heritage of Word and song while incorporating recent work from prominent LCMS hymn writers such as Stephen Starke. While the book is doctrinally pure, to Schalk's mind, the choice of hymns in some instances reflects a lack of theological subtlety.

"There is one hymn (of Schalk's) which is in *ELW* but not in *LSB*," he says. "That is 'God of the Sparrow.'[200] I know why that is, although it's not a good reason. It's typical: They think it's not explicit enough. 'God of the sparrow, God of the whale'—the first stanza is good creation from the smallest to the largest. The second stanza deals with creation in its more ominous, threatening aspects—'God of the earthquake, God of the storm.' Stanza 3 is central: 'God of the rainbow, God of the cross, God of the empty tomb.' How much more explicit can you be other than saying, 'Jesus was raised on the third day?' So I think that is an unjust criticism."[201]

Schalk objects to the inclusion of so much Hispanic and African American hymnody in *ELW* as well as changes in language from that in *LBW* that are intended to avoid the use of gender-specific

---

[197] Changes were intended to accommodate passages excluded by the RCL which Missouri leaders considered important. These include Eph. 5:22–33; Rom. 13:1–7; 1 Cor. 10:16–17; 11:27–32; Gal. 2:11–14; 6:1–6; Phil. 4:10–20; Heb. 12:4–13; 1 John 4:1–6; and Luke 13:22–30. Many Old Testament readings and psalms are different from the RCL as well, although the Gospel readings are usually the same. See lcms.org/page.aspx?pid=448.

[198] Introduction, *Evangelical Lutheran Worship* (Minneapolis: Augsburg Fortress, 2006), 7.

[199] Introduction, *Lutheran Service Book* (St. Louis: Concordia Publishing House, 2006), ix.

[200] This hymn is a Vajda/Schalk collaboration and appears as *ELW* 740.

[201] Conversation with the author, September 3, 2012.

pronouns. "People are not thinking male, paternal," Schalk contends, arguing the issue from the congregation's perspective. "They're thinking, 'I learned it that way,' and it irks them to have it changed unless there is a compelling theological reason, although of course [the hymnal editors] think there is a compelling theological reason."[202]

He also takes vigorous issue with attempts by the ELCA since publication of its new hymnal to discourage use of *LBW*—indeed, to banish it altogether from places of common worship. Schalk vividly recalls an article in the ELCA resource newspaper *Seeds of the Parish*, which reads in part:

> Because the ELCA is encouraging all congregations to acquire and use the new hymnal it would not be helpful to donate your copies of the *Lutheran Book of Worship* to struggling congregations. Nor should you pack them up and send them to missions overseas. If you want to help under-funded ELCA congregations, purchase and donate the new hymnals. This would truly be a Godsend for many churches that are finding it tough to make ends meet these days. Likewise, what better way to support the various missions of the ELCA than to help defray the cost of the new hymnals? That way they can allot more of their precious resources to helping others and proclaiming the gospel of Christ.[203]

"This is probably good marketing advice," Schalk says, "but morally, I don't know how they can say this. I understand that your song is partly what you hope the Church will become. But to dump all that African American hymnody, some of which I have theological problems with, on a bunch of Norwegian bachelor farmers, is missing the point. The idea that white Anglo-Saxon Lutheran congregations should be singing spirituals because they are part of the wider Church, I understand that argument. But what I would like to see is for them to equally push that Hispanic and African American congregations should also be learning 'What God Ordains Is Always Good.'[204] But they say, 'No, that's not our kind of music.'"[205]

---

[202] Ibid.
[203] *Seeds for the Parish* 20, no. 1 (January–February, 2007): 2.
[204] *LSB* 760; in *LBW* 446, the title is "Whatever God Ordains Is Right"; in *ELW* 776, it is "What God Ordains Is Good Indeed."
[205] Conversation with the author, September 3, 2012.

One Church. One book. One hope? We read in Ephesians 4:5, "There is one body, and one Spirit, just as you were called to the one hope of your calling." For Carl Schalk, this one hope is centered in the embrace of the historical identity that has been the strength and substance of Lutheran hymnody since the earliest days of the Reformation.

"Building on the basis of an historical perspective rooted in the Lutheran tradition, and of a knowledge of where it has been and how it got there, Lutheran hymnody in America can build on its impressive accomplishments, avoid the repetition of past mistakes, and move toward the future, solidly grounded in the spirit and the content of Lutheranism's beginnings in the sixteenth century," he writes. "Only in this way will the completeness of Muhlenberg's vision—whatever shape it may take in the years ahead—become a reality. Only in this way will Lutheranism in America find its way beyond the mere appearance of a common hymnody to one that captures both the spirit and the substance of Lutheranism's unique contribution to the Church's song."[206]

[206] *God's Song in a New Land*, 19.

CHAPTER FOUR

The Practice of Church Music

> Wherever and whenever God's people have gathered to hear his Word and celebrate the sacraments they have sung songs, songs of death and rebirth, songs of sin and salvation, songs of repentance, renewal, and new life. In Christian song words and music join together to rehearse the story of God's deliverance and to proclaim his Word to all the world.[207]

Church music, Carl Schalk never tires of saying, is both proclamation and ministry. The call of the church musician is to enable music to faithfully reflect "in its own terms the honesty, integrity, truthfulness, and winsomeness of the Gospel message."[208]

Key to this faithfulness is the understanding that music is not an object of beauty, reverence, or awe to be admired as it is performed and then cast aside. Rather, music reveals new truths about God's Word in just the same way as does a sermon. "Music in the Church can never be seen simply as part of the wrapping," Schalk asserts. "It is part of the unwrapping, an unwrapping that either contributes to or detracts from a faithful proclamation and witness."[209]

Integral to that witness is the embrace of the understandings that enabled Lutheran worship and church music to achieve such a rich history. With this in mind, he advocates "a parish practice that is both faithful to Lutheran traditions and, in returning to Lutheranism's roots, help to realize a more vital worship practice in our parishes."[210]

Schalk makes the most of every opportunity to address the centrality of corporate worship in our lives as Christians.

---

[207] *God's Song in a New Land*, 13.
[208] *Luther on Music*, 51.
[209] Ibid.
[210] *A Handbook of Church Music*, 13.

> Corporate worship is the fundamental, indispensable, and central work of the gathered community—that glowing center from which all other aspects of the Church's life arise. I see the grounding in tradition as critical and we must rely on the tradition of the church through the ages rather than in the ingenuity, cleverness, or the resourcefulness of creative church leaders. . . . Our challenge as church musicians is to take the traditional rites and employ them with richness and variety of their tradition. The problem is not a lack of new resources. It's that we are not mining the tradition enough.[211]

In addition to *what* is done, Schalk urges musicians to pay attention to the *way* it is done. It is not enough to replicate the traditions; musicians, charged with their various responsibilities, must bring them to life. Schalk affirms that the congregation is the chief musical instrument in corporate worship. The cantor is the conservator, the "hander-on," of tradition, as well as the one who moves the tradition forward. Schalk was head of the group that wrote the text for the Association of Lutheran Church Musicians' original "Role of the Cantor" poster, below, which has since been released in revised form.[212]

[211] "Basic Lutheran Understandings of Music in Worship."
[212] The revised "Role of the Cantor" is available from the Association of Lutheran Church Musicians. alcm.org.

When Christ's people, the baptized,
gather for worship
they receive God's love
in word and sacrament,
and through the gift of music,
praise, pray, proclaim, and recount
the story of God's grace in song.

THE ROLE OF THE CANTOR

The cantor--
the historical
term among
Lutherans--
is the leader
of the
people's song.

The cantor
is responsible
for leading the
musical expression
of the
people--
the assembly,
choral
groups,
solo singers,
and
instrumentalists,
among whom organists
have been especially
important
for
Lutherans.

The cantor uses
whatever musical resources
are available,
using them
in a manner appropriate
to the talents
of those serving
and the needs
of the people who are served.

The cantor leads
the earthly assembly
in a foretaste of
John's vision of the heavenly assembly
in which all creatures give
praise, honor, glory, and power
to the Lamb.

The cantor's work
is a worthy service to God,
God's people,
and the world.

It is a high and holy calling.

The organist is charged primarily with the unique art of accompanying the congregation. Although the role of the organ in Lutheran worship has been greatly expanded since the Reformation to include preludes, postludes, and anthem accompaniments, it is good to keep in mind that the organist's chief role in liturgical worship "is that of serving the gathered assembly as it sings its liturgy." In this way the organ, like the assembly, becomes the "living voice of the Gospel."[213]

The choir supports the congregation and sings the assigned parts of liturgy, including psalm, verse, and offertory, in addition to attendant music, that which attends upon or serves the liturgy. This includes "the entire spectrum of motets, anthems, Passions [and] cantatas," which should not only be chosen thoughtfully for the appropriate Sunday, festival, or season, but which also should give priority to the traditional Lutheran practice of *sub communione*, music sung or played during the distribution of Holy Communion.[214]

"In the Lutheran tradition the choir functions liturgically as helper and servant of the gathered assembly," Schalk affirms, "assisting, enlivening, and enriching the worship of the entire congregation. Without the leadership of the choir, the liturgies and hymns are often sung indifferently, in a manner lacking vitality, and without enthusiasm. Where a choir is present and effectively leading in worship, congregational singing is usually more confident, assured, vital, and vigorous." He adds that regular rehearsal time devoted to practicing both the liturgies and hymns is indispensable.[215]

The Role of the Choir in Liturgical Worship

One of the principles of what Lutherans believe about music, ratified at the ALCM biennial conference in 2003 in a series of statements spearheaded by Schalk, is that "Lutheran worship stands unashamedly in the liturgical tradition." Within that tradition, the role of the choir is critical.

"In the Lutheran tradition of worship the choir functions liturgically as a helper and servant to the congregation," Schalk asserts, "enlivening and enriching the worship of the entire assembly."[216] Neither the *Lutheran Book of Worship*, *Lutheran Service Book*, nor *Evangelical Lutheran Worship*[217] make any prescription for the singing of a stand-alone choral number during the

---

213 "Music and Liturgy: The Lutheran Tradition," 256–57.
214 Ibid., 255.
215 Ibid., 252.
216 *A Handbook of Church Music*, 19.
217 *ELW* does allow that as the offering is taken and the table is set, "assembly song or other music may accompany or follow the gathering of the offering," and it refers users to options in the liturgical music section of the hymnal.

service. This stands in contrast to the widespread practice today in which the choir's main involvement consists of providing an anthem as "special music," usually during the offering or between the appointed readings.

It is a battle, however, that the Lutheran tradition still seems to be losing.

"This whole business of the anthem," Schalk says, shaking his head. "I remember vividly when *LBW* came out and every choir director asked, 'But where shall we sing the anthem?' because there *is* no rubric, 'Here shall be sung the anthem.' So, after giving them the smart answer—'maybe we shouldn't be singing all these many anthems'—I would always say that the traditional Lutheran position for 'special' music, which I call 'attendant' music, music which attends to the liturgy, is during Holy Communion. You don't stop the whole liturgy and do a big anthem. Then, the pastor says, 'And now we will continue our worship,' which essentially means the worship was interrupted."[218]

It's not that many musicians don't know what the proper role of the choir is in Lutheran worship, Schalk says; it's just hard to follow through. "Many pay lip service to the idea that the choir's basic job is to assist the congregation in the singing of liturgy and hymns. We say yes, absolutely, that is what a choir is for. But when we plan our services, we end up spending most of our time on some big anthem, because we don't know it. Then at the end, if we have five minutes, we'll run through a hymn or two. In practice, we invert what we ought to be doing."

The problem is compounded, Schalk argues, because church musicians are receiving little reinforcement from publishers about what music the choir should be doing in Lutheran worship.

"In general, we aren't getting any help from the publishing houses in choral music," Schalk says. "There is little or nothing from our tradition. Most denominational publishing houses have a mission statement that is something like, 'Our purpose is to provide materials to our churches so they can properly do this and that.' But pretty soon, you have a broadening of that mission: 'Well, there are other Lutherans besides the ones we represent . . . and there are other Christians . . . and there are broader markets . . .' Imagine a series of concentric circles which gets wider and wider. As you move into the

---

[218] Conversation with the author, September 2, 2012.

outer circles, you ask, 'What will be appealing to the Missouri Synod? to all Lutherans? to other Christians?' The farther out you go, the more watered down it will get. Pretty soon, you are gearing your purpose not to what you should be doing but to selling music to Methodists and Episcopalians. From a marketing point of view, that makes perfect sense."[219]

This puts musicians in great need of new liturgical resources and makes it more important than ever to teach well how choir rehearsal time should be allocated. The rehearsal strategy in many parishes, Schalk believes, is to focus most of the time on the anthem. Rehearsing hymnody and music for the liturgy, including psalmody, is "what you do if you have time left over after you work on the anthem."[220]

A major obstacle to a greater interest in music for the liturgy, Schalk points out, is that anthems are mostly what denominational publishing houses now produce. This genre "is not designed for Lutheran services, and in many ways is antithetical to the kind of thing you ought to be doing in a Lutheran service," he says. So when that repertory is all that is presented at church music workshops, "it is understandable when people say, 'Well, I guess this is what we're supposed to be doing.'"[221]

As an illustration, Schalk recalls an all-day church music workshop he offered with Paul Bouman some years ago at Concordia University, Ann Arbor. "For the last session, we asked people to bring fifty copies of something you have found to be very useful in your church and we will have a reading session using those. Well, we got in the car afterward and shook our heads: Everything we'd said during the workshop had been destroyed by the music that they brought. That was the music they felt their choirs really liked." There had been no effort on those musicians' parts, in the course of their parish work, "to say 'we need to help people experience things that they haven't experienced and learn to love them.'"[222]

This doesn't mean Schalk is not sympathetic to the typical music director's way of thinking.

---

[219] Ibid.
[220] Ibid.
[221] Ibid.
[222] Ibid., July 26, 2012.

"I understand that mindset because I had it myself," he admits. "When I got out of college, I wanted to replicate all the things I did with the college choir. That's probably the wrong thing to do, because most of the literature sung by college choirs—even good choirs—is not what you need to be singing in church on Sunday. There's no reason you need to be singing 'Beautiful Savior' in eight parts with your church choir. That's not where your first attention should be."

He reminds musicians to keep three things in mind. "The role of the choir is to assist the congregation to sing the liturgy and hymns. Secondly, you sing music pieces which are attendant to the liturgy—introits, graduals, psalmody, gospel acclamations. Thirdly, you sing attendant music—pieces which are attendant to the liturgy, not big pieces that you sang in your college choir. Everyone has that experience of doing [the latter] to some extent; I know, because I did it. But now I *know* that I did it and that I shouldn't have done it!"[223]

To those who would complain that such a body of work might not be "exciting" enough—after all, most attendant music lacks the "six flags over Jesus endings" about which Schalk likes to good-naturedly scoff—he has a solid rejoinder.

"We think we need to get people excited about what we are doing. One of the ways you do that, the thinking goes, is by picking up the tempo. Or we choose music with good syncopation that you think will appeal to kids. But what (church musicians) need to be doing is learning a basic repertory. Paul Bouman taught 'Lord, Thee I Love' to the congregation at Grace Church. They can sing it in their sleep, and he taught it to all the kids as well. The choir 'pieces' are the last things you should worry about. Every choir wants to sing pieces! I understand that. But they have to be weaned into understanding that it's just one of the many things we do and that it's not the first thing."[224]

Schalk learned well under Bouman's tutelage in his many years at Grace as music associate. "Paul understood that all the time I worked with him," Schalk says. "We were forty minutes into the rehearsal, and someone would ask, 'When are we going to get going on the big piece for Sunday?' He would reply, 'Well, we have six things connected with the liturgy we need to do. We'll work on the anthem,

---

[223] Ibid., October 24, 2012.
[224] Ibid.

if we get to it.' And now in most parishes, no one thinks twice about that. Focusing on the anthem is just what they do."[225]

For those who might think liturgical music is not arresting enough to compel the interest of choir or congregation, Schalk has a clear remedy: "Do what you do well, and if you do it well enough, others will be attracted to that."[226]

The Fourfold Pattern of Worship

Schalk is also troubled by a recent trend toward a fourfold pattern of worship—Gathering, Word, Meal, Sending—which serves as the standard order of service in many congregations, so much so that some apparently assume it represents the recovery of an ancient Latin rite.[227]

As far as Schalk knows, these designations have no basis in Lutheran historical tradition. "We always have had a 'gathering' hymn, but it wasn't called that," he points out. "Lutheran tradition gave pride of place for that first hymn as a 'hymn of invocation of the Holy Ghost.' To Luther, it was the Holy Spirit who calls, gathers and enlightens, as He does the whole Christian Church. So you don't have to make a big deal about 'Now we're gathering to worship.'"

Schalk also takes to task the designation itself. "To call the first hymn a 'gathering' hymn makes it sound like a revival situation. 'There's a Meetin' Here Tonight' is a gathering song which says, 'Let's all get together.'" Therefore, he adds, "'O Holy Spirit, Enter In' (*LBW* 459) is much better than 'Gather Us In' (*ELW* 532)."[228]

Schalk has similar concern about the notion of the way the fourfold pattern concludes. "The dismissal, 'Go in peace, serve the Lord'[229]—that's what we do when we go out," he says. "That sends us forth into the world." What is commonly designated as a "sending" hymn, he contends, often ends up being a general hymn that lacks the exhortation of the dismissal.

"Is it sinful to have a 'Gathering' song and a 'Sending' song?" he asks. "No. But the trouble is, suddenly Gathering and Sending are of

---

225 Conversation with the author, July 26, 2012.
226 Ibid., September 3, 2012.
227 A quick search on the Internet will provide many examples of congregations and organizations that support this understanding of the structure of the liturgy.
228 Conversation with the author, July 26, 2012.
229 *Lutheran Book of Worship*, 117.

equal importance with Word and Meal. What you call things is important—words are important."[230]

Richness of the Rites of the Church

"Lutherans have sought stability within the traditions of worship," Schalk says. "But the rites of the church, when used in their richness and fullness, provide interest and richness and variety. Because we have not always taken advantage of this potential, we are accused of being dull. Therefore we need to employ them with the richness and variety of their tradition. Then they are enriching, satisfying, engaging and nourishing."[231]

Chorales provide a fine avenue for opening before worshipers the richness and variety of historical Lutheran practice. Far from sounding dull or old-fashioned, these proclamatory hymns "should be winsomely introduced so that congregations may welcome them into their tradition," Schalk urges.[232] Many dancelike chorales benefit from being sung faster than they are often heard, while those derived from Renaissance dances often gain greater life and definition, paradoxically, in *slower* tempos than one often experiences. "When you hear recordings of Praetorius dance tunes, they are very sprightly," Schalk explains. "But that doesn't mean we should sing them that fast. Sometimes, they're done at tempos faster than the congregation can bear. True, they shouldn't be dull, slow, and dirgelike, but they need to have the proper rhythmic space." Schalk the conductor makes a familiar point: "The effect of any kind of syncopation is enhanced the slower you do it—up to a point."[233]

Gospel Motets

Another musical genre with a strong liturgical purpose in Lutheran worship, to which Schalk is committed, is the Gospel motet. The authoritative source for the history of the genre is none other than Schalk's *Key Words in Church Music*, in which Carlos Messerli authors the entry.[234] Messerli explains that these polyphonic settings of texts from the Gospels of Matthew, Mark, Luke, and John assigned

[230] Conversations with the author, July 26 and October 24, 2012.

[231] "Basic Lutheran Understandings of Music in Worship."

[232] Ibid.

[233] Conversation with the author, September 2, 2012.

[234] *Key Words in Church Music*, revised and enlarged edition (St. Louis: Concordia Publishing House, 2004), 273–76.

for specific Sundays in the liturgical year flourished in Protestant Germany in the sixteenth and seventeenth centuries, first as individual works and later as a series of Gospel motet cycles.[235] The intent then, as now, is that they be used during or in place of reading the Gospel to provide a deeper window into the meaning and drama of the text. Messerli notes that Gospel motet cycles created for use in Protestant worship through the end of the seventeenth century included more than nine hundred individual settings, or an average of sixty motets in each collection. The apex of the genre in that era was the *Geistliche Chormusik* of 1648 by Heinrich Schütz.

Schalk recently completed a set of thirty-five Gospel motets to celebrate the 100th anniversary of Grace Lutheran Church. (See chapter 9 for a discussion of this collection.) He admits there is scant awareness of the genre today.

"CPH published some Gospel motets by Jan Bender,[236] and they didn't sell well," Schalk reflects. "Also, some by [Gerhard] Krapf and Hillert—same result. Hardly anybody bought them because they didn't know what they were for. So the publishers say, 'Our experience with that is not good, so we are skeptical about our involvement.'"

Grace Church's 100th anniversary in 2004 involved many projects dedicated to that milestone, including a building addition. As his contribution to the centenary, Schalk offered to do three things: (1) to write a short history of music at Grace, focusing on its organ and organists; (2) to do an adult education presentation; and (3) to write a series of Gospel motets. Schalk completed the set of fifty early in 2012, pared it down to thirty-five, and presented a copy to Cantor Michael D. Costello.

"If you ask where I might send them, I can tell you that nobody is interested in publishing thirty-five Gospel motets," Schalk acknowledges. "The history of Gospel motets has been a disaster from a publishing point of view." He suggests, however, that they could be marketed by releasing them in groups of four to six, each bundled according to liturgical season so purchasers could buy only those in which they were interested. Once they can be experienced periodically, people will gain greater familiarity with this inventive

---

235 Ibid., 275.

236 Jan Bender's Opus 32 lists twenty-seven Gospel motets, published by CPH between 1963 and 1984.

genre and will be more open to other ways in which liturgical worship can be life-giving.

"Ideally what should occur is that a congregation should become so accustomed to the idea of a Gospel motet interrupting the readings, or repeated after the reading, that it is no longer novelty," Schalk says. "And that can only happen if they are used more than infrequently."[237]

Carols

Carl Schalk has long had an uncommon interest in the genre of the carol. In addition to many he has composed and continues to write, some of which have drawn from him the most inspired music he has yet written, he compiled and edited *The Concordia Book of American Carols*.[238] Schalk drew its delightfully varied contents from early New England psalmody; shaped-note music; nineteenth-century American carols; those from Canada, the African American, and Hispanic traditions; and newer carols from the twentieth century.

As employed in that volume, Schalk writes in its preface, the term *carol* "is meant to include a broad sweep of material in which the textual content is essentially strophic in form, and narrative, contemplative, dramatic, or celebrative in spirit." He adds, "It is unfortunate that the uniquely American contributions to the carol literature have sometimes been overlooked or ignored. This may reflect the fact that much of our interest in and celebration of Christmas—including the carol itself—has been so strongly influenced by the nineteenth-century revival of the Christmas celebration in England. At its best, however, both texts and the music of the American carol reflect a unique perspective and a genius distinct to its American origins."[239]

We have Schalk to thank, therefore, for adding significantly to the body of American carols. Pressed on the difference between a hymn and a carol, Schalk explains that it largely derives from the text. "In general, a carol can be a lot looser in content," he says, "such as the 'The Cherry Tree Carol,' You say, where is that in the Bible? There is a freedom to do things in the text that you might not do in a hymn. In

---

[237] Conversation with the author, July 26, 2012.

[238] *The Concordia Book of American Carols* (St. Louis: Concordia Publishing House, 1996). The volume is dedicated to Schalk's three children, Jan Marie, Rebecca Lee, and Timothy Scott.

[239] Ibid., 5–6.

a hymn, the content should be more proclamatory, it should stick to proclaiming the Gospel in the broadest sense."[240]

Steward of the Mysteries

Carl Schalk's unwavering legacy to the Church encompasses a deep grasp of the ministerial purpose of the musician's vocation. Among the titles one might bestow, such as cantor, music director, and minister of music, Schalk suggests one with Biblical overtones—that of "steward."[241] He cites the common usage of a steward as "one called to exercise responsible care over possessions entrusted to him." Understanding that "the work of the church musician is a 'calling,' a ministry," he notes that musicians are therefore "personally accountable—accountable, that is, first to the one who has given us this great gift of music. Such 'responsible care' includes both the conservation and the development of the gift."[242]

The church musician is a responsible steward of the mysteries of faith, Schalk writes, when that person models four essential understandings about his or her vocation.

First, the musician understands that the Church—before it is anything else—is a worshiping community.

Second, the musician understands that the music in corporate worship is a vehicle for the common praise and prayer of the entire worshiping body. "In a very practical sense, music is the glue that helps hold together the action of the liturgy, that gives it more discernible shape and form, and that projects in a unique way its varying moods and emphases." Sagely, Schalk testifies to the way in which music can bind or separate members of that body. "Music is a uniting force when it helps the Christian community focus its attention where it belongs—on Christ and what he has done for us. Music becomes a dividing force when its focus is on lesser or secondary concerns—on musicians as performers or on the congregation as a group to be entertained or manipulated."

Third, the musician understands that music in the Lutheran tradition finds its most comfortable home in the liturgy. "It is in the

---

[240] Conversation with the author, December 4, 2012.

[241] "This is how one should regard us," writes the apostle Paul in 1 Corinthians 4:1 (ESV), "as servants of Christ and stewards of the mysteries of God."

[242] "The Church Musician as Steward of the Mysteries," 59–66. Schalk adds that the emphasis with a given individual is usually on conservation *or* development of the gift of music, not both.

liturgy in all its richness and fullness that God's people can best express their common worship and praise. For Luther, certainly, and for Lutherans at their best, music in worship is liturgical song. The church musician understands that it is the liturgy—that living tradition of praise, proclamation and prayer and mutual edification—that disciplines our use of music and best determines how it is used in worship and for special occasions."

Fourth, the church musician understands "that God is praised and people are edified when the Word is proclaimed through texts, which speak the Gospel clearly and distinctly, and through music, which in its honesty, integrity and craftsmanship, reflects that same Gospel. . . . The truly great songs of the church share traits that make them simultaneously uncommon and truly popular: texts that speak of the heart of our faith, and music that reflects the character of faith in its simplicity, directness, suitability to its function, and in its careful craftsmanship."[243]

The Composer as an Agent of Renewal

Schalk's grasp of the musician's vocation is grounded in the concept of a practice that is constantly being renewed and revitalized. Lutherans receive their heritage of worship forms and practices with thanksgiving and appreciation, he stresses, yet they do not accept it uncritically. Lutherans also "see their heritage as a basis for moving toward the future. Thus Lutheran worship is simultaneously conservative and open to the future."[244]

Over the course of his career, Schalk has vigorously encouraged and supported the work of living composers, supporting those who respond to the story of salvation "with the best of their musical and poetic gifts."[245] If past experience is any indication, he suggests, "the treasury of the Church's song will continue to build on the song which has nourished God's people through the centuries, all the while incorporating new songs reflecting the gifts of God's people of each new age."[246]

Because worship is a living tradition, the nature of the hymnody of each new age cannot be easily predicted.

---

[243] "The Church Musician as Steward of the Mysteries," 61–64.
[244] *A Handbook of Church Music*, 14.
[245] *Praising God in Song*, 7.
[246] Ibid., 53.

"What is the new song everybody asks—and there is no answer. Nobody knows . . . . There are no answers and no standard forms. The answers and standards come *after* the song. What all this means is that the church musician—particularly the church musician in the small parish—is free. . . . Because God made him free. . . . God has simply said to us, 'Sing to Me. The words and music are up to you.' What a glorious freedom! And also, what a frightening freedom! For it is not easy to be free. We would much rather be right.

"But, easy or hard, risky or not, it is in this freedom that our opportunity lies. Here, and particularly in the small parish, we have the opportunity to start fresh and to fashion a music in worship which can rise anew out of the shared Christian faith and life of the people who love the Lord."[247]

The Composer's Craft

In Schalk's view, the music of the Church must reflect the qualities of the very Gospel it proclaims. This embodies Luther's own understanding of music as a gift and creation of God. "To speak about music as craft means to be concerned with its fitness *as music* for the purpose for which it was intended, its suitability *as music* for its function, its 'well-madeness' *as music*. For the church to be concerned about the craftsmanship of music it uses in its praise and prayer is a direct reflection of its care in the use of this great and good gift of God."[248]

He dismisses those who claim they require "artistic inspiration" in order to create and who seek beauty as the highest quality. Aside from the fact that any two people may not agree on what constitutes beauty, "such a view stresses the *effect* rather than the *rightness of the thing made*. If music is indeed God's good creation and gift to people, then to proclaim the Gospel in music that reflects cheapness, superficiality, banality, shoddiness and—perhaps worst of all—pretentiousness is to contradict in our art the truth, honesty, and integrity of the Gospel itself."[249]

In parishes both large and small, the calling for those who compose music is a high one.

---

[247] "The Opportunities for Music in the Small Parish," *Church Music* 68.2, 38.
[248] *Luther on Music*, 51.
[249] Ibid., 52.

"The task of the musician who is a Christian is to be faithful to both the content of the communication and the integrity of his art," Schalk writes. "He guards the content by being faithful to the Word. And he guards his work by letting it reflect the honesty, simplicity, and integrity of the Word—whether his chords are built in thirds or fourths."[250]

What should those who write music for the Church bring to their task? Paramount in Schalk's view is the integrity of heart, mind, and spirit that can come only from the Gospel itself. "For Lutherans, the substance of what is proclaimed is intimately connected with the way it is proclaimed. The honesty and integrity of the Gospel itself must be matched to the honesty and integrity of the craftsmanship of the musical vehicle to which it is united. Music cannot be just a sincere expression of an individual statement."[251]

The flip side of this is an awareness of "the dangers and pitfalls to which all of us who write music for the church are susceptible. The lack of attention to the study of one's craft, the striving for the easy effect, the subtle notion that piety can somehow substitute for competence, or that cleverness and flair can replace mastery and skill—all these are very real temptations for young and old composers for the church."[252] One must also guard against using music to promote an individual's point of view. "When liturgy and hymnody are used as opportunities to advance personal agendas, everyone suffers."[253]

Craft is essential as well. "It is not enough, I believe, to simply want to write music for the Church," Schalk suggests. "Many have that desire, but, unfortunately, no ability at the craft of music. For that, good training in theory and counterpoint is necessary, not simply to replicate the music of another time, but also to develop the discipline of writing itself, however the music turns out to sound. Good part writing and voice leading are essential, no matter what kind of music one writes."[254]

Schalk's prerequisites for the church composer can be gathered into a series of basic points:

---

[250] *Lutheran Hour Music News* 2, no. 4 (April, 1961): 6.
[251] "Basic Lutheran Understandings of Music in Worship."
[252] "The Church Musician as Steward of the Mysteries," 65.
[253] "Basic Lutheran Understandings of Music in Worship."
[254] Conversation with the author, July 26, 2012.

- The composer should have a solid grounding of the craft of musical composition in all its technical, theoretical, and formal aspects.
- The composer should be aware of the uniqueness of the congregation as a singing group. "Some things it does well, musically, and other things it does less well. The composer needs to remember (and congregations and pastors need to be reminded) that a hymn tune intended for congregational singing should never be a simplistic, undistinguished melody whose only purpose is functional. Nor is congregational song . . . best approached and understood as either art song or as choral music. A congregation is neither a soloist nor choir in disguise."[255]
- The composer should be part of a regular hymn-singing community. This will help them develop a sense of "what is possible, practical, of how far the boundaries can be stretched before they break, and what should probably be avoided." Common pitfalls include "trite rhythms, colorless melodic patterns, lackluster harmonic progressions," none of which are able to "stimulate, ennoble, and excite congregations into great singing." Good tunes, on the other hand, are those that wear well with age.[256]
- Composers are well advised to study the great hymn tunes of the Church with special attention to form, cadence, word emphasis, melodic high points, and harmonic settings that strengthen or weaken the melodic line.[257]

The Danger of Contemporary Styles

Schalk has regularly identified and commented on trends in church music during the remarkable flowering of modern hymnody over the past half century. His stance moderates over the years from openness to a variety of styles to sharp criticism when he did not perceive that proclamation of the Gospel was being served.

---

[255] "Some Thoughts on the Writing of Hymn Tunes," *CrossAccent*, no. 7 (January, 1996): 8.

[256] "Approaches to Hymn Tune Writing," *The Hymn* 35, no. 2 (April, 1984): 86–93.

[257] "Some Thoughts on the Writing of Hymn Tunes," 8.

Early in his time as editor of the *Lutheran Hour Music News*, Schalk encouraged the Church to be more open toward a variety of contemporary styles and voices.

"One of the very real dangers in an overemphasis of the role of the Christian heritage," he wrote in a 1960 editorial, "is that confronted by the giants of the past, the contemporary poet or musician is either frightened into silence, convinced that he can contribute no valid additional insight, or else that he is content to imitate the form of what has gone before, usually losing the spirit that moved that form into being."[258]

A few months later, Schalk wrote, speaking for church musicians, that "to shut ourselves off from serious consideration of new contexts, new forms, new approaches to the music of the church is to continue the peculiar musical inbreeding which has tended to stifle new creative efforts in the church in its use of music to reach out with the message of the Gospel. To shut ourselves off from such considerations is to lay ourselves open to the danger that in 'defending the faith' we do no more than maintain the Establishment."[259]

At the same time, he urged that the same standards of integrity must be applied within these other forms and approaches. "Where what we find is distorted, sentimental, or offensive, let us not hesitate to reject. Where we find what is good, let us not hesitate to take to ourselves the valid musical expressions of other Christians that our musical witness may more truly become what it ought to be . . . a reflection to the world of the song of the Christian faith throughout the world."[260]

He had little patience for self-serving efforts steeped in sentimentality. He considered that music for the Church, which is geared only toward the emotions or which strives mainly for effect, "is quite far removed from the message of the New Testament" and risks losing "the Biblical concern for faithfulness." Above all, it enables us to "forget that the most perfect communication of the Gospel (by Christ himself) was still a stumbling block and foolishness without the work of the Spirit." Efforts of this kind, he wrote impatiently, frequently reach people "with words and music which

---

[258] *Lutheran Hour Music News* 1, no. 5 (May 12, 1960): 6.

[259] *Lutheran Hour Music News* 2, no. 1 (September 16, 1960): 6.

[260] *Lutheran Hour Music News* 1, no. 3 (January 14, 1960): 6.

only serve to reinforce distortions of the Christian gospel, the very gospel it pretends to present."[261]

Some of his most withering criticism was directed at "schmaltz," which he dismissed as "a detour—a detour which prevents us from facing up to the basic Christian facts of life and death. A detour from both the Word and the work of art. A detour which reduces Christian anxiety to a diminished seventh chord and the joy of the Christian life to a waltz in a major key. A detour which divorces the musician from his work by insisting that the music—whether simple or complex—is unimportant as long as the words are 'right.' Denying the Christian musician the right to carry into his work the honesty and integrity of his faith, it forgets that Christ is Lord over all, and that no work can be called Christian unless it is first of all a good work."[262]

In a blistering 1975 editorial in the journal *Church Music*, Schalk openly denounced the "romance with relevancy," which had infiltrated church music over the preceding decade.[263] That was, he wrote, "a period of disposable hymns and whimsically contrived liturgies; a time of collections like 'Hymns Hot and Carols Cool,' stream-of-consciousness devotional pamphlets, and books designed to tear apart" and "a time when many Protestant and Catholic church musicians feared for their jobs in the face of an invasion of guitar-playing, bass-plucking, tambourine-banging enthusiasts."[264]

In retrospect, he continued, "it seems quite clear that the church never really took its romance with relevancy to heart. Not that it was uninterested in being truly relevant. What turned it off was the slowly dawning realization that relevance was not to be found in the slickly merchandised packages of pop liturgies and jazz masses. To be perfectly honest, the church was rarely confronted with the real thing. Instead, in all but a few instances, watered-down imitations (both textual and musical) were offered as panaceas for the problems of the Church's worship."[265]

---

[261] *Lutheran Hour Music News* 2, no. 4 (April, 1961): 6.
[262] Ibid.
[263] "The Search for a Usable Tradition of Church Music," *Church Music* 75.1, 2.
[264] Ibid. Elsewhere, he wrote that the 1960s was "a period of largely undisciplined and often bizarre experimentation throughout American Christianity generally." "Lutheran Hymnody in America: Problems and Possibilities," *Church Music* 76.1, 19.
[265] "The Search for a Usable Tradition of Church Music," *Church Music* 75.1, 2.

Because this music carried its own "seeds of decay," few of the offending items found their way into mainstream denominational resources. Nonetheless, the listing of these "seeds of decay" serves today as a useful yardstick for our evaluation of the worthiness of new resources. Foremost among these trends of which to beware is the emphasis on individualistic and subjective approach to the music of worship that centered on a solo singer or a performing group, which in turn led to a greater passivity on the part of the congregation; an overabundance of texts and settings "that, while they were different, were at best mundane and mediocre"; and a general "carelessness and insensitivity in the handling of both words and music."[266]

By the late 1980s, Schalk's concern had heightened over the impact of work that was poorly conceived and crafted.

"Much of the music heard in churches today," he wrote in 1988, "can be characterized by the banal melody, the trite rhythm, the treacly harmony, and a striving for the easy effect. Such basic dishonesty, lack of integrity, and contempt for craftsmanship in dealing with the materials of music, often overlaid with a patina of superficial attractiveness, does a disservice to the Gospel in which service such music pretends to be."[267]

Psalmody

At Grace Church, Schalk and Bouman developed a tradition of psalm singing that they considered authentically Lutheran and that accorded the highest respect to the psalm itself.

"I felt what we did was right. It wasn't the only way, but it's the better way. That was to have the congregation sing the verses and, if there was a refrain, to let the choir do that. This way, the people were singing the actual words of the psalms."[268]

The practice Schalk developed with Bouman and continued with Bouman's successor at Grace, John Folkening,[269] was to compose a

---

[266] Ibid., 2.

[267] *Luther on Music: Paradigms of Praise*, 52.

[268] Conversation with the author, September 3, 2012.

[269] Folkening was also the first graduate of the Master of Church Music program that Schalk helped start at Concordia Teachers College. Schalk's friends and former students still treasure a spot-on parody of a typical Schalk anthem that Folkening concocted titled "How!?" With words and music ostensibly composed by "Harvy

short antiphon for four-part choir and to have the congregation sing the verses using a Gregorian-style psalm tone—all unaccompanied.[270] That practice persists at Grace today under Cantor Michael D. Costello. "The congregation has never sung the psalms accompanied," Schalk says proudly, except for a month or two under an interim organist. "They've never experienced that, unless the kids are singing the antiphon, in which case they need a little accompaniment." This stands in contrast to the widespread use today of the responsorial psalm, in which a soloist (or the choir) sings the verses and the congregation responds with a short refrain. Although the practice dates from ancient times, it vaulted into general use, Schalk theorizes, with the Vatican II reforms when the worshiping body suddenly was commanded by the pope to sing. "They had no repertoire, they didn't know what this idea of singing was," Schalk says. "So the congregation was given a little snippet of song to sing a couple of times." For Lutherans who are accustomed to singing all the verses of a psalm, however, it is a retrenchment to sing only the refrain. "All that people get is one phrase repeated a few times," Schalk laments. It is doubly unfortunate, he added, that many psalmody resources promote this habit. "No one does this out of mean spirit; they just say, 'it seems like what everybody is doing. So we'll go along with it.'"[271]

Music in the Smaller Parish

Encouragingly, for the vast majority of working church musicians, Schalk has always been convinced that the most

---

Foonman," it is to be played "with great sincerity" and notes that "instrumental parts will be available if sales are good enough."

[270] Given the practice of psalmody supported by Schalk and standardized in the *Lutheran Book of Worship*, which is centered on the congregational use of ten psalm tones, it is interesting to note that a decade before the publication of *LBW*, Schalk discouraged the embrace of any one style of psalmody. "Basic to any consideration of congregational involvement in singing the Psalms is the need to actively encourage and support experiments with the formation of new musical systems to carry the textual forms of the Psalter available to us today," he wrote in 1969. "The very danger in the mere presence of any overarching musical system of psalmodic material is that, in its very comprehensiveness, it tends to inhibit further thought or development." While being an expression of the church's unity, the development of a single musical system for singing the psalms also "tends to negate that stimulating variety which is an equally essential characteristic of the church." *Church Music* 69.1, 43.

[271] Conversation with the author, September 3, 2012.

exhilarating opportunities for music ministry reside in modestly-sized congregations, great though the struggles may be in those situations.

"Making music in the smaller parish can be one of the more exciting, challenging, and simultaneously frustrating and discouraging experiences of the church musician's life," Schalk observed more than three decades ago. "Typical frustrations are easy to enumerate: resources perceived to be less than adequate, small or nonexistent budgets, modest musical resources, largely volunteer leadership. Easily intimidated by the 'successful' church music program of the larger parish down the block, many smaller parishes too easily give up in the face of such 'competition.' Rather than building on their unique strengths and shaping a church music program based on those strengths, they content themselves with the fact that they are, after all, 'only a small parish.'"[272]

Whatever one's situation, Schalk cautions music directors against preparing larger works that make week-to-week worship duties seem less consequential. Those often become the focus of the choir season, overshadowing the importance of the church at worship.[273]

"What you ought to be doing is concentrating on writing music for the forces that you have available," Schalk advises. From a publishing point of view, concentrating on writing music for one's specific context "may not always ensure that you get published, because sometimes your forces are peculiar to your situation," but he still encourages the creation of music to meet specific needs of an individual congregation.[274]

To mine the great potential for worship in the smaller parish requires great creativity and resourcefulness on the part of the musician.

"It is relatively easy to make music where the resources are great," he writes. "Smaller parishes with more limited possibilities need a particular measure of enlightened and ingenious musical leadership. But it is within reach where the vision of what might be is present."[275]

Tools that can be used to help get started include taking a detailed inventory of available musical talent within the congregation;

---

[272] "Getting More for Less," *The Christian Ministry* 13, no, 4 (July, 1982): 20–23.
[273] Conversation with the author, September 2, 2012.
[274] Ibid., July 26, 2012.
[275] "Getting More for Less," 20.

scrutinizing past bulletins to discern the core hymnody of the congregation with an eye toward gradually broadening it; and mining the hymnal for new liturgical or worship materials. An understanding of the true role of the choir in Lutheran worship relieves the director from having to prepare a steady stream of anthems and frees the choir to function more effectively as a body that serves a leadership role in the worship service. Where attendant music is needed, the director may investigate the serviceable body of music for unison or two-part choir both from the Lutheran heritage and the present day.

For the organist too, the smaller parish means less pressure and a greater invitation to be creative.

"Organists, perhaps more than any other church musicians, need to see that less is more," Schalk writes. "Living in a culture in which we are bombarded with music at every turn, we increasingly hear but no longer listen. Organists—like everyone else who lead in worship—should function only where there is a clear and appropriate need. To clear the service of the sometimes oppressive and continuous presence of the organ will not only relieve the organist of an unnecessary responsibility; it will help focus on the proper function of the organ in worship: to introduce and accompany the congregation's singing with sensitivity and effectiveness."[276]

This means less pressure in terms of technique as well as repertory.

"Where the primary function of the organist is seen as assisting the congregational singing of the liturgy and hymns, organists will be drawn back to basics: correct and rhythmic playing, appropriate introductions to hymns, and playing which focuses attention where it belongs—on the corporate singing of the people, not on the virtuosity of the player."[277]

Today, Schalk continues to steer musicians away from the concept of the big anthem and emphasizes opportunities in the small parish.

"Every choir director asks: 'What's new that we need to know about?' The answer is: 'You just need to know the old stuff—because you don't know it!' A lack of available resources: This is a perfect description of a small parish. You've got eight singers, maybe, and you're lucky if you have a high school trumpeter who can play a

---

[276] Ibid., 22.
[277] Ibid.

descant on Easter. What that ought to do, if you care about it and you really think about it, it forces you back to say: 'What are the essential things?' And not to say, 'But with our eight singers and our organist who can barely play the hymns, we want to do Handel's "Hallelujah Chorus."' So then you do the big P.A. thing, play a recorded sound track and sing along. That is exactly what you *don't* want to do.

"But the fewer resources you have, the more you are forced to ask: 'What am I really about as a church musician?' And what you're really about is teaching the congregation the liturgy and the basic repertoire of hymns. When you are introducing a new hymn, if you have the choir there and they've learned it in rehearsal and they really know it, then they can lead the congregation vigorously."

This invests the church musician with the new responsibilities of "teaching and learning that broadens the horizons of the church's music for all involved." Not only does this avoid allowing the congregation to endlessly sing what it already knows, but it also deepens the spirituality of worship.

"Church music as a participatory medium does not aim simply to give people something to do," Schalk emphasizes. "It means involving them in more faithful and effective *singing of the liturgy*, thus expanding their understanding and participation in the total prayer life of the Church."[278]

[278] *Luther on Music: Paradigms of Praise*, 54.

CHAPTER FIVE

Under the Discipline of the Liturgy

> At its root, the church's tradition refers to what the church essentially is and does—a community that baptizes, proclaims the Word, celebrates the meal. In a broader context it can include other aspects which assist and support these essentials. From the very beginning, the church's song has been closely allied with what the church is and does.[279]

The world knows Carl Schalk primarily through his music. In evaluating the entirety of his service to the Church, however, one discerns that the qualities that define his compositional voice find their origin not only in the craft of the great masters of Reformation hymnody and their forbears but in the very precepts that define the music of the Reformation.

"Lutheranism's genius—based on Luther's understanding of music as gift of God to be used for the praise of God and the proclamation of the Gospel—that understanding made possible the combination of the most sophisticated art music of the day with popular congregational song," Schalk affirms. "And at the heart of that combination was the Lutheran chorale, those sturdy texts and strong, vigorous, rhythmic melodies which sang their way into the hearts and minds of Lutherans everywhere."[280]

Schalk's music is direct and engaging, accessible yet artful, deeply felt yet never sentimental. It supports the texts and draws from

---

[279] "Worship: Through Alice's Looking-Glass," *First Person Singular* (St. Louis: MorningStar Music Publishers, 1998), 93.

[280] Excerpt recorded for *Celebrating the Musical Heritage of the Lutheran Church*, CD-ROM and five-disc set produced in 2002 by Thrivent Financial for Lutherans. One may hear the excerpt at www.lutheransonline.com/lutheransonline/music/16/index.html.

them new dimensions of expression in a way that always proclaims and never overwhelms.

Offering one of the highest compliments available for those engaged in the weekly practice of sacred choral music, Evangeline Rimbach, Schalk's longtime colleague at Concordia Teachers College (now Concordia University Chicago), praises Schalk's music as "easily singable. Carl was not trying to do anything difficult," she says. "He wanted the little parish choir to be able to sing most of his music. It was always very lyrical and always singable."[281]

Above all, his music serves not the composer's ego but rather the needs of the Church in worship. As noted earlier, Schalk calls the process of this realignment "placing oneself under the discipline of the liturgy." It requires from the musician the practice of "radical simplicity."[282]

What defines music of "radical simplicity," then, which is created under the discipline of the liturgy?

Above all, it reflects a clear sense of purpose. Returning to Schalk's analogy that music is part of the "unwrapping" of the Gospel rather than a component of the "wrapping" of the service, music created under the discipline of the liturgy draws the worshiper more deeply into the intersection of time and eternity that is the locus of our life in worship. As the words of the liturgy proclaim the story of salvation and as the service itself leads us from confession and forgiveness to the Word read and proclaimed and the Eucharist received and celebrated, so music mediates the living God in a way that is unique to each individual. Too much glamour and the words become irrelevant; too much austerity and the presence of Christ is dulled.

There may be those who claim the latter is sometimes the case in Schalk's music. This is where thoughtful musical leadership is critical. Each of Schalk's works is carefully gauged to proclaim the Good News of salvation using the combination of line, harmony, and texture that Schalk deems most appropriate to the text at hand. When this proclamation is found wanting in the context of a service, chances are that the piece was played either too fast (as is often the case with "Thine the Amen"), too slow ("Now the Silence," which can assume a dirgelike quality when it is used during communion

---

[281] Evangeline Rimbach, conversation with the author, December 19, 2012.

[282] See chapter 1.

instead of the processional tempo most appropriate for this entrance hymn), or that central characteristics of line and shape were left untended.

Composing Is Hard Work

"Whoever said it had it right when they said it's 1 percent inspiration and 99 percent perspiration," Schalk says. "I view writing music as a craft, a craft that you work at. Whatever your craft, you work at it to improve it—playing golf or whatever. You don't sit there waiting for a blinding flash of inspiration."[283]

So how does an aspiring composer improve his or her craft? As with any skill, practice is the key.

"The more you do it, the more you learn. Jan Bender pretty much did this: write ten measures before breakfast every day. It's like exercising; you practice it. You don't expect a great pianist to rely on inspiration, although hopefully that's in there somewhere! But it builds on the craft that you nurtured by all those exercises."

Another key, Schalk suggests, is to be authentic. "I have never set out to write something strikingly contemporary," he admits. "I don't know what that means. What you want is a good melody. If you don't have a good melody, you don't have anything."

Schalk identifies two qualities that, in his estimation, make a good melody: shape and character. Both, he says, are determined by the text.

In terms of shape, Schalk emphasizes that a melody must have a form that coincides as closely as possible with the form of its text. From this, one comes to understand that the long, arching lines that remain a hallmark of Schalk's style emerge not of their own accord but in response to the kind of texts he likes to work with.

"I once heard A. R. Kretzmann, who was then the pastor at St. Luke's in Chicago, deliver a paper. I don't remember the topic, but he quoted this hymn from *The English Hymnal* from 1906. What it had was *long* lines, four lines of fourteen syllables each: "Behold the bridegroom cometh in the middle of the night." It ended, "But woe to that dull virgin whom the bridegroom shall surprise, with lamp untrimmed, unburning, and with slumber in her eyes."[284] These big

---

[283] Conversation with the author, September 3, 2012.

[284] "Behold the Bridegroom cometh in the middle of the night, / and blest is he whose loins are girt, whose lamp is burning bright; / but woe to that dull servant, whom the

soaring lines! I've always been partial to long lines. Because when you have those, you've got room to develop a good melody."

In beginning work on a new hymn, Schalk dedicates plenty of time to becoming familiar with the text. "My practice in setting a hymn text is that I take the first line and commit the first line or the whole first stanza to memory," he says. "I mull that around in my head for several days or a week and try to figure out what melody would reflect that line and would work with those words. I might sit at the piano and work out some tentative harmony."

Once he establishes the first line and possibly its harmonization, he then tries to discern the character of the new tune. "Should it be slow moving, more quickly moving? Is it a barn-burner or a quiet and more meditative text? I try to work from there. Let's say it has four lines. I'll sketch out a melody for the whole thing knowing it's probably not the way it's going to end up. I sort of know the general harmony that might go with it; I'll write out a bass line."

The next step is important—making sure the tune works with the accentuation of the text.

"I work with that first stanza of text to make sure the accents are right," he says. "What you don't want to have is unaccented syllables on either of the strong beats of the measure or on high points. In 'Thine the Amen' the high point is raised at the penultimate measure. You wouldn't want that to come any sooner: 'only THEE only Thee!' If you do it in poor way, with unaccented syllables on a high point, if anyone has any sensibility at all, people singing it will notice that. If it all falls properly, it just seems right."

There is always the danger, familiar to any composer, that music thought to be original is inadvertently borrowed from pre-existing tunes lodged in the subconscious mind. "I've never had the experience before of realizing that 'this is the same as another melody,'" Schalk says. But in working recently on a setting of a newly written text, something about his tune was bothering him, he said. Suddenly, he realized the first half of the melody was "pretty much a steal" from "Like the Murmur of the Dove's Song" (BRIDEGROOM, by Peter Cutts), necessitating a significant rewrite.

Master shall surprise / with lamp untrimmed, unburning, and with slumber in his eyes." It is contained in many hymnals from that era, including the Norwegian Evangelical Lutheran Synod's *The Lutheran Hymnary* (1913).

Gauging the hymn tune for use by the singing assembly is a tricky business as well. "You have to think in terms of congregations singing these," he points out. "That imposes certain musical limitations—range, for example. You have to work within whatever you think is possible. On the other hand, most congregations are capable of doing musical things which they think are beyond them. That is not a license to do crazy things, but it does mean that maybe you can stretch them a little beyond what is comfortable."[285]

Getting the hymn tune to the point where it feels exactly right is hard work. "You can write a tune, and people like it. They say, 'Look how nice that is, and it isn't hard to do.' It may look easy, but what they don't know is that you've gone through ten versions before and dismissed them. Paul Bunjes used to say that the worth of a piece is directly in proportion to the amount of paper in the wastebasket."[286]

The Importance of Self-Criticism

Self-criticism is a tool Schalk considers vital to the conscientious composer's trade and one he often finds lacking in aspiring composers. "I certainly don't think of myself as a great composer who has reached all these heights. But one of the things I've learned is the art of self-criticism. I haven't mastered it yet, but I do know that you have to be very self-critical of what you do. I constantly tinker with a melody if there is something that doesn't feel or sound right. You either can fix it, or at some point, you have to let it go. But I don't let it go very easily. If there's something about it I don't like, I'll try to fix it in some way or other. That's something that a lot of younger composers don't have: As objective as you can be, self-critical—how do you do that? You've got to just say, 'I think I can find a better way to do what I want to do, and this is not it.' Others just say, 'Well, I wrote this; let's just throw it against the wall and see if it sticks.' I don't like to do that."

He suggests a process for others that he has found to be helpful, which encourages this quality of self-criticism.

"When I have a hymn text and harmonization that is where I want it to be at a given time, I'll put it away for a week and try to forget about it," he says. "Then, I'll come back to it, play it though; at that point, it's clearer what doesn't work or what does work. It's a

---

[285] Conversation with the author, September 3, 2012.

[286] Ibid.

perspective in which I try to forget what I did. It's just like writing. If you're writing an article and get to a certain point, you think it's pretty good. If you come back after a day or two and read it fresh, you can see what is missing or what it needs."[287]

Working with Hymn Writers

If Schalk is collaborating with a hymn writer with whom he is comfortable, and finds that his tune doesn't quite fit the text, he may request slight alterations.

"If I'm working with an author and I know them well enough, I may ask if they can readjust it so they don't have odd accents," he says. "The guy who was most ready to do that was Herb Brokering. He would tell me, 'If you can think of another way to word it, just go ahead.'"

Jaroslav Vajda, the other hymn writer with whom Schalk frequently collaborated, was just the opposite. "It wasn't that he said 'Don't change a word I've written,'" Schalk notes. "But he had thought through his texts so well that he answered all the questions you could raise and fixed them even before you raised them. He had solved the problem before it became a problem."

In any collaborative process, there are variables that can't always be controlled, and occasionally, projects crop up that Schalk can see are likely to never be well received no matter what he does. Recently, for example, he undertook another carol project concentrating on the slaughter of the innocents. "There is not a big market" for settings of that story, he admits. The same is likely to be true of another commission that he received for the celebration of an ordination anniversary. "The text is by a legitimate British writer," Schalk says, "but the first line was 'Thankless for favors from on high.'[288] I thought, 'That is a downer!' With that title, I know it is going to just fly off the shelf."[289]

---

[287] Ibid., September 2, 2012.

[288] By William Cowper, the opening stanza reads, "Thankless for favors from on high, / Man thinks he fades too soon: / Though 'tis his privilege to die, / Would he improve the boon."

[289] Conversation with the author, December 4, 2012.

What Makes for a Good Hymn Tune?

Schalk resists calls to provide a formula for writing a good hymn tune. Instead, he prefers to identify certain areas with which the conscientious composer should be concerned.

Most importantly, an effective hymn tune should be written with "liturgically grounded congregational song" in mind. He emphasizes that one must bring to the task "the understanding that congregational song possesses a distinct uniqueness which sets it apart from all other musical writing."[290] Among these is the realization that the music will be sung "by largely untrained singers who do not ordinarily rehearse, but who long to sing their faith in songs that are theologically rich, challenging, and musically satisfying."[291]

This may be one of the most difficult assignments facing the composer in any genre. If the hymn tune is too simple-minded—"a simplistic, undistinguished melody whose only purpose is functional"[292]—the singing body will lose interest. If it's too complex, they will lose their place. A congregation, Schalk cautions, "is neither a soloist nor a choir in disguise, a soloist or choir which unfortunately happens to sing rather poorly most of the time." Hymn tunes that strive to emulate the complexity of art music risk losing sight of the purpose of hymn singing. "If our basic musical commitment is simply to 'personal self-expression'," Schalk reflects, "it will ultimately prove a commitment untrue to the goal of true congregational song."[293]

The greatness of a hymn tune does not depend on a wide tessitura. Schalk points to HAMBURG as one that sports a restricted melodic range (that of a fourth) and is also very simple rhythmically but that is nonetheless widely beloved and perceived to be spiritually rewarding. More common are the grand, expansive tunes such as SINE NOMINE and CRUCIFER. Noting wisely that "not every new hymn tune needs to be a blockbuster," Schalk acknowledges that many strong hymn tunes do "stretch the boundaries of rhythm, melody, harmony and form beyond the point where most congregations may think it is allowable or even possible to go."

---

290 "Some Thoughts on the Writing of Hymn Tunes," 7.
291 Ibid.
292 Ibid., 8.
293 Ibid., 7.

> A successful hymn tune will demonstrate just how far the musical or formal boundaries can be stretched before they break. By extending these boundaries beyond what many congregations would regard as possible, a new hymn tune can help congregations realize the thrill of singing beyond what they may think are their limits, but not beyond what they can actually do. The result can be the establishment of a new and broader musical horizon within which new voice can be given to the unique song of the church which is congregational hymnody.[294]

Distinctive Characteristics of Schalk's Hymn Tunes

Carl Schalk's contribution to the life of the Church lies not just in his dedication to a deeper understanding of Lutheran musical history in all its many aspects but also in his desire to establish a means through which this great heritage can be expressed and celebrated through the musical language of the Church today. Schalk's friend Carlos Messerli puts it well in his assertion that Schalk is "an advocate for the preservation of the historical Lutheran music and liturgical heritage and the development of an equivalent contemporary practice."[295]

Nowhere is the nature of this contemporary practice more clearly crystallized than in Schalk's hymn tunes. Approaching 120 in number, Schalk's settings possess a style that is distinctive and easily recognizable. These stylistic characteristics exist not to cajole, impress, or sway, but simply to serve the purposes of congregational song in the Lutheran tradition.

- They are defined predominantly by stepwise quarter-note motion, generally with one note assigned to each word. In this way, the music serves primarily to proclaim the text rather than calling attention to itself.
- The form of the tune is derived directly from the structure of the text. Creative or unusual formal features always constitute a response to unorthodox or irregular qualities of the text, and in that way do not draw attention to themselves.

---

[294] Ibid., 8.

[295] Carlos Messerli, conversation with the author, November 13, 2012.

- The expressive gestures are restrained, but because Schalk uses them sparingly, they are also deeply affecting. Most idiomatic is his appropriation of the *échappée* (or "escape note"), a melodic turn in which a nonharmonic tone is approached by step from a chord tone and left by skip in the opposite direction.[296] (See * in Example 1.) So characteristic of Schalk is this winsome gesture that one could almost call it his signature flourish (if one dared to use the word "flourish" at all in connection with the music of Carl Schalk).

Example 1: Where Shepherds Lately Knelt

296 For a more thorough definition, see any standard music dictionary.

- Schalk's harmonic language serves to underscore the melodic shape and formal structure. While expressive, it does not call attention to itself as an independent musical element.
- There is usually some element of surprise in his tunes. These range in scope from an unexpected interval that is judiciously placed to underscore a feature of the text, to a wholesale internal modulation that fleetingly opens to the singer new harmonic panoramas before seamlessly returning to the original key. A good example is Schalk's setting of Timothy Dudley-Smith's "O Christ the Same" to his tune RED HILL ROAD, found in *Evangelical Lutheran Worship*. Compare this to the enervating sentimentality of LONDONDERRY AIR, to which this text had previously been sung.[297]
- Schalk betrays a fondness for starting his tunes on the second beat of a measure, whereas less artful settings might simply begin on an upbeat. This carries the subtle suggestion that the song has been going on for some time, perhaps through all eternity, before the singer happens to join in—an image that a simple upbeat cannot satisfy.

As with all his endeavors, hymn writing is not undertaken for its own ends but simply to serve the purpose of the worshiping body.

"In writing these tunes, there has never been a conscious attempt to carve out new musical territory," Schalk notes in the preface to his hymnary, "but simply to provide songs which are both singable by

[297] See chapter 7 for a detailed discussion of this tune.

largely untrained congregations, and which reflect as faithfully as I have been able the texts to which they are set.

"Whatever its musical characteristics may be, true congregational song must never be merely simplistic, undistinguished melody whose only purpose is functional; neither is it essentially choir music simplified for the purpose of group singing. True congregational song operates within the parameters of largely amateur singers, yet—hopefully—has a character and integrity all its own."[298]

---

[298] Introduction to *The Carl Schalk Hymnary* and reproduced in *Thine the Praise*.

CHAPTER SIX

Hymns and Carols with Jaroslav Vajda

> After all, the gift of language combined with the gift of song was only given to man to let him know that he should praise God with both word and music, namely by proclaiming [the Word of God] through music and by providing sweet melodies with words.[299]

One cannot approach a discussion of Schalk's hymn tunes without considering his relationship with the prominent hymn writers with whom he has collaborated during the course of his career. Foremost among these is Jaroslav J. Vajda, with whom Schalk enjoyed a fruitful partnership for nearly three decades.

In his foreword to Vajda's comprehensive hymnary, Schalk writes that Vajda's background as pastor and preacher, and later as editor and book developer, "helped hone the crucial skills necessary to both the translator's and the hymn writer's art: clarity of imagery and the ability to convey that imagery with economy and power."[300]

Schalk came to know Vajda during his St. Louis years. At the time, Vajda worked at Concordia Publishing House and served as the editor of *This Day* magazine; later, he became head of the editorial department for book development. "His wife sang with me in the Lutheran Hour Choir," Schalk recalls. "She was a good singer, from Milwaukee, and used to sing in the Lutheran A Cappella. That's how I first met Jary."

---

[299] *Liturgy and Hymns*, vol. 53 of *Luther's Works*, 323–324.

[300] Foreword to *Sing Peace, Sing Gift of Peace: The Comprehensive Hymnary of Jaroslav J. Vajda* (St. Louis: Concordia Publishing House, 2003), 10.

Schalk singles out three aspects of Vajda's writing that clearly served to inspire him as one who would bring these texts to the people of God through song. First in Schalk's estimation is Vajda's ability "to fashion a striking new image, or to reshape an older image, recasting it in a way which brings fresh insight and understanding. To mention such lines from his carol "Before the Marvel of This Night" as 'Then tear the sky apart with light' or 'Give earth a glimpse of heavenly bliss / A teasing taste of what they miss' is simply to begin to touch the surface of writing consistently marked by fresh, sparkling turns of phrases and vibrant imagery," Schalk asserts.[301]

Noteworthy in Schalk's eyes as well is the author's "affinity for less usual textual forms and meters, less usual at least in the context of traditional hymnody." Interestingly, Schalk argues that Vajda's most successful texts are those that embody unusual metrical patterns while acknowledging that this aspect of Vajda's style "presents a challenge to musicians who would attempt to set these texts to music intended for congregational singing."[302]

Schalk is also inspired by "the strong theological thrust" of Vajda's texts, with their frequent use of trinitarian language. He also praises "the significant number of texts designed for particular liturgical purposes," including those for Baptism, Holy Communion, and dismissal; fresh Psalm paraphrases; Entrance, Kyrie, and Credo hymns, as well as hymns for various times of the Church Year.[303]

Now the Silence (NOW)

This beloved hymn represents the first collaboration between Schalk and Vajda, launching what was to be an uncommonly fruitful partnership. It is one of only a few hymns of Schalk's which has transcended denominational boundaries: "Now the Silence" has appeared to date in fifteen hymnals, representing a wide variety of church bodies.

Schalk's setting was written in 1969 for *Worship Supplement*. The way the assignment came about was anything but auspicious.

---

[301] Ibid., 10–11.
[302] Ibid., 11.
[303] Ibid.

The LCMS Commission on Worship's Music Committee had a new text of Vajda's they wanted to include, Schalk recalls.[304] "That was unusual for this supplement because most of the hymns were those widely used in other denominations which had not made it into any Missouri Synod publication, such as 'At the Name of Jesus.' So there were maybe just three or four new hymns."[305]

The task for writing new tunes for these texts fell to members of the committee.[306] "Of course there wasn't one extant which fit it, and no one on the committee was that interested in giving it a try. Because I was the newest member of the committee, I got the assignment."

Schalk made three or four tries that ended up in the wastebasket. "Finally, something clicked."

Vajda had given Schalk a specific instruction that might have proved daunting to a less creative mind.

"The idea was that it's an entrance hymn for the Order of Holy Communion," Schalk explains. "When the hymn is over, it goes right into the opening of the liturgy. So Jary said, 'Whatever you do, it should end on a G, so that you will be giving pitch to the pastor for the beginning of the liturgy.'"[307]

Schalk's ingenious solution was to harmonize this G as the fifth degree of the chord of the dominant in F major—which never resolves to the tonic. "So it ends kind of up in the air," Schalk notes. "It isn't over when it's over. What I mean is, when the hymn is over, it goes right into the opening of the liturgy. That's why you can end it on the dominant and it doesn't sound completely unfulfilled, because it carries on at that moment into the liturgy. So it was part of a bigger whole."[308]

---

[304] Vajda has said that the text came to him one morning while shaving. See Jaroslav Vajda, *Sing Peace, Sing Gift of Peace: The Comprehensive Hymnary of Jaroslav J. Vajda* (St. Louis: Concordia Publishing House, 2003), 175.

[305] Conversation with the author, December 4, 2012.

[306] Other new tunes for *Worship Supplement* were Hillert's setting of William Danker's missions text, "The Sending, Lord, Springs from Thy Yearning Heart" (761) and Paul Bunjes' tune for Vajda's "Thank the Lord, for He Is Good" (773), couched uncomfortably in 5/4. Neither made it into subsequent hymnals, although the Danker text has appeared elsewhere to both SINE NOMINE and ENGELBERG.

[307] This works precisely for The Order of the Holy Communion in *The Lutheran Hymnal* (1941), which directs the pastor to start on a G (see page 15) and in *Common Service Book* (1917; see page 12). It also works with Setting One from *Evangelical Lutheran Worship* (see page 98). It is also appropriate for the Communion service in *Service Book and Hymnal* (see page 18).

[308] Conversation with the author, December 4, 2012.

While gratified by the hymn's popularity, Schalk is dismayed that it is almost never sung at the position in the service for which it was intended. "It's rarely done as a processional hymn for reasons which escape me," he says. "Because when it first appeared, it was clearly the intention, and the text anticipates everything you're going to experience in the service: Confession, Absolution, Word, Eucharist, and Benediction with the reverse order in the text."[309] Having surveyed what is about to come, it ends with the words, 'Now, Now . . . and here we go!'"[310]

Nor is the hymn appropriate for weddings. People request it, Schalk says, "because of the words 'Now the wedding Now the songs,' but that's talking about the marriage feast of the Lamb, which is what Communion is a foretaste of."[311]

The tune itself stands as an extraordinarily innovative response to an equally creative subject. "Carl Schalk must be given the credit for recognizing the potential of this unusual text as a hymn," Vajda writes. "Its subsequent acceptance convinced me (and evidently many others) that hymns could take on new forms and yet perform their function in congregational worship."[312]

Schalk readily admits that his setting of the text constitutes "an odd shape. The lines of text are short, but I conceive the first line [in his setting] as one long phrase, through 'the empty hands uplifted.' It's in an arch shape. Then, there is a dual high point: 'Now the hearing / Now the power' and 'Now the Body / Now the Blood.' That

---

[309] Instead of Father, Son, and Holy Spirit, Vajda's text sings of "Now the Spirit's visitation Now the Son's epiphany Now the Father's blessing . . . ." Vajda writes that "this not only expressed the order in which I pictured the Trinity coming to us in worship, but also the order in which the Incarnation took place: the visitation of the Virgin Mary by the Holy Spirit, then the Son's epiphany as the incarnate Word, followed by the universal blessing that is bestowed upon all in whom this same process occurs." *Sing Peace, Sing Gift of Peace*, 175.

[310] While it is subtitled "An Entrance Hymn" in *Worship Supplement*, it was included in the *Lutheran Book of Worship* in the Holy Communion section. Since then, usages continue to vary: In *Christian Worship* (1993), it turns up in the Opening of Service section, and in *Lutheran Service Book*, it is restored to the "Beginning of Service" section. But it appears in *Evangelical Lutheran Worship* as the first of the hymns for Holy Communion, where it is subsequently placed by other hymnals, including Hope Publishing Company's *Worship & Rejoice*. And in Hope Publishing's *Renew!* (1995, 221), the rubric says the hymn "may be sung either during communion or at the close of a worship service."

[311] Conversation with the author, December 4, 2012.

[312] Vajda, *Sing Peace, Sing Gift of Peace*, 175.

is the peak of the melody. Then it goes down to where it began from. So the high point is not at the end; it's in the middle, because that's what the text does."[313]

Both melodically and harmonically, Schalk exquisitely captures the sense of heightened anticipation, which is at the heart of Vajda's text.[314] The first two arching phrases, exactly parallel melodically, are constructed of rising fourths that gently settle back onto the scale's second degree. Because Schalk chooses to begin on the fifth degree, *below* the tonic, this allows the tune ample room to expand. The harmonization of the first chord, containing a pair of appoggiaturas evoking the subdominant that resolves on the next beat, immediately generates an aura of expectancy.[315]

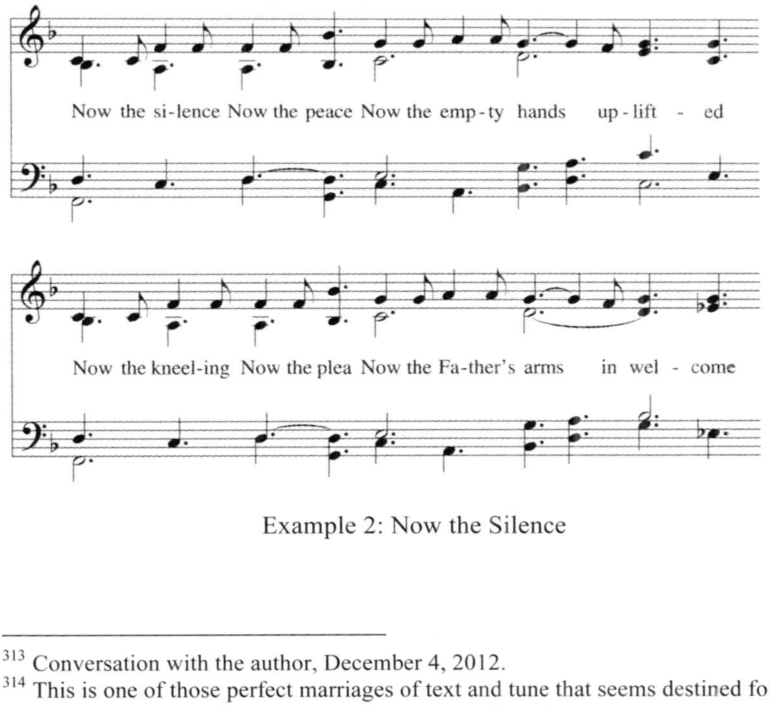

Example 2: Now the Silence

[313] Conversation with the author, December 4, 2012.

[314] This is one of those perfect marriages of text and tune that seems destined for the ages. Few since have dared to set this text; among them is Gerald Near, who pairs the "Now the Silence" with Vajda's companion "Then the Glory" (Aureole Editions, Hope Publishing Company, 1991) in a series of broad melodic lines whose general shape cannot but help mirror Schalk's setting, since Schalk responds so closely to the shape of Vajda's text.

[315] This same quintessentially Schalkian harmonic device surfaces again three decades later at the beginning of "Day of Arising" (RAABE), *ELW* 374, again conveying the idea of anticipation as the travelers in Susan Cherwien's text journey on the Emmaus Road with the risen Christ, who is about to be made known to them.

Harmonization of the end of the second phrase with the chord of the flat seventh degree (an E-flat major triad in the home key of F major) instead of the customary dominant not only tells us that we have embarked on a great journey but also presages the surprising turn to the key area of the subdominant, B-flat, for the third phrase ("Now the body, now the blood . . ."), in which the pattern of rising fourths begins anew in this new region. It is repeated precisely in the fourth phrase in this higher region, with another telling harmonic turn at the end as the introduction of the E-natural signals the dominant of the home key.

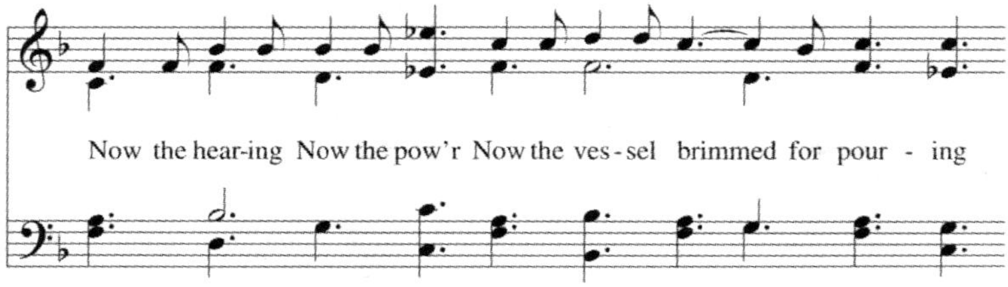

This "joyful celebration" returns us to the point of melodic origin for the final three phrases. Richer harmonies in the first of these closing three phrases, including the introduction of the dominant seventh at the end ("Now the heart forgiven leaping"), signal to us that fulfillment is on the horizon and that we shall, at last, reach that resting place on the journey toward which the entire hymn, in its succession of rising fourths and pregnant textual images, has been leading us.

Truncated motivic repetitions in the penultimate phrase heighten this expectation. Then, in a striking move, the hymn does not end after all: Instead, it concludes with a threefold repetition of the very word with which it began ("Now"), which Schalk perfectly locates on the *supertonic* and harmonizes with the dominant. The tonic, we are amazed to discover, eludes us both melodically and harmonically. But of course, this is the entire point of the hymn, for it signals not an ending but a beginning.

It is worth noting as well that a fluidity of metric rhythm contributes to the sense of heightened anticipation. In a sense, we are also waiting for a downbeat that never arrives. At the beginning, the absence of bar lines prevents the opening gesture from being interpreted as either upbeat or downbeat. Melodically, one is tempted to hear the first dotted quarter beat of the tune as a weak beat, but the harmonization with its subdominant appoggiaturas tells us it is a strong beat. And, knowing what we do about the purpose of the hymn, we cannot hear the last note as a downbeat because we know its purpose is preparatory. This is a true foretaste of the feast to come.[316]

God of the Sparrow, God of the Whale (ROEDER)

Arnold Schoenberg reportedly said that "there is still much good music to be written in C major." Schalk has said he is reluctant to write in C major, yet this tune in C is good indeed.

Vajda notes that his text was conceived in 1983 as a response to the invitation from Concordia Lutheran Church in Kirkwood, Missouri, "to provide an opportunity to compose a hymn text that would provoke answers from the users of the hymn as to why and how God's creatures (and children) are to serve him. . . . God's adopted family responds both as creatures and as children, thus fulfilling the expectations of the Law with the fruits of the Spirit, and in doing so 'saying' with actions something of significance to God and the world."[317] The first tune was supplied by Concordia's organist and choir director, David Christian, and Schalk's followed soon after.

Named to honor his wife Noël's father Paul Roeder, a Lutheran pastor in Chicago, Schalk's tune captures the childlike eagerness of Vajda's engaging imagery; in its second half, the ardent quality of the invitation to prayer is as if one was singing with hands uplifted. Richard Hillert deems the tune "at once sweetly charming but never simplistic and alarmingly simple but replete with tiny surprises."[318]

---

[316] It is interesting to trace the history of the notation of this conclusion in the various publications in which it has appeared. In *Worship Supplement* (1969, 770) the hymn concludes with a single "Now", notated with a dotted quarter and fermata. In Vajda's own book *Sing Peace, Sing Gift of Peace* (St. Louis: Concordia Publishing House, 2003, 174), and in the *Lutheran Book of Worship* (1978, 205), *The Carl Schalk Hymnary* (1989), and *Lutheran Service Book* (2006, 910), it ends with a threefold repetition of "Now" with those hymnals notating the last word with a dotted quarter with no fermata. *Evangelical Lutheran Worship* (2006, 460) renotates this last note as a dotted half to conform to the preceding two statements of the word.

[317] Vajda, *Sing Peace, Sing Gift of Peace*, 105.

[318] Richard Hillert, "Composers for the Church: Carl F. Schalk," 9.

Example 3: God of the Sparrow, God of the Whale

The antecedent phrase, which rises in gentle stepwise motion to a pregnant pause on the seventh degree of the scale, invokes the image of God that the singer is addressing: God of the sparrow, of the earthquake; of the rainbow, the hungry, the neighbor; and finally the God of the ages.

From this vantage point of great expectancy, the singer's image of God is lifted before God; then, prayer erupts from the depths of the singer's heart. It is phrased powerfully as a question—for we know that at the heart of our faith journey lie refined questions instead of clear answers—although it lacks the specificity of punctuation ("How does the creature say Awe / How does the creature say Praise"). Schalk shapes the gesture of this consequent phrase as a sigh breathed out, all the way down through the octave to the tonic (which we have experienced only in passing so far, since the tune began on the third degree of the scale) and back up to the fifth. The end of each stanza is harmonized by the dominant in the first five stanzas as befits a question and by the tonic after stanza 6.

Someone Special (EISENBERG)

A Vajda/Schalk collaboration commissioned by the LCMS Board of Parish Education to celebrate "The Year of the Child" in 1979, this carol appeals to young and old alike in a simplicity that is endearingly childlike. In the first two four-measure phrases, the singer reflects on the wonders of God's creating hand and then in the third, pondering further, comes to the sudden realization that all these marvelous things are signs of God's love for all humankind: "Someone special I must be, since You made it all for me!"

Using the most elemental of means, Schalk underscores musically the parallelism of the first two phrases while in the third, on the critical eye-opening word "I," lightly touches the upper sixth degree for the first time before playfully leaping down again into the middle register for the tune's conclusion.

Before the Marvel of This Night (MARVEL)

Cherished wherever it is heard and sung, this carol and "Where Shepherds Lately Knelt," written a few years later under identical circumstances, stand as twin pillars of the Schalk/Vajda collaboration.

The impetus for "Before the Marvel" came as a request from Augsburg Publishing House for a new Christmas carol for the 1981 issue of *Christmas, The Annual of Christmas Literature and Art*, an elegantly produced publication that included original music and poetry along with substantial articles relating to the season.

At first, Vajda wasn't sure how to respond, Schalk recalls. "Jary said, 'What is there left to say about Christmas that hasn't already been said better by someone else?'"

What, indeed! No one except a hymn writer of Vajda's caliber could have come up with such a poetic solution. For here, in "Before the Marvel," we find ourselves singing the story of the angels receiving their instructions as they are about to go out and announce the birth of Christ.

Schalk hazards that "99 percent of people who have sung it don't understand this: the angels are getting their marching orders!" He points out as well that the title phrase is a subtle play on words. "Before the marvel of this night' has the dual meaning of 'in front of' but also 'previous to.' 'Before the marvel of this night / Adoring, fold your wings and bow, / Then tear the sky apart with light / And with your news the world endow.' It's telling the angels what they should be doing. 'Give earth a glimpse of heavenly bliss, A teasing taste of what they miss,' which is a great line."

This explains how "Before the Marvel" falls into the genre of a carol rather than a hymn. A carol typically embellishes a story from Scripture with details drawn from the poet's imagination. For example, explains Schalk, "How do we know what the angels' marching orders were?"[319]

Schalk wraps his setting in the velvety key of B-flat major. Like so many of his finest tunes, it begins on the second beat and in so doing subtly suggests that we are being invited to join the Church's endless song.[320] Like two other Schalk hymns that open to us cosmic depths of mystery and wonder, "Now the Silence" and "Day of Arising," its first note falls on the lower fifth degree.

The structure of Schalk's melody is simple yet profound. The first six phrases, three measures each, project a quiet confidence as if three-measure phrases have always been the norm. Each consists of two measures of quarter notes followed by a whole note. The long note offers a welcome period of repose, which allows the wonder of Vajda's imagery to blossom in the singer's imagination. Within these phrases, the sphere of activity opens gradually. The first traverses a fourth from F to B-flat; the second expands to a sixth, up to D; and in the third the heavens open onto the fifth above the tonic, all the way up to high F ("Then tear the sky apart with light"). Moving through the fifth and sixth phrases, the harmonic motion arrives on the dominant.

It is in the seventh phrase that the great surprise occurs. Instead of simply resolving to the tonic, Schalk brilliantly uses the unusual structure of this last part of Vajda's text ("Sing peace, sing peace, sing gift of peace") to prolong a sense of fervent hope and expectant yearning by using a series of subdominant inversions over a dominant pedal. At the same time, he quickens the pace by shifting the meter from duple to triple and moving forward on quarter-note beats instead of half-note beats.

---

[319] Conversation with the author, December 4, 2012.

[320] In the choral version, a four-measure introduction contributes to the impression of endless song already in progress.

Example 4: Before the Marvel of This Night

At the melodic climax on the high D, we remain filled with anticipation of what is to come. Because we reach the high point of this last section ("sing gift of peace") on a second-inversion tonic chord,[321] this tells us we are not yet "home" and therefore invites us to exhale the final statement as a prayer instead of a pronouncement, as the tonic is finally reached: "Sing peace, sing gift of peace!"

Even this final cadence, as natural as it sounds, is anything but conventional. Here again we encounter Schalk's harmonic resourcefulness. The penultimate chord contains elements of the dominant seventh (F, C, E-flat), which on their own would call for simple resolution to the tonic. But Schalk combines these with

[321] Actually, this is at first a first-inversion chord on the minor third degree that resolves to the second-inversion tonic two beats later.

elements of a first-inversion subdominant chord (G in the tenor, B-flat in the melody). The effect is a proleptic revelation of eternity, for placing the B-flat in the melody for this penultimate chord means we have arrived on the tonic a beat too soon. At the same time, the G that glows in the tenor voice points ahead to the distant horizon. This recalls in our mind's ear the repetition of that same note in the tune's second measure. So this, too, points us toward what is to come.

Therefore, by means of a single five-note chord, Schalk gives us the past, in the already-arrived-at tonic; the present, in the dominant seventh demanding immediate resolution; and the future, in the expectant G.

Among hymnals in common usage, "Before the Marvel" is represented only in *With One Voice* (1995). Schalk, however, does not regret that it is not included in later hymnals. This is frequent water-cooler discussion, so to speak, among Lutheran church musicians: "I can't understand why that wonderful carol isn't in either of our new hymnals," one often hears it said.

Schalk offers a reasoned explanation. "In that Christmas annual, it is set for soprano and keyboard," he points out. "That's the way I envisioned it, as a carol to be sung at best by all the [choral] trebles or by solo voice. Augsburg asked me if I would mind making it into a choral setting. So I did; both the original and the choral setting are in B-flat. It got to be very popular. When they were planning *With One Voice*, they wanted to include that in there. But the carol goes up to an F, which is too high. So the key was transposed down to A-flat, meaning the high note is just E-flat. But I never really thought of it as a congregational song. That was not the intent."

At the time that they wrote the carol, did Schalk and Vajda know they had one for the ages? Schalk demurs. "You try to do your best on whatever you're working on," he says. He adds with a laugh, "Once in a while, you think, 'This is going to be a winner,' and then it falls flat on its face."

Where Shepherds Lately Knelt (MANGER SONG)

A greater achievement still is "Where Shepherds Lately Knelt," the most deeply affecting setting of a text Schalk has yet created, yet one that is relatively unknown even among many Lutheran congregations.[322]

For the 1987 issue of the same *Christmas Annual*, Augsburg Publishing House asked Schalk and Vajda "to write another one just like ['Before the Marvel']," he recalls, but cannot resist adding, "If they wanted one just like the previous one, I could have just given them that one again."[323]

Vajda and Schalk obliged, and as before, Augsburg asked for a choral setting. The result, again, was a timeless masterpiece. Richard Hillert hails the carol as "a triumph of poetic and melodic elegance."[324]

Like "Before the Marvel," it was conceived for soloist (or choir). "I think of them as carols, not really for congregation," Schalk says of MANGER SONG and MARVEL, "although 'Where Shepherds Lately Knelt' is in a number of hymnals."[325]

As with the earlier assignment, Vajda was faced with the challenge of trying to say something new in a genre that was already overwhelmed with texts. "Once again I wondered what fresh approach and contemporary application could be made of that central event in history," Vajda writes.[326]

Once again, his solution was revelatory.

"Rather than report the event again in the third person, as so many Christmas songs do, I placed myself in spirit at that poor manger bed and reviewed the implications of that visit in my life and future and in that of my fellow human beings," Vajda continues. "I have struggled, and more so as I grow older, with the incomprehensibility of that event and of my connection with it, and with each commemoration of that miracle becoming more routine,

---

[322] Schalk shares that an experienced Lutheran choral conductor recently acknowledged, after making "Where Shepherds Lately Knelt" the centerpiece of his institution's Christmas festival, that he had learned of the setting only the previous year.

[323] Conversation with the author, October 24, 2012.

[324] Richard Hillert, "Composers for the Church: Carl F. Schalk," 11.

[325] It is included in *Christian Worship* (1993) and *Lutheran Service Book* (2006). In both publications, one again encounters the misfortune of transposition from its original and distinctive key. The original is set in E major, but in both hymnals, it is transposed a half-step up to F. While relieving the organist of the worry of four sharps, the blandness of F major compromises the setting's luster. It also asks the congregation to rise to a high E at its high point instead of to a D-sharp.

[326] Jaroslav Vajda, *Sing Peace, Sing Gift of Peace*, 289.

though its impact on God's heart remains the means of my salvation. I pictured myself at the opposite side of the event from Isaiah and his prophecy (9:6, 7), applying the same promise to myself as a late-arriving pilgrim."[327]

In its third and most memorable stanza, the text affirms its status as a carol rather than a hymn in its introduction of new images with which to experience the manger story:

How should I not have known
Isaiah would be there,
his prophecies fulfilled?
With pounding heart, I stare:
A Child, a Son,
the Prince of Peace—
for me.

Schalk still finds this insight breathtaking. "How did you know Isaiah would be there?" he wonders, marveling at the thought. "In the world of poetry, you imagine him coming back to see if his prophecy was fulfilled."[328]

Noteworthy as well about this setting is that it represents a rare instance in which Vajda welcomed suggestions for both theological and structural revisions of his original text. In terms of the theological revision, "the original text of the last stanza ends: 'To live, to die and not alone for me,'" Schalk noted. "At some point, I said, 'Okay, but I think it makes more sense theologically to say: to die, to live.' He said, 'Oh yes, that makes much more sense,' and he changed it. But that *never* happened otherwise with Jary Vajda."[329]

In terms of the structural revision, the magnificence of Schalk's setting of Vajda's text lies not simply in the character of the tune, but also in the creative way Schalk altered the structure of Vajda's original. The metrical structure of its original form, represented in the stanza quoted above, is 6 6 6 6 4 4 2. But Schalk's comes out as 12 12 10 10. The numbers don't add up, so what happened?

Schalk arrived at this through two epiphanies. One was the realization that he could compile Vajda's shorter phrases into the

[327] Jaroslav Vajda, *Sing Peace, Sing Gift of Peace*, 289.

[328] Conversation with the author, October 24, 2012.

[329] This is how it appears in all published versions, but Schalk's original manuscript, housed in the archives of Grace Lutheran Church in River Forest, contains Vajda's original—which is how the Grace choir first sang it.

long, arching phrases that he loves so much. In this way, the two pairs of six-syllable lines become two twelve-syllable phrases, and Vajda's three short phrases (4 4 2) become a ten-syllable phrase.

The second epiphany was to repeat that entire ten-syllable phrase.

"I asked him if I could do that," Schalk explains, "because I had a certain musical solution." Vajda, who rarely allowed for any alterations of his texts once they were completed, agreed. The poet writes admiringly, "Once again Schalk captured the mood and style of the text, while making the lines more fluent and giving additional attention to the crucial refrain."[330]

If one could identify a hymn tune and harmonization that discloses all of Schalk's most distinctive, engaging traits, those which have opened to him a place in the hearts of all those who treasure the proclamation of the Church through song—then MANGER SONG would be that tune. Foremost among these traits as manifested here include the following.

- Long, arching lines.
- A developmental structure that opens gradually through each phrase onto the high point in phrase 3, which is also the high point of the text; the location of the achingly expressive *échappée* at that very point ("but there is room, and welcome there *for me*") in which the line, seemingly at its apex, reaches unexpectedly one degree higher to a non-harmonic tone that then resolves by means of a sweetly expressive major third;[331] and then a gentle return to the tonic scale degree in phrase 4, seemingly uttered as a prayer.
- A melody that begins on the measure's second beat, suggesting the ongoing eternal song—also hinted at in the transition between stanzas and by the accompaniment's melody following the tune's first whole note, before the next vocal entrance.
- A harmonization rich in thirds and sixths that is lit from within by the brightness of E major, and whose forward progress is propelled by two warmly expressive and astutely

[330] Jaroslav Vajda, *Sing Peace, Sing Gift of Peace*, 166.

[331] In Schalk's anthem setting of this carol, the expressivity of this phrase is heightened as it reaches from the sixth degree of the scale *above* the upper tonic to the supertonic, and back down to the dominant via the seventh degree.

placed secondary dominants (respectively in the third and fourth measures).[332]

- An unconventional cadential formula in the accompaniment, which, like that of "Before the Marvel," moderates the feeling of finality when the cadence is reached—for, as we know, the song goes on. The penultimate chord of the cadence combines elements from a seventh chord built on the minor second degree (F-sharp in the tenor and E in the soprano) with a first-inversion subdominant (C-sharp in the bass and A in the alto, approached as an appoggiatura from B). It is, as one often finds in Schalk, a refreshing alternative to the typical V-I cadence.

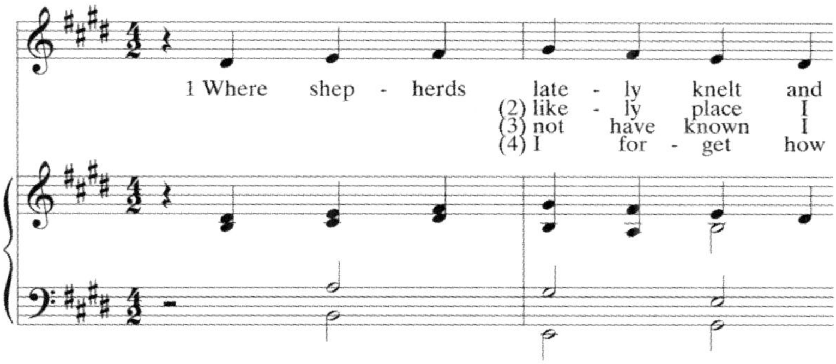

Example 5: Where Shepherds Lately Knelt

[332] Note the vibrant color of the last chord in measure 3 that features a raised root, G-sharp in the midst of this first-inversion secondary dominant.

kept the an - gel's word, I come in
find him as they said: Sweet, new - born
- sa - iah would be there, His pro - phe -
Love was born and burned Its way in -
half - be - lief, A pil - grim strange - ly
Babe, how frail, And in a man - ger
cies ful - filled? With pound - ing heart I
to my heart: Un - asked, un - forced, un -
stirred; But there is
bed: A still, small
stare: A Child, a
earned. To die, to
room and wel - come there for
voice To cry one day for
Son, The Prince of Peace for
live, And not a - lone for

The anthem version by Schalk follows the straightforward pattern typical for him in arranging his hymns and carols in choral settings, but remains nonetheless a marvel in its infusion of creativity into the economy of means.[333] Following just a measure and a half of

---

333 At the invitation of William Raabe, Paul Bouman, Schalk's longtime colleague at Grace Lutheran Church, created a graceful setting of this text and tune scored for TTBB chorus, strings, and organ to honor the ministry of the Rev. David V. Koch and the Concordia Seminary Chorus. It remains unpublished. Other composers, including Joseph Herl and Craig Courtney, have set Vajda's text to newly composed music, but these versions have not achieved the popularity of Schalk's setting.

introduction, stanza 1 is sung in unison, stanza 2 weaves the women's and men's parts together in elegant two-part counterpoint, stanza 3 is richly scored for four-part choir *a cappella*, and stanza 4 places a descant in the sopranos above the unison lower voices. A breathtaking embellishment of melody captivates the imagination where at the high point of this final stanza, where the sopranos soar from the repeated C-sharps up to an F-sharp, a third above the pitch the melody had previously attained, providing a powerful climax of the phrase "To die, to live, and not a*lone* for me."

This Touch of Love (TOUCH OF LOVE)

This post-communion hymn by Vajda, in existence several years before Schalk's tune was written in 1987, is based on the institution of the Lord's Supper in Matthew 26:26–29 and Luke 22:14–20.

Vajda's words offer insight into the music Schalk created. "Not always, not even often, much less often enough am I aware of what is happening in that high and tender meeting between my Lord and myself in the Sacrament of Holy Communion," Vajda writes.[334] Such a meeting is what one experiences in Schalk's setting. Starting on his trademark second beat, the tune ushers the singer with consummate compassion into the mystery of this encounter, first by gentle ascent to the third degree ("this touch of love"), then to the fifth ("this taste of peace") and still higher to the seventh degree to voice Vajda's tender question ("how can it last and still increase?"). Returning then to the fifth degree, the singer yearns upward once again, this time all the way to the tonic in the upper octave ("I cannot bear to have this air of wonder cease"). As with so many of Vajda's unusual meters, Schalk has identified a solution to 4 4 8 4 4 4, which one imagines was waiting inside the text all along, yearning for its own release.

There through Endless Ranks of Angels (FIRST TUNE)

A fascinating constellation of circumstances attends the history of this hymn. Schalk originally wrote it for inclusion in *Lutheran Book of Worship*, but it was published there in a setting by someone else and with a significant alteration to the text Schalk had been assigned.

Schalk explains that his setting of Vajda's Ascension text was "written at the request of Augsburg Publishing House for a series of new hymns published [as] inserts to acquaint congregations with a

---

[334] Jaroslav Vajda, *Sing Peace, Sing Gift of Peace*, 255.

number of new texts which would appear in the *Lutheran Book of Worship*."[335] The text he was given began, "There through endless ranks of angels." Those familiar with the hymn as it appears in the *Lutheran Book of Worship* and *Lutheran Worship* will note, however, that the hymn begins with a different first word, "Up." This was actually the word Vajda originally used, and in the ensuing back-and-forth over the word lies the story of what became of Schalk's setting.

Vajda explains that during preparation for *LBW*, "Augsburg Publishing House asked for an Ascension hymn to go with OUR LADY TRONDHEIM, [sic][336] hence the metric structure of the text. Into that format I gathered a number of implications of the Ascension as they apply to the followers of Christ, who recall his departure and await his promised return. Taking the Scriptural phenomenological viewpoint, I originally began the text with the word 'Up.'

"The publishers, however, preferred to avoid the three-tiered universe imagery and so substituted the word 'There,' in which version they published [in provisional resources] a setting by Carl Schalk," Vajda continues. "When the Inter-Lutheran Commission on Worship chose the text as the hymn of the day for Ascension, the original opening preposition was restored and a last-minute substitution for both OUR LADY TRONDHEIM and the Carl Schalk tune was made: ASCENDED TRIUMPH by Henry V. Gerike, the festive tune almost always used with the text since that time."[337] It subsequently appeared as 152 in *Lutheran Worship* and 172 in *Christian Worship*.

Schalk tells the story from his perspective. As Vajda suggests, after Augsburg first asked him for the tune, he completed it and made it into a choral arrangement. "This was published, and it was usable," Schalk says. When it came time for *LBW* and the original preposition had been restored, "they decided not to use my tune, because it was gentler. When you start a text with the word 'There,' you probably don't want to put that on a strong beat. So I put that first word on the second beat." Schalk accepted the turn of events in characteristic

---

[335] *Thine the Praise*, 9.

[336] OUR LADY, TRONDHJEM, 8 7 8 7 8 7, is found in *Service Book and Hymnal* (1958) as 160, as an alternative for Henry Lyte's beloved text, "Praise, My Soul, the King of Heaven" to which the standard tune PRAISE, MY SOUL is listed as the first option. It is also found under the name HER VIL TIES in *Lutheran Book of Worship* as 481 with the text "Savior, like a Shepherd Lead Us."

[337] Jaroslav Vajda, *Sing Peace, Sing Gift of Peace*, 271.

good humor. “That’s the joke,” he says, “that a tune by my student, Henry Gerike, supplanted mine.”[338]

The truth is that Gerike’s tune is compelling for this text in a way that Schalk’s is not. FIRST TUNE[339] is characteristic of Schalk in its careful shaping of phrases and well-sculpted ascent to the upper octave in the penultimate phrase. Gerike’s tune, on the other hand, emulates Christ’s ascension in its vault through an entire octave in just the first three notes and commands our attention to the text from there on.

The Schalk-Vajda collaboration is among the richest in modern hymnody. Its legacy lies not in the sheer volume of hymns created but in the continuing freshness of those that have endured. In the ideal artistic partnership, each party is challenged creatively in ways that would not have been otherwise possible. Vajda has honored Schalk for his ability to couch highly poetic textual forms in musical forms so singable (“Now the Silence”) that they become part of the very fabric of a community’s worship life. And Schalk has honored Vajda for providing the “stimulation and generative force of textual forms requiring new and different musical solutions.”[340] Together, they continue to invite the Church to “Catch the vision! Share the glory! Show the captives, tell them: Christ is here!”[341]

---

[338] Conversation with the author, December 4, 2012.

[339] The tune name comes from the original inserts published by Augsburg. Each of the hymns in the series was presented with two tunes: a new first tune and an older second tune. A header at the top, right of each page indicated a “FIRST TUNE” or “SECOND TUNE.” Perhaps the header was later adopted as a tongue-in-cheek tune name after the hymn became associated with ASCENDED TRIUMPH.

[340] Jaroslav Vajda, *Sing Peace, Sing Gift of Peace*, 11.

[341] “Catch the Vision! Share the Glory!” *Thine the Praise*, 58–59.

CHAPTER SEVEN

Hymns with Herbert Brokering and Other Writers

> Next to the Word of God, music deserves the highest praise. . . . Thus it was not without reason that the fathers and prophets wanted nothing else to be associated as closely with the Word of God as music.[342]

Carl Schalk's path intersected with that of Herbert Brokering during an auspicious two weeks in the summer of 1981 spent together at Holden Village in the good company of theologian Walter Bouman.

More precisely, their paths crossed on the long voyage across Lake Chelan, which provides the only access to the remote outpost nestled among the Cascades in North Central Washington.

At the time, Schalk knew Bouman well from their years together at Concordia Teachers College, but he had never met Brokering nor did he have any idea what he looked like.

"I knew that the three of us [with Bouman] were going to be out there and that we were all taking the boat that day," Schalk recalls. "I knew that Herb had to be on the ship because it went just once each day. So Noël and I were walking around thinking, 'Which one of these people looks like a Herb Brokering?' We settled on one guy, and sure enough, that was him."

The collaborative plan for this trio was intense. Each morning, Bouman was to lead a Bible study geared to the topic for the week. Based on that study, Brokering was to complete a new text by noon. Schalk then had a couple of hours to create a musical setting. The

---

[342] *Liturgy and Hymns*, vol. 53 of *Luther's Works*, 323.

product had to be deposited at the only available copy shop by 3 p.m. so that copies for the next morning's worship could be printed up.

In this way, ten new hymns were written in two weeks. For those present in the Holden community during that period, the outpouring of creative energy was something they will probably never forget. This is hinted at in Holden's audio archives, where some of Bouman's lectures from that summer are preserved. Near the beginning of Bouman's "Eucharist, Part 3: The Meaning," one hears Brokering and Schalk presenting, for the first time, the hymn "Take the Bread, Children, Take the Bread." From Bouman's comments, we gather that on the preceding Friday the pair presented the five new hymns they had written that week—the last of which was probably "Thine the Amen." One hears Bouman exult, "As we sang about the fourth one, someone next to me said, 'They can't get any better!' And then we did the last one, and it *was* better!"[343]

Schalk soon discovered at Holden that, in contrast to Vajda, Brokering was relatively easygoing about the structure of his hymn texts and the nature of their collaboration.

"With Herb Brokering, you really had the chance to take part in shaping the text in a way that you didn't, for example, with Jary Vajda," Schalk explains. "Herb used to type out the text on the left-hand side of the page, and on the right-hand side, he'd sometimes put an alternate reading of a line. I'd ask him which he'd prefer, but he said he didn't care, whichever one seemed to me to work better. In 'Thine the Amen,' I remember I even moved some of the stanzas around; I'd always show it to him and tell him why I did it. Or if I said, 'I need another stanza for this purpose,' then he'd write one."[344]

Brokering participated fully in the life of Holden Village, Schalk recalls.

"Peace, justice, and those kinds of issues were big there. Of course, Herb had done a lot of that kind of thing in his life, so it was a good fit. A number of his texts were written for specific occasions there. One time, they were pouring a slab of concrete for a building, maybe a shed of some kind. And they wanted Herb to cook up some kind of song everyone would sing. He first said that everyone had to bring a rock and said we would have a 'rock festival' in which everyone would throw their rock into the cement mixer so that

---

[343] These can be accessed at /audio.holdenvillage.org/year/recordings/1981.

[344] Conversation with the author, September 3, 2012.

something from everyone would be part of the new floor. He came up with a song that was on the pattern of the Kyrie in the liturgy, 'Lord have mercy,' although we sang other words. He entered right into the spirit of whatever the occasion was. Not everyone would want to do that, but Herb—that's the kind of thing he lived for."[345]

Even though Brokering's texts were often playful and tied to specific events, they had an uncommon theological richness that Schalk came to admire. "Someone was asking what his place is in the grand scheme of things, and they were trying to describe him as the only twentieth-century mystic that they knew. In a sense, that was correct."[346]

Thine the Amen, Thine the Praise (THINE)

This hymn is the most enduring of those that emerged from the Holden experience. The topic that week, as Bouman's son Luke remembers it, focused on the catechism.

"The particular lecture for 'Thine the Amen'—and the original hymn title might have been 'Then the Amen,' at least my memory suggests that might be the case—was part of a series that I think was on the catechism. My best recollection of the lecture in question was that it was on the Lord's Prayer and especially on Luther's teachings on the 'Amen' of the prayer."[347]

As with "Now the Silence," this hymn was also conceived with a specific liturgical function in mind. In this case, it was intended to be a Post-Communion Canticle. In fact, Schalk thought of it as counterpart to the earlier hymn.

"I envisioned this as something which could be used at the very end of distribution, as it is winding up, or just as it is concluded, because it points to the future," Schalk notes. "So those two hymns of mine which have gotten a lot of play, 'Now the Silence' and 'Thine the Amen,' are bookends in the service of Holy Communion."

This explains the original tune name, THEN, which when paired with NOW at the beginning underscores this concept of these twin pillars.

"When it was to be included in *With One Voice*, (editor) Martin Seltz wanted to know why it was called THEN when the main word in

---

[345] Ibid., December 4, 2012.
[346] Ibid., September 2, 2012.
[347] Luke Bouman, communication to the author, December 5, 2012.

the text was 'Thine,'" Schalk remembers.[348] "I explained the concept to him, and he said, 'Well, that's kind of an inside joke that few people will get.' So he asked if they could change the name to THINE." Thus the tune has the former name in *The Carl Schalk Hymnary* and in its expanded edition, *Thine the Praise*,[349] but appears as THINE in *With One Voice* and subsequent hymnals.

Nowhere are Schalk's dual penchants for matching a word or syllable to every note and for progression through stepwise motion put to better use than in what has become one of the Lutheran church's most treasured modern-day hymns.[350]

Example 6: Thine the Amen, Thine the Praise

---

[348] The word "then" does occur prominently in alternation with "thine" in stanzas 3–5.

[349] Chicago: GIA Publications, Inc., published respectively in 1989 and 1996.

[350] One puzzles over why the hymn does not appear in other mainstream Protestant publications. At present, it occurs only in *With One Voice*, *Hymnal Supplement 98*, *Lutheran Service Book*, and *Evangelical Lutheran Worship*.

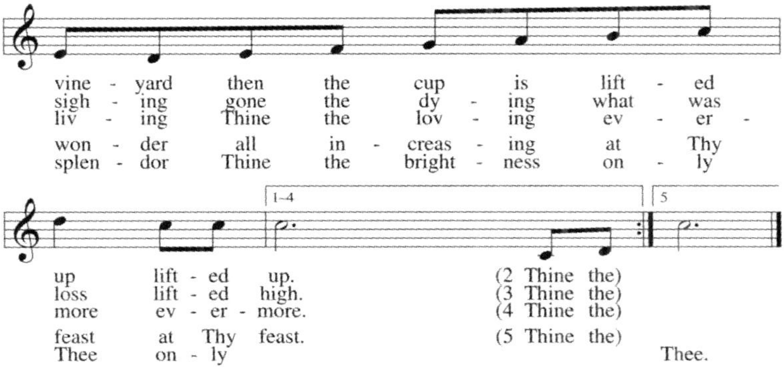

It begins on the tonic and rises in the first phrase before gently settling back onto the second degree. The second phrase opens with the same gesture, but this time reaches through the complete scale all the way to the tonic in the upper octave and settles back this time onto the fifth degree.

What comes next in the third and fourth phrases is astonishing for the profundity that is encased in the simplest of means. In the third phrase, within the first movement of nonstepwise motion, the tune leaps from the fifth to the upper octave and proceeds to cascade all the way down to the lower tonic and then back up to the fourth degree. In the fourth phrase, this note is essentially left suspended in midair as the tune returns once again to the lower tonic; employing the by-now familiar opening gesture, it moves purposefully upward by step and—in its final arching gesture—takes us by surprise in surpassing the upper tonic and attaining the note above before moving down to the tonic directly below for the conclusion. How unusual it is, as well, for a tune to end on the tonic in the *upper* tonic instead of the lower tonic on which we began! It is a powerful metaphor for the journey we are on in singing this text: it transports us, truly, into new planes of new musical and spiritual dimensions.

Most breathtaking about Schalk's tune is the way it gives life to Brokering's mystical stream-of-consciousness images relating to Holy Communion, entirely lacking in punctuation, which are graced by playful touches so characteristic of Brokering ("Thine the *wonder full* surprise").[351] The musical gesture that rises above the tonic at the end gives ardent voice to the crowning image in each stanza: "lifted

[351] "A kind of hymnological perpetuum mobile," Hillert writes admiringly. "Composers for the Church: Carl F. Schalk," 11.

up," "what was *loss*," "ever*more*," "at thy *feast*," and most of all "only *Thee*."

So that the text can shine forth, Schalk's harmonic language is straightforward, firmly supporting the stepwise motion of the tune and allowing the singer to focus on Brokering's imagery without the distractions of harmonic manipulation. The only secondary dominant occurs at the midpoint and provides the impetus for smooth movement through the second-inversion dominant seventh to the gentle first-inversion tonic for the beginning of the third phrase; a root position tonic at this point would constitute a premature arrival.

And yet, forthright as it is, one still finds surprises hidden in the setting. As all organists know who have worked through Schalk's carefully crafted accompaniment, there is a delightful contrapuntal idiosyncrasy in the tenor line of the penultimate measure. There, a middle C on the second quarter-note beat appears to clash with the tonic D-flat on which the tune has arrived but is actually a product of the fine arch of the tenor voice as it moves toward the cadence. This is a good illustration of Schalk's concern for integrity of line.[352]

Two performance-related aspects of Schalk's setting are important to note.

The first is tonality. The original key, D-flat major, offers a luminous context for the mystical qualities of both text and tune. That the congregation is required to reach slightly above its comfort level in the penultimate measure to E-flat also serves the purpose of both text and tune at that point. For these reasons, one laments the decision of the editors of *With One Voice* (1995) and *Evangelical Lutheran Worship* (2006) to present the hymn a half-step lower in the commonplace key of C major. *Lutheran Service Book* (2006) restores the key of D-flat but only as an option in the accompaniment edition; in the pew edition, it still appears in C. This solution, however, allows the organist to play the hymn properly in D-flat while the congregation is permitted the convenience of reading it in C.

The other concern with "Thine the Amen" relates to tempo. One often hears it sung too fast because the musician sees that the setting is primarily written in eighth notes. This greatly diminishes the communicative power of this perfect marriage of text and tune. Because of the intensity of Brokering's images, it is critical that the

---

[352] This idiosyncrasy stands out in the choir-only stanza of Schalk's 1983 setting for SATB choir and congregation (Augsburg Fortress, ED002909).

organist select a tempo moderate enough to let these images take root in the singer's imagination. The ideal tempo would be majestic, but not ponderous, and would convey a sense of breadth while preserving the tune's sense of forward motion.

Take the Bread, Children, Take the Bread (BREAD)

This simple yet deeply affecting hymn, also a product of that fruitful summer of 1981 at Holden Village, focuses on the simple actions during Holy Communion by the children of God. The hymn is not merely about taking and eating, but addresses the source of the meal and the expression of love by which it is offered. "We don't start with the meal; the meal is given to us, and we take it, as children, as those baptized to come into the presence of their God," Brokering explained at the beginning of the third lecture presented on the Eucharist that summer by Walt Bouman.[353] The people, almost like children, engage in and receive actions of simplicity—take, bless, break, give, and eat the bread, in each of Brokering' five stanzas.

Schalk's tune, BREAD, embraces the gentle, dancelike rhythm of Brokering's accentuations. The end of the second phrase turns toward the minor in an attitude of gentle reflection as the singer moves to the tune's embracing high point on the relative minor before returning home—but not quite. Each stanza ends on the dominant, providing the momentum for the next stanza, coming to rest in the tonic only on the final phrase.

Oh, the Wailing and Lamenting of the Woman by the Tree (RACHEL)

This carol constitutes a kind of dark parallel to "Thine the Amen." Also written in 1981, Brokering's text explores the implications of the massacre of the innocent children in Matthew 2. Schalk's minor-mode tune RACHEL assumes an exotic cast from the use of the scale's lowered seventh and raised fourth.

The text is metrically organized as 15 15 15 15 14. Normally, this would be a boon for Schalk, who loves to work with long lines. But here, they prove burdensome. The assignment of one note to each word or syllable lends to the carol a quality of relentlessness,

---

[353] The link to Bouman's lecture that features the Schalk-Brokering hymn, about seven minutes into the sound file, is found at audio.holdenvillage.org/year/recordings/1981.

particularly with the inclusion of the additional phrase of 14 syllables. While relentlessness may have been Schalk's intent—after all, that defined the massacre Herod ordered—whether that quality serves the singing assembly is open to question.

Holy Spirit on the Earth (HOLDEN)

This arresting pairing of text and tune was hatched during a second Holden Village stay by Brokering and Schalk in 1987.[354] The annual theme at Holden that year was "There is something afoot in the universe." Brokering's refrain addresses the Holy Spirit as the stirring force—"Holy Spirit on the earth, afoot inside the universe"—while images of divine justice and the forces of creation so ingrained in the mission and ministry of Holden Village tumble forth in his six stanzas.

Schalk's choice to frame the refrain as a single expansive gesture set in the major mode and the stanzas as a series of staccato outbursts in the relative minor sets off the bracing freshness of Brokering's imagery. Both components of Schalk's setting employ a transparent simplicity of means that focuses the singer's attention directly on the text.

Christ Be Our Seed (WHEAT RIDGE)

In retirement, Herb Brokering served Wheat Ridge Ministries as a staff associate for more than a decade, with a special interest in the healing arts. The organization commissioned text and tune from Brokering and Schalk in 1998. Brokering's text (11 10 11 10) features the long, arching lines that Schalk finds most appealing. He responds with a setting based on a four-note motive that gradually opens toward the third phrase, where the upper octave is attained, and then gradually closes down toward the tonic just as would a loving physical embrace.

A minor issue concerns the last three measures, for which the meter changes from 2/2 to 3/2. The accentuation of both the text and tune during those measures, however, remain in duple meter. One wonders whether Schalk is looking for a way to convey visually the effect of broadening at the final cadence of which he is so fond.

---

[354] Recordings of Brokering talks from the 1970s are also featured in the Holden audio archives at audio.holdenvillage.org/node/679.

OTHER HYMN WRITERS

Rise Again, Ye Lion-Hearted Saints of Early Christendom (ZION)

As his first formal hymn-writing effort, Schalk set a translation by Martin Franzmann of an anonymous eighteenth-century text, "Rise Again, Ye Lion-Hearted Saints of Early Christendom," to a decisive tune that foretells the strength of his great FORTUNATUS NEW. This setting was written in 1958 shortly after he began his ministry at Zion Lutheran Church in Wausau, Wisconsin, for the church's Fifth Annual Day of Spiritual Music. Previously, the text had appeared in *The Lutheran Hymnal* with an early nineteenth-century tune by Bernhard Klein which, in Schalk's judgment, "had little use in congregations."[355]

Driven by the strong forward impulse of the opening fifth, Schalk's ZION betrays qualities of a mature compositional voice that would serve him well down through the years. These include confident quarter-note motion, a clear structure, and a firm sense of purpose by which the tune ascends in its third phrase to the upper octave and then to the supertonic above for the climactic phrase. The violent imagery of the text, however ("Mid the lion's roaring / Songs of praise outpouring, / Joyously they take their stand / On th'arena's bloody sand"), probably accounts for its demise in popularity over the years, more so than Klein's lackluster earlier tune. Schalk's longtime colleague Richard Hillert writes admiringly of ZION, "It is a solid, classical tune, full of spirit and reflective of its text. It is a model of economy with no wasted notes in its setting. I have long regarded it as one of his best tunes."[356]

Sing, My Tongue, the Glorious Battle (FORTUNATUS NEW)

Written in 1967 as a Lenten carol for the St. Louis–based youth magazine *Spirit*, Schalk's angular, sharply chiseled tune breathes new life into Venantius Fortunatus' great Good Friday text, which had been known before through PANGE LINGUA and PICARDY.[357] First

---

[355] "Some Thoughts on Writing Hymn Tunes," 6. It appears as *TLH* 470, and the text also turns up in the *Evangelical Lutheran Hymnary* to a tune by Alfred Fremder.

[356] Richard Hillert, "Composers for the Church: Carl F. Schalk," 6.

[357] *Evangelical Lutheran Worship* provides both PANGE LINGUA (355) and FORTUNATUS NEW (356). The text was set to the tune PICARDY in *The English Hymnal* (1906) and *The United Methodist Hymnal* (1989).

published in *Worship Supplement* (1969), FORTUNATUS NEW continues to enjoy a vigorous life in various hymnals and has since been paired with other texts.[358]

In place of the contemplative attitude of the earlier tunes, Schalk's urgent setting urges us to look, with Fortunatus himself, beyond Good Friday to Christ's victory over death. As Schalk puts it, "We acknowledge on Good Friday that the story isn't over."[359] The forward momentum of the tune encourages all Christians to "sound the loud triumphant lay" (stanza 1) while its stark harmonic language and strong modal flavor reaches across centuries into the era of the hymn writer.

Example 7: Sing, My Tongue, the Glorious Battle

In tandem with Schalk's desire to create a contemporary language for hymnody, we find in the last phrase a fleeting yet highly expressive move to the relative major ("Tell how Christ, the world's

[358] "Christ, the Lord of Hosts, Unshaken," 521 in *Lutheran Service Book*.
[359] Conversation with the author, December 4, 2012.

redeemer") that attains the upper sixth degree of the scale, which tells us that we are not in the sixth century but in the modern era. This makes all the more powerful the text of this phrase in its closing stanza: "While the timeless ages run."

Richard Hillert writes insightfully of Schalk's setting that "tune and accompaniment are hewn with exceptional beauty and precision" and notes that "the music seems throughout to be so persuasive that it is easy to overlook the climactic high note in the final phrase, coming in at least four of the stanzas, on a weak syllable."[360]

As the Dark Awaits the Dawn (LUCENT)

Written in 1997 for this Susan Cherwien text, Schalk once again chooses to begin the tune on the second beat so that we are ushered gently into the ongoing cosmic song. His uncommonly expansive setting features many long notes during which Cherwien's lustrous, mystical images are invited to flower in the singer's imagination. The whole notes at the end of each of Cherwien's phrases, each tied over into the next measure, also create a riveting sense of expectancy: "As the dark awaits the *dawn*, / so we await your *light*."

Another noteworthy feature of the tune concerns its uncharacteristically wide intervals. In the second half, these include leaps of a downward sixth followed immediately by an upward fifth, then from the scale's second degree to the fifth and then all the way up to the upper octave before plunging down to the lower tonic. To the singer, these suggest that we are scanning the entire panorama of the heavens as we "long to see your day arise, / whole and wise, whole and wise, / O lucent Morning Star."

How Good, God Said (BENISON)

This modest setting represents yet another assignment whose realization perfectly meets the needs of the project. In 1993, William Raabe commissioned Gracia Grindal to write a hymn celebrating Christian marriage. Upon its completion, he submitted it to Schalk for a setting. The resulting tune is BENISON. Grindal said at the time that the graceful leap from lower to upper octave and then down by thirds to the scale's second degree in the fifth and sixth measures, set in the

---

[360] Richard Hillert, "Composers for the Church: Carl F. Schalk," 8. The syllables in question, in stanzas 1, 2, 3 and 5, are "a," "as," "the," and "the"—transgressions, indeed, at which most composition teachers would probably frown!

first stanza to "in Eden's sparkling dew," is the loveliest musical turn of phrase that had yet been written for any of her texts.[361]

Schalk uses Western music's most basic building blocks, the notes of a major scale, to fashion a melody that is utterly idiosyncratic and yet which sounds as natural as the sparkling dew it sings of. So logically do the tune's two five-measure phrases unfold, one is led to think that melodies have always been structured that way.

The anthem version of this hymn is compromised by the underlay of a second text, "How Sweet the Name of Jesus Sounds" by the eighteenth-century Evangelical hymnist John Newton. The piousness of the text does not suit the discreet character of the tune, nor do its contents fit the tune's shape. The high point in Grindal's stanza 1, for example, is sung poignantly to "*E*den's sparkling dew" but to a weak syllable in the Newton text ("*a* believer's ear"). If a second text was deemed necessary, a far better choice would have been a companion hymn by Grindal written for BENISON a year later and also commissioned by Raabe, "How Good It Is to Praise the Lord," which serves as the official hymn of the Lutheran High School Association of Greater Milwaukee.[362]

Day of Arising (RAABE)

William Raabe also commissioned both text and tune for this hymn. With Susan Cherwien's evocative poetry and the contemplative lyricism of Schalk's setting, the hymn has become a favorite whenever the Emmaus Road story from Luke 24 is read.[363]

As in "Now the Silence," the commonplace key of F becomes window to revelation. Here, we are not only onlookers but also participants in the two apostles' life-changing encounter with the risen Christ. It is perhaps not by coincidence that the opening chord sequence and melodic gesture are strongly reminiscent of NOW, with its rich suspension melting into the root-position tonic on the next beat.

---

[361] Undated communication to William Raabe. The hymn is found in Schalk's *Our Voices Raise: Twenty New Hymn Tunes for Congregation, Choir, and Accompaniment* (Chicago: GIA Publications, Inc., 2003) and was published in anthem form by Augsburg Fortress in 1996 (11-10678).

[362] Raabe commissioned Kenneth Kosche, Jonathan Kohrs, and John Behnke to create contrasting settings of the hymn. The one by Behnke is used by the Association on most major ceremonial occasions.

[363] *Our Voices Raise*, 24.

Each half of RAABE features an identical opening-up of the initial rising fourth motive (to the fifth and then the octave); the only difference being the resolution to the tonic at the end instead of the conclusion on the half-cadence in the middle. Considered apart from its text, one might say the repetition on the upper octave in the tune's second half is redundant since we have already been there. Yet the tune serves the text beautifully in that it opens the way before us, clearly and simply, just as the dusty roadway opened before the weary travelers as they journeyed down it that life-changing evening.

The delightful unsteadiness of measure 3 warrants mention. Here, the first syllable of Cherwien's fourth phrase finds itself on the last note of Schalk's third measure, creating a syncopation in the tie across the bar line. For the singer, this creates a moment of hesitation, or uncertainty of foot, that is entirely in keeping with the journey down a dusty road, especially given the astonishing "things about Jesus of Nazareth" (Luke 24:19) that the two travelers have experienced and heard about in Jerusalem during the past few days. True to form, Schalk does not replicate this little surprise in the tune's second half, where the phrase receives more conventional treatment.

Look, Now He Stands! (PARSONS)

This problematic tune appears in the Easter section of *Lutheran Book of Worship*. That PARSONS did not make the cut into subsequent hymnals does not surprise Schalk (or anyone else, probably, who has sung it).

The text was written by George Utech, a graduate of St. Olaf College and Trinity Lutheran Seminary who went on to become an ELCA pastor and chaplain at Texas Lutheran College. His stanzas consist of four lines of twelve syllables each, plus alleluias. The obstacle for the composer is that the accentuations within each line of twelve are irregular. For Schalk, that made the assignment of writing a good tune, given to Schalk by the Inter-Lutheran Commission on Worship's Hymn Music Committee, a difficult one. He acknowledges that the effort took him out of his comfort zone.

"My goal has never been to do something strikingly modern," Schalk says. However, he continues, "I thought the text called for me to do something *really* modern. The text was assigned to me, and I remember Ludwig Lenel[364] was there. He was the one who used to correct me like a student." The pressure to do something original was considerable. "I was trying to be something that I didn't know how to be," Schalk admits.

PARSONS is primarily in 4/4 but incorporates surprising measures of 5/4 and 6/4. Its melodic shape can best be described as jagged. In Schalk's defense, the tune was surely a faithful effort to reflect Utech's irregular accentuations. Those aside, the poetic meter is still very unusual. The only other hymn in common usage in the Lutheran corpus which has that meter is "Where True Charity and Love Abide," a ninth-century text that possesses no discernible meter. (In fact, it is set in *Evangelical Lutheran Worship* to Plainsong mode VI.)

Schalk's solution in PARSONS is to avoid phrase structure altogether. As a result, the tune consists of one long, shapeless phrase until the Alleluias are reached and a greater sense of purpose emerges. The high point on D, for example, is attained in the first measure and repeated in the seventh, tenth, and eleventh measures. Neither is there much clarity in the harmony. Set in G minor, it has a modal feel, but occasional cross relations create tonal confusion.

Schalk agrees the result is unsatisfying. "I have heard congregations try to sing it," he says with a chagrined laugh. "I'd just as soon they didn't."

Lord God, the Holy Ghost (DES PLAINES) and Spirit of God, Unleashed on Earth (DONATA)

These represent two more hymns of Schalk's included in *Lutheran Book of Worship* that did not make the cut into subsequent hymnals. Both texts are appropriate for use at Pentecost.

Named for the Illinois town of his birth, DES PLAINES was written to James Montgomery's "Lord God, the Holy Ghost." Conventionally structured in short meter (6 6 8 6), the text has appeared in a variety of hymnals to predictable tunes including ST. MICHAEL and ST. PHILIP.

Schalk seems to have been attempting to do something different. Instead of the regular phrasing of those earlier tunes, which consist of two phrases of two measures and one of four measures, he structures the new tune in two five-measure phrases. In the last phrase, the tune

---

364 Lenel was a composer and longtime professor of music at Muhlenberg College in Allentown, Pennsylvania, who served on the ILCW's Hymn Music Committee from 1966 to 1972.

springs from the lower tonic to the upper seventh, back down again and back up to the tonic in the upper octave before making its final descent. The effect may have been intended to represent the first stanza's plea for the Spirit to "Descend with all your pow'r" or to capture the drama of stanza four's "tongues of fire."

Bearing his wife Noël's middle name, DONATA offers a striking alternative to more conventional tunes, such as TRURO, which have been paired with John W. Arthur's text, "Spirit of God, Unleashed on Earth" (*LBW* 387). Schalk's tune vaults in the second measure from the tonic to the upper sixth and conveys the image of unbridled power cut loose.

By the third return to that upper sixth degree, however, the setting feels redundant. A lack of metrical consistency in the motive marking the beginning of the two halves of the tune also creates uncertainty. Initially, the tune begins on the downbeat, but when the motive recurs at the tune's midpoint, it begins on the upbeat. Which is its "real" form? The upbeat motive also is ill-suited to the beginning of stanza 3, "*Let* new lips, *tast*ing vict'ry won."

Schalk acknowledges this quirk. "In DONATA, the skips are all sixths; that is the Spirit of God, un-*leashed* on earth. The problem is, in the way it starts, I began with the first stanza and ran into problems with subsequent stanzas." He adds, however, that these are pitfalls of the composer's trade and points to the John Ireland tune for "My Song Is Love Unknown" (featured in both *Lutheran Service Book* and *Evangelical Lutheran Worship*) as problematic in this respect. "I think it's in the second to last stanza the accents are way off," he reflects, "and they occur several in a row, although they work fine for stanza one."[365]

We Meet You, O Christ (STANLEY BEACH)

This setting offers an interesting example of a hymn that has become established in several mainline Protestant hymnals but not Lutheran ones. The author is the passionate ecumenist Fred Kaan. Composed in 1987 on request from the hymnal revision committee of the General Conference of the United Methodist Church, Schalk's setting appears in the *Chalice Hymnal*, *The United Methodist Hymnal*,

---

[365] The tune emphasizes the first note and places less stress on the second, but works well actually only for stanza 7: "Here might I stay and sing . . . ." See *LSB* 439 or *ELW* 343. *LBW* fits the tune more comfortably to RHOSYMEDRE.

and *Worship & Rejoice*. Its simple melodic structure perfectly suits the straightforward setting in C major, which moves gradually by step to the upper octave and then descends again just as gently. Its tender harmonization, sweetened by a single secondary dominant, allows Kaan's uncluttered, heartfelt images to project their age-old wisdom, as in stanza 4: "You choose to be made at one with the earth; the dark of the grave prepares for your birth. Your death is your rising, creative your word: the tree springs to life and our hope is restored!"[366]

As the Sun with Longer Journey (NAGEL)

This lovely 1981 text from John Patrick Earls of St. John's Abbey appears in *Voices United: The Hymn and Worship Book of The United Church of Canada* to the tune PICARDY, but finds a gentler, more welcoming home in Schalk's tune NAGEL (his daughter Rebecca's married name). It was written on request by the committee for the supplement *With One Voice* and was first published there. In place of the stark solemnity of PICARDY, the luminosity of Schalk's setting with its shimmering rising sixth gives life to the text's opening image: "As the sun with longer journey melts the winter's snow and ice, / with its slowly growing radiance warms the seed beneath the earth."

While assigning a note to every word or syllable in the manner that is typical for Schalk, the tune never feels rushed because the harmonic rhythm by quarter notes maintains a calm steadiness of pace. The tune contains subtle surprises: while the melodic movement of the opening phrase is strictly stepwise, suggesting at first this is to be the pattern for its remainder, the more complex character of the tune is slowly revealed by the gradual opening up of the range of motion. The end of the second phrase surprises with its upward and downward vaults, followed by an octave leap for the opening of the third phrase (instead of the sixth experienced in the two previous phrases).

Throughout, Schalk capitalizes on the deep expressivity of these wide intervallic gestures. These constitute a telling journey in themselves, giving powerful voice to the prayer at the end of the first

---

[366] Fred Kaan, copyright © 1968 Hope Publishing Co., Carol Stream, IL 60188. All rights reserved. Used by permission. The hymn may be found in *Worship & Rejoice* (Carol Stream: Hope Publishing Co., 2001), 616, where the tune is also paired with Brian Wren's baptism text "In Water We Grow" (678).

stanza: "may the sun of Christ's uprising gently bring our hearts to life."

Cradle Hymn (LA GRANGE)

Schalk is in his element when pondering images of the infant Jesus. The tunes he has written at the foot of the manger are consistently engaging, endearing, and heartfelt. Perhaps this is because it allows those winsome aspects of his own personality to blossom. This gentle lullaby offers a case in point. Written in 2001 to an Isaac Watts text for St. John Lutheran Church in La Grange, Illinois,[367] Schalk's setting features rocking motion in both the measure-to-measure rhythm and in the very shape of the arching melody itself. It moves gently by step to the upper octave, partway back down, up and down again, and then proceeds to weave back and forth through the octave in an achingly sweet series of Alleluias that are spun out for a few blissful additional measures beyond what the ear expects. The harmonic language is rich in thirds and sixths, which are well-employed in the anthem setting and incorporates a lilting flute part.[368]

O Christ the Same (RED HILL ROAD)

Every so often, a well-known text receives a new setting of such originality and freshness that it is impossible to return to the text in its former guise. Schalk's FORTUNATUS NEW did that for "Sing, My Tongue." His RED HILL ROAD accomplishes this again for Timothy Dudley-Smith's beloved 1984 text, formerly sung to the folk song LONDONDERRY AIR.

Schalk's tune came about not as a result of a commission or request, but because of a situation with a loved one that turned him toward the deep truths articulated by the text. In its three arching stanzas (11 10 11 10 D), Dudley-Smith affirms Christ's faithfulness to humankind in all its aspects and ages: "O Christ the same, beyond our brief tomorrows, / we bring our thanks for all that is to be."[369]

After Schalk composed the setting, he sent a copy to the person for whom it was intended and then promptly put it away in a drawer. "I wasn't going to do anything with it," he says.

---

[367] *Our Voices Raise*, 5.

[368] Augsburg Fortress, ED004678.

[369] Timothy Dudley-Smith, copyright © 1984 Hope Publishing Co., Carol Stream, IL 60188. All rights reserved. Used by permission.

A few years later, Schalk received a batch of hymn texts from the editors of *Evangelical Lutheran Worship*, for which they were seeking new tunes. "Several people got the letter," he recalls. "It said, here are a bunch of texts; if you want to set any, give it a try."

Among them was "O Christ the Same." "They didn't want to put it in *ELW* to 'O Danny Boy,'" he continues. "I just happened to have my setting lying around, so I sent it in. I think it is a very nice tune; it will probably last a little while."[370]

Before our very eyes, RED HILL ROAD opens to us, through a variety of means, entirely new realms in which we may encounter this text and be moved by it.

- More so even than LONDONDERRY AIR, it emphasizes Dudley-Smith's long, gracious lines. In the earlier tune, all phrases except the last are weighed down by a dotted half on the downbeat (see *With One Voice* 778). Each of Schalk's phrases, on the other hand, are composed of moving quarter notes, one word or syllable per beat, with longer notes at the end of each phrase. In this way, each constitutes a single gesture that reaches compellingly forward and yet has clearly articulated resting points that allow us to ponder the meaning of each phrase of text.
- Set in the key of D major, the tune's first four phrases constitute an elegantly sculpted unit whose overarching goal is the arrival at the midpoint of the setting on the tone of the dominant, A. Although parallel in length (seven half-note beats) and structure, these four phrases do not sound redundant because each has its own clear purpose and distinct shape. Schalk's gracious harmonization, which draws sensitively on the poignant minor chords of the key (built on the second, third and sixth scale degrees), lends character to each phrase as well.
- Every good hymn tune contains an element of surprise. The astonishing wonder of RED HILL ROAD comes at this midpoint of the tune as it is poised on A, the scale degree and key of the dominant. Staying on the same pitch for the next measure, we suddenly find ourselves in an unrelated key. What had

370 Conversation with the author, September 3, 2012. It appears in *ELW* as 760. One must consult the accompaniment edition to see the full setting.

been the scale degree of the dominant is now the third degree in the new key of F major. This move is accomplished by the simplest of means; the bass line of the accompaniment moves from A through a single quarter note G and comes to rest on F. Yet in so doing, it transports us to an entirely new tonal plane. Moving from a sharp key to a flat key, the tune at this point conveys qualities of grace, peace, and timelessness.

- In the second phrase of this new key, we experience a relaxing of the tightly held stepwise character of the tune as the singer not only reaches through a fifth but also finds respite on a dotted half ("who spread the *skies*, and set the stars ablaze") as the phrase comes to rest again on the pitch A to prepare for the return home.
- Every good hymn tune also constitutes a journey in which we venture out and then return, the richer for our experience. Perched on this A on our journey down RED HILL ROAD, how are we to get home again? Schalk's solution is obvious yet startling in its very simplicity: We return home by the same way that we left. In a compositional *tour de force* all the more remarkable for its economy of means, the A is reinterpreted from the third degree in F to the fifth degree in D, and the bass line moves again from A, down through G, to F-sharp (which supports a first-inversion chord in the home key of D).
- The final two phrases of the tune are almost identical to third and fourth phrases of the first half, except that we descend home to the tonic instead of pausing on the dominant. However, we experience them in a new and refreshed light as a result of our voyage into a different key. The effect is that we are welcomed home to that which is unchanging and ever-faithful: "O Christ the same."
- Another of this tune's great gifts is that it is deeply expressive while avoiding altogether the syrupy sentimentality of LONDONDERRY AIR. While that earlier tune labors under the weight of secondary dominants and a high point that can only be experienced as crooning, Schalk's simple and warm harmonies, clean lines, and carefully-crafted structure permit the text to occupy center stage as we breathe this offering of gratitude ("we bring our thanks for all that is to be").

"Talking about structure," Schalk muses about RED HILL ROAD, "it's 11 10 11 10 and then the same again—nice long lines, but a lot of them. That's why I thought, when we get to the third group, we're going to change key. If you look, the shape of the tune is exactly the same each time, but [in the F major section] it's in a different key, which gives it a different flavor. Instead of starting on the fifth, you're starting on the third."

So well constructed is this breathtaking transition that congregations are able to sing it flawlessly, even on the first time they encounter it. "The average singer is not going to notice," Schalk adds with a grin. "They don't know why they don't stumble over the key change—and they don't need to know!"[371]

On Christmas Morning Children Sing[372] (AARON MICHAEL)

This is an engaging carol that deserves to be more widely known. Its playful tune and the original text by Henry Lettermann were written for the December 1983 issue of *Lutheran Education*, the journal of the faculty of Concordia University Chicago. With a tune named for his grandson, Schalk's setting boasts a high-spirited lilt and forward momentum generated by a strong bass line and stepwise phrases that sweep the singer along in their dancelike swirl. It is a fine contribution to the genre of hymnody that children can enjoy and that also has a strong theological message. Lettermann's stanza 2 is particularly memorable: "Christmas tree, Calvary, / crossing in God's most awesome plan, / Sin and grace, face to face, / bringing together God and man!"

With Head on High (RED HILL)

This is the third in a trio of tunes by Schalk written on texts by J. R. Peacey[373] for Hope Publishing Company's 1992 publication *100 Hymns of Hope*. It illustrates the hazards of straining too hard to extract a theological interpretation from the text.

Peacey's Christmas/Epiphany stanzas fall into a conventional meter, 8 6 8 6 D. The first half of each stanza deals with the story of Christ's birth from a worldly perspective, and the second half shifts

---

[371] Conversation with the author, September 3, 2012.

[372] *Thine the Praise*, 169–171.

[373] Peacey lived from 1896–1971 and is best known for his hymn "Filled with the Spirit's Power;" *Worship & Rejoice*, 331.

the perspective to the divine plane. For example, in stanza 2, we sing first of the "frantic race to get first place" in the census that night in Bethlehem, and then we recount in the second half the angels' song of peace, which trumps the preceding frenetic activity in the town.

The tune sets these two halves apart. Schalk couches the first half of each stanza in a dancelike 6/8 propelled forward by the steady beat of the dotted half notes in the bass line. However, poised at the midpoint of the tune, on the scale degree of the dominant, he abruptly shifts the meter to 4/4, yet directs that the quarter note should remain equivalent in both meters. This has the effect of slowing the pace for the second half of the tune and creating the sensation of dissociation between the two halves. The effect of slowing down is further drawn out by the half notes in the penultimate measure.[374]

I Greet Thee, Who My Sure Redeemer Art[375] (WAUSAU)

Sometimes, the particular characteristics of a tune result from an inside joke or hidden commentary. This is the case with Schalk's tune WAUSAU, a commission for a Texas congregation. In 1979, Russell Schulz-Widmar asked Schalk for a setting of this John Calvin text for a small hymnal companion his liturgically proper Episcopal congregation was assembling. The joke lies in the first three notes. "The first two intervals are fourths," Schalk points out, "and are little reminders of 'Dear Christians, One and All, Rejoice'—and in this Calvin hymn. So that was kind of my little protest," Schalk says, clearly enjoying the idea of Luther's exuberant hymn resonating deep within this Calvinist framework.

Indispensable Quality

Throughout this selective journey through Schalk's hymns, we find him continually occupied with those qualities of hymn writing he considers indispensable.

- The text must be one worth setting, "a text which reflects the understandings and the faith of the church, which possesses

[374] It will require an astute musician to make the transition properly from the end of each to the beginning of the next. Because Schalk indicates the quarter note remains constant, that means eighth notes are equivalent. The temptation will be for the musician to equate the quarter of the 4/4 section with the dotted-quarter beat of the 6/8 section. In that case, the 6/8 section will be played too fast (or that the 4/4 section is played too slowly).

[375] *Thine the Praise*, 40–41.

intrinsic poetic worth, and which, for whatever reason, calls for a new tune."[376]

- The tune must be well crafted. "How does one judge a chair to be well crafted, well made? If a chair falls to pieces the first time one sits in it, it is probably not very well made. On the other hand if one can sit in it comfortably for long periods of time without tiring, it is serving the purpose for which it was intended." More to the point: "Does [a piece of music] fit the purpose for which it was intended? Does it bear repeated use without becoming boring or trite? Does it observe appropriate patterns of melodic, harmonic, rhythmic and formal construction? Is the text effectively reflected in the music?"[377]
- The tune must be appropriate for congregational singing. The effort must reflect musical honesty and integrity as well as craftsmanship. For Schalk, this means his hymns are clear about the purpose for which they are intended—proclamation of the Gospel of Jesus Christ—and they embody a genuine concern for the well-being of the Church and its people.

Even today, Schalk continues to explore new avenues for hymnody. As in other aspects of his life's work, his hymns stand at the intersection of past, present, and future. "To treasure our musical heritage as Lutherans," Schalk has said, "we need to see that it is kept alive in a living parish practice. That is what I have, in a variety of ways, been about."[378]

---

[376] "Some Thoughts on the Writing of Hymn Tunes," 7.

[377] "The Church and the Composer," *CrossAccent* 8, no. 1 (Spring, 2000): 4.

[378] Richard Hillert, "Composers for the Church: Carl F. Schalk," 18.

CHAPTER EIGHT

Choral Music (Octavos): Critical Analysis of Selected Works

> Walter's style was closer to that of the earlier Renaissance than to his own time, his models being such composers as Josquin des Prez, Heinrich Isaac, and Ludwig Senfl. Walter's music reflects Luther's concern that music in Lutheran worship serve as proclamation.[379]

Just as Carl Schalk wrote these words about Johann Walter, the "first cantor of the Lutheran Church,"[380] so they could have been written of Schalk himself. Schalk's most distinguished choral music emulates in approach and intent the great motet style of the high Renaissance, particularly Josquin and Palestrina. One discerns a similarity with the work of those masters in Schalk's high regard for craft, in the music's single-minded devotion to the text, in the finely wrought points of imitation, and in reverence and gravity of purpose. Yet—with only a few exceptions—one experiences him as a creature of his age in those qualities that have earned his music a lasting place in the repertory. These include a lyricism that melts the heart but never draws attention to itself, a glowing harmonic palette rich in triadic constructions, and a generosity of spirit that is solely focused on the praise and worship of God.

---

379 *Lutheran Choral Anthology: The 16th Century* (St. Louis: Concordia Publishing House, 2010), 131.

380 *Johann Walter: First Cantor of the Lutheran Church* (St. Louis: Concordia Publishing House, 1992).

Lamentations of Jeremiah (SATB, Unaccompanied, 1957; Published 1961, Reissued 2000)[381]

These four somber choruses constitute one of those rare exceptions. Succinct and finely wrought, they were completed in 1957 as a project at the Eastman School of Music during Schalk's Wausau years. Schalk's first choral publication, they remain central to the choral repertoire. One frequently encounters them not only in worship environments but also on the repertoire list of high school choral contests because of their fine yet challenging part writing.

Schalk has said that he modeled the writing on that of Randall Thompson, the composer who was the focus of his research during that course at Eastman. For the project, he chose four passages from the Book of Lamentations, authored by the prophet Jeremiah.

These dark ruminations on the destruction of Jerusalem, approached with an urgency of musical witness, are not for the faint-hearted. Schalk brings sharp dimension to the gripping King James Version of these verses. In the third chorus one finds "they have polluted themselves with blood" in place of the New Revised Standard Version's "so defiled with blood." Similarly, his staccato setting of "Depart ye!" rings out as the NRSV's "Away!" could never do. The settings are remarkable for their boldness of vision. They reveal stylistic hallmarks that would serve Schalk in the decades to come—even at this early stage. These include the following.

- The careful craftsmanship of each chorus, each with its own clear structural pillars, as well as a compelling overall vision for the four-chorus cycle centered in the region of E minor (and secondarily that of its minor dominant) that mandates they be sung as a unit.
- The way in which the music gives life and dimension to the text, always elucidating it and never obscuring it. In the second chorus, for instance, one can almost literally feel the searing flames in the rising tonal plateaus. These are designed not for mere effect but instead to lead us up to that anguished high level from which the prophet cries, "He has made me desolate," and leads to the world-weary sigh of resignation, "and faint all the day" (Lamentations 1:13).

---

[381] Concordia Publishing House, 98-3601.

- A harmonic language that derives its energy from superimposed fourths. The result calls us back to an ancient time while positioning us firmly in the currents of the mid-twentieth century. Especially notable in this way is the last chord of the first chorus, which suggests a suffering that is never ending, and the tumbling fourths in the last line of the final chorus, which cascade downward almost in free fall: "The crown is fallen from our head" (Lamentations 5:16).

Joyous Light of Glory (SATB, Unaccompanied, 1995; Published 1997)[382]

Written for Schalk's longtime friend and colleague Carlos Messerli upon Messerli's retirement from the directorship of Lutheran Music Program, this setting of Roger Petrich's translation of the late third-century Greek lamplighting hymn "Phos hilaron" attests to Schalk's ability to craft clear musical structures from through-composed texts.

Light emerges gradually in the first section, emanating from the unison tonic and filling the heavens in one long, arching phrase until it comes to rest ("heavenly, holy, blessed Jesus Christ"). Closely following the text in a free homophonic declamation, Schalk then moves to points of imitation ("We sing to God") before returning to the music of the opening with the text, "You are worthy of being praised." An imitative section similar to the first ensues, and the setting gradually comes to rest on the tonic in a luminous scoring. In this way, we experience the hymn as a single broad gesture that unfolds organically with elements of repetition and development that create a well-integrated unit.

Centered in D major, the setting also demonstrates a command of harmony and counterpoint that owes much to the motet style of Palestrina and other late Renaissance masters. Yet subtle but distinctive touches locate us in the present era. Among these is the half-note chord in measure 20 by which Schalk approaches the half-cadence at the setting's midpoint, where the soprano and alto have already moved to the dominant but the tenor and bass linger on notes of the subdominant.

---

[382] Concordia Publishing House, 98-3354.

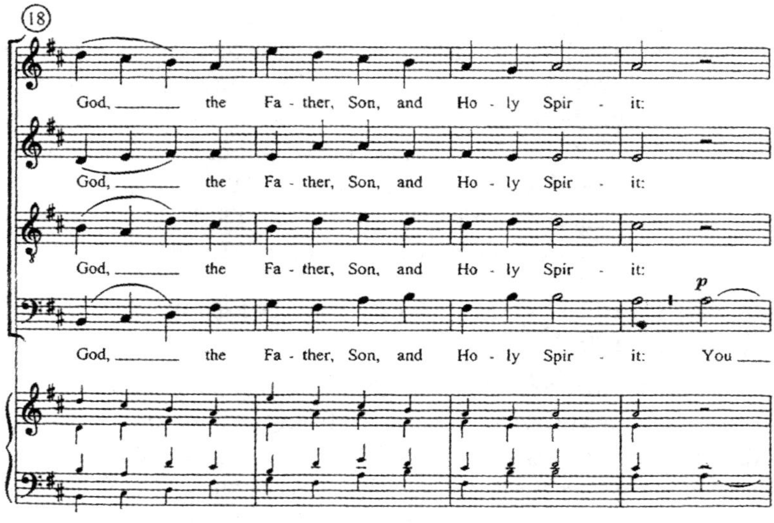

Example 8: Joyous Light of Glory

This creates a luminous sense of expectancy, for the ear detects the chord as a second-inversion minor seventh—an E minor chord with B in the bass—with a suspension on the fourth degree, begging for resolution down to the third, which never comes since the harmony moves instead onto the tone of the dominant.

Blessed Are the Dead Who Die in the Lord (SATB, 1995)[383]

It is a testament to Schalk's humility of purpose that what may be his most perfectly constructed choral work is one of the least ambitious in scope.

Written upon the death of a longtime member of Grace Church as "A Motet for All Saints' Day" and set in the contemplative key of D-flat, this setting of Revelation 14:13 clearly, simply, and eloquently accomplishes its purpose to raise the single verse of text as an offering to God and a prayer on behalf of mourners on earth.

Schalk's great care with every aspect of this setting begins with the translation he selected. His choice of the RSV provides him with a crucial element integral to the classic A-B-A′ form he favors in so many of his settings. Because he assigns the first words of the verse

[383] Concordia Publishing House, 98-3214.

as a tenor solo in the manner of an evangelist, a clear structure then emerges:

[Solo] And I heard a voice from heaven saying, "Write this:
[A] "Blessed are the dead who die in the Lord henceforth."
[B] "Blessed indeed," says the Spirit, "that they may rest from their labors, for their deeds follow them."
[A'] "Blessed are the dead who die in the Lord."

It would not have worked as well with the NRSV and other commonly used versions, which read this way or similarly:

> "And I heard a voice from heaven saying, "Write this: Blessed are the dead who from now on die in the Lord." "Yes," says the Spirit, "they will rest from their labors, for their deeds follow them."

The RSV thus allows Schalk to begin each section firmly with the same word, "Blessed." It also represents a more faithful translation: In the Greek, the phrase of text that begins Schalk's B section is not just "Yes" but the equivalent of "Yes, indeed!" The RSV finds a way to elegantly render that amplifier as "Blessed indeed."

Schalk employs to magnificent effect the same opening up of vocal register that serves him so well in *Joyous Light of Glory*. For the first choral entrance, the sopranos and altos take up the unison A-flat of the last note of the tenor solo. As the sopranos intone the first syllable over an entire measure, the other voices enter imitatively on the remaining notes of the tonic triad to create a shimmering, richly triadic texture that resolves in measure 7 after an elegant suspension to a first-inversion tonic flows toward a partial cadence on a first-inversion tonic in measure 7.

Example 9: Blessed Are the Dead Who Die in the Lord

Schalk's interpolation of a word from the KJV to the repetition of the last five words ("who die in the Lord *henceforth*") then allows this first section to move toward a full cadence. At the moment of resolution, however, we are surprised to find that the music comes to rest not on the tonic but instead through a deceptive cadence on the chord of the minor third. This sets up the contrasting middle section starting in measure 11, in which the affirmation "Blessed indeed" is uttered with quiet urgency as the tessitura reaches above the upper tonic. The phrase comes to rest on the dominant of the relative minor in measure 17, setting up an exquisitely calculated sequence of points of imitation on the phrase "for their deeds follow them" that extends through measure 28 as the music arrives on the dominant.

As the sopranos remain on the note on which they ended, the fifth scale degree, the music moves seamlessly into an abridged reprise of the first section. A less resourceful composer might have simply extended the cadence throughout measure 28 and begun the repeat of the A section on the downbeat of measure 29, to replicate exactly how the piece began. Instead, Schalk has the sopranos enter with the first note of the return on beat 3 of measure 28 while the other voices are still sustaining the last note of the previous phrase as a vision, full of expectation, of what is to come. The other voices then enter as they did at the beginning, marking a return of the entire first section. This time, though, in place of the word "henceforth," Schalk simply repeats the words "who die" and brings the setting to a full cadence in the home key.

Noël, Noël (SATB, Handbells or Celeste, and Organ, 1991)[384]

While "Blessed Are the Dead Who Die in the Lord" may represent Schalk's finest craftsmanship, this delightful piece—with which Schalk honored his wife at Christmas in 1989—shines with what may be his most elegantly spun melody. It embodies all the traits that make Schalk's voice distinctive:

- The line rises elegantly and compellingly to its high point and descends again with well-calculated ease.
- It is constructed as a long arch spanning a full twenty-eight measures (with one dotted half note per measure), without a single rest.
- Moving in gentle half notes and quarter notes, it is almost entirely stepwise in motion.
- It is harmonized with chords rich in thirds and sixths that are all drawn from the family of the tonic, E-flat major. The tune never ventures beyond these bounds yet continually compels the listener's ear.

The melodic handbell part lends to the texture a glistening luster. In Schalk's typical economy of means, the setting consists simply of a bell introduction that is later recalled twice, followed by four repetitions of this melody—by the women, by the men, by the four-

[384] MorningStar Music Publishers, MSM-50-1022.

part choir unaccompanied, and finally with the melody in the three lower voices with the sopranos soaring above through a descant. Even so, each time it sounds new.

It is infinitely touching that the text consists solely of the two words in its title, repeated over and over during the course of 130 measures and that this also happens to be the name of Schalk's beloved wife, Noël, to whom—of course!—the work is dedicated.

Lord, It Belongs Not to My Care (SATB and Organ, 1978)[385]

This timeless hymn by Richard Baxter, penned in 1681, has experienced a wide variety of musical settings over the ensuing three centuries. It has found its way into more than two hundred hymnals by means of tunes including EVENTIDE (by Henry Thomas Smart, not the familiar one by William H. Monk), HOLY TRINITY, TALLIS' ORDINAL, ST. FRANCES, BURLINGTON, ST. AGNES, FROME, EASTLAND, NOX PRAECESSIT, RAMSEY, YORK, and more recently, ST. BERNARD (*The Lutheran Hymnal*, 1941), CHESHIRE (*Service Book and Hymnal*, 1958), and ST. FULBERT (*Lutheran Service Book*, 2006).

It is not hyperbole to say that if the world had known Schalk's setting first it would be hard to think of the text in any other musical guise. (While conceived for choir, it could work as a hymn.) It is not only the elegant melodies and rich harmonies that compel the ear but also the creative structure that incites the imagination.

Schalk combines two of Baxter's stanzas into one well-ordered melodic arc, with antecedent and consequent periods of five and four, and then four and five, measures each (the additional measure lending expressive impact to the text at those points), which in its entirety spans eighteen measures. This is a fine concept because it allows us to experience Baxter's second and fourth stanzas as responses to the first and third. Every hymn writer will agree that the progression through stanzas is crucial to the theology of the text, but often, worshipers consider each stanza as a separate thought. Here, the progression is laid beautifully before us. Particularly powerful is the move from stanza 3 to stanza 4. The poet muses that every burden we bear, Christ has also borne—and that by grace alone God's kingdom is opened to us, where we will see the face of Jesus in a splendor that is only hinted at in all earth's magnificence.

---

385 Augsburg Publishing House, ED002894.

Schalk's middle section unfolds thus:

Christ leads us through no darker rooms
than he went through before,
He that unto God's kingdom comes
must enter by this door.
Come Lord, when grace has made me meet,
thy blessed face to see;
For if thy work on earth be sweet,
what will thy glory be!

He calls special attention to the theological weight of this section by means of an *a cappella* setting that highlights the achingly poignant dissonance on "sweet," after which he indicates a breath as the music then expands outward, arms stretched, to ponder "what will thy glory be!"

Omitting Baxter's fifth stanza, Schalk concludes with the sixth stanza. Here, the women proleptically enter ahead of the men (see measure 44), two measures before the tune is set to begin while the transition out of the *a cappella* section is still cadencing.[386] Schalk adds an additional layer of expectancy as the organ anticipates this soprano-alto entrance an octave higher in the preceding measure.

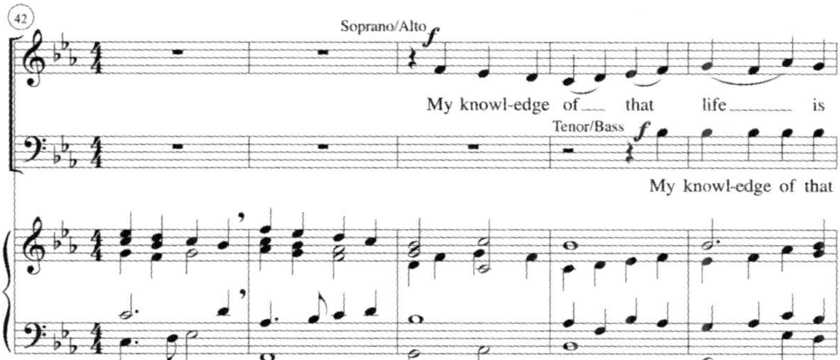

Example 10: Lord, It Belongs Not to My Care

[386] This move calls to mind the great moment in the first movement of Beethoven's "Eroica" Symphony, when the horn calls out the main theme in the tonic just before the recapitulation while the cadence on the dominant has just reached its climax.

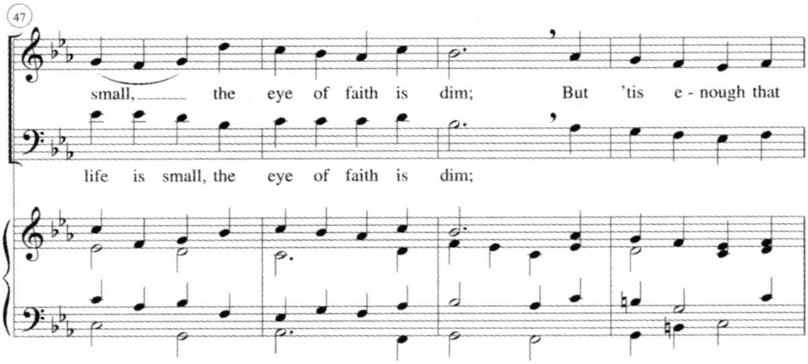

My Song Is Love Unknown (Two-Part Mixed, Keyboard, 1969)[387]

This modest setting, also published the same year in *A Second Crown Choir Book*, is another example of an effort that accomplishes its purpose simply and effectively, with quintessentially Schalkian expressive touches shining through its economy of means.

Samuel Crossman's text, omitted from *The Lutheran Hymnal*, had been known to RHOSYMEDRE in *Service Book and Hymnal*. *Worship Supplement* (1969) paired it with John Ireland's LOVE UNKNOWN, a practice that continued in *Lutheran Service Book* and *Evangelical Lutheran Worship*. In *Lutheran Book of Worship*, however, it appears again with RHOSYMEDRE. Schalk's setting, including just stanzas 1, 2 and 6, is geared toward teaching the words with this tune.

The approach may seem formulaic at first glance. It features stanza 1 scored for unison voices, stanza 2 in canon at one measure between women's and men's voices, and stanza 3 (6) back to unison with the addition of an instrumental descant. But a closer look at stanza 2 reveals that the tune has been altered not only to suit the purposes of the canon but also to highlight the acknowledgment of the aching truth that Christ, our friend, spent His life because of our need. Most poignant is the second half of that stanza, where Schalk reaches beyond the fifth scale degree ("But O my Friend") up to the expressive sixth degree to highlight the interjection ("my *Friend* indeed"). He then proceeds to spin out that welcome reminder of Jesus as our dearest companion for two additional measures before

[387] Concordia Publishing House, 98-2236.

allowing the line to rise all the way to the upper octave and back home again for the exclamation, "who at my need his life did spend!"

One also notes the distinctive harmonic touch with which the stanza concludes. Instead of a simple plagal cadence, we find the tonic approached through a second-inversion major seventh chord built on the flat seventh degree (E-flat, in the key of F), which allows us to reflect somberly on what has just been sung.

Jesus Is Born Tonight (SATB, Organ, 2007)[388]

Original in text as well as tune, this lovely Christmas anthem is conventional in both melodic and harmonic structure yet abounds in elegant touches so characteristic of Schalk.

Set in the pastoral key of D major and starting on the lower tonic, the eight-measure tune rises to the upper octave twice before coming to rest. However, the harmonization of the upper tonic note, both times by the chord of the minor sixth, maintains the harmonic momentum through the end of the period.

The shape and harmonization of the tune underscore the words with glistening clarity. The first high D is attained by the unison women on "stars in the *heavens*" and the second by the unison men at "All earth in wonder longs for the *sight*." Similarly, the sudden plunge to the lower octave for the last phrase of the tune, "Jesus is born tonight," emerges from the amazement of the first three phrases as a simple pronouncement of the reality that has transpired.

Example 11: Jesus Is Born Tonight

[388] Concordia Publishing House, 98-3940.

Following a contrasting middle section in F-sharp major, the music turns delightfully back to the tonic by way of the re-interpretation of that scale's fifth degree, C-sharp, as the third degree of the dominant chord in the home key (C-sharp being the third of the A-major chord). This is accomplished by the simplest device available. As the C-sharp is suspended in midair at the end of measure 18, the dominant seventh chord in D major enters below on the downbeat of measure 19, and we find ourselves, suddenly yet gently, returned to that key area.

A stellar example of the poignant melodic beauty and subtle surprise that is so characteristic of Schalk, yet which never descends into the sentimental, is found at the end of this contrasting middle section just before the return to D major both times where it occurs in the setting. The first three phrases consist of simple stepwise excursions up a portion of the scale and back down again (measures 15–20 and again in measures 33–38). Naturally, we expect the same for the fourth phrase. But Schalk surprises us in the second measure of this fourth phrase (see measures 22 and 40), where the melody springs up a note higher than expected—to D instead of the C-sharp that we have been led to believe is coming next—and then winsomely descends by a string of glistening thirds, rather than by simple stepwise motion, to prepare for the reprise of the main section. Tellingly, this occurs on phrases of text that reveal much to us about the nature of this child: "born in this boy" in measure 22 and "conquered our fears" in measure 40. They are moments to treasure.

Christ Be Our Seed (SATB, Oboe, Organ, 2000)[389]

It has been said of Schalk that his own anthem settings of his hymns are nothing special and perhaps are best left to be undertaken by others. While many are indeed modest in scope, their economy has more to do with the overarching purpose at hand, to simply find a faithful means by which a choir may come to better know the texts through the lens of his music, rather than to impress or to devise distractions.

This elegant choral setting of the 1998 hymn jointly commissioned from Schalk and Herbert Brokering by Wheat Ridge Ministries amply demonstrates that Schalk is willing and able to undertake more expansive arrangements. Remarkably, this one opens with three entire pages of introduction, encompassing twenty-three measures in 4/2 time (which if notated more conventionally would have amounted to forty-six measures in 2/2 time). The scope of this prefatory section is all but unmatched in the entirety of Schalk's catalogue.

Why? Once heard and experienced, the answer is clear. Schalk has chosen the oboe as a voice integral to the setting, the instrument mastered by his daughter Rebecca. His eloquent tune for Brokering's hymn lies perfectly in the sweet middle register of this instrument. But Schalk's resourcefulness goes far beyond simply assigning the tune to the oboe during this long introduction. In fact, in the course of the statement of the entire tune, along with ten measures of prefatory music that precedes its beginning, that melody is never once heard in the oboe. Instead, that voice gently and gradually opens to us the lustrous tonal landscape of D major for seven measures before settling into a dreamily reflective motive in measures 8–10, poised on the dominant. The organ then intones the tune with similar gentleness

[389] Concordia Publishing House, 98-3602.

of spirit starting in measure 11. Around this, the oboe weaves a counterpoint of aching beauty.

This is, in fact, the pattern for the entire setting. What is perhaps Schalk's most finely sculpted instrumental part never once assumes the assignment of the melodic line, although it functions as a voice part equal in weight to those of the choir. And always there are winning surprises, each subtle in its splendor. These include the oboe's partnership with the men's voices in the second half of the third stanza, which includes an ardent ascent to the third above the upper tonic in measure 49.

Example 12: Christ Be Our Seed

All Creatures of Our God and King (SATB, Organ and Optional Strings, 2005)[390]

Schalk's brilliant new tune and setting for the well-known text adapted by William H. Draper from Francis of Assisi, widely sung to

[390] Augsburg Fortress, ED005045.

LASST UNS ERFREUEN, captures the range of character that we associate with this beloved saint. This is a creative take on a familiar text that embodies the very meaning of what it is to proclaim a text through song and to tell a story—the story of our salvation through Christ.

Locating his setting in D major, Schalk conflates into each of his long phrases two stanzas from the hymn as most of us know it, wisely omitting the alleluias so as not to arrest the progression of thought. The product is a single, ecstatic outpouring of praise in running eighth notes that arches across nine measures. In the tenth measure, the progression suddenly comes to rest and time seems to stand still as the choir intones, "O praise him, O praise him, alleluia!"

But even still there is the pregnancy of expectation, for we have come to rest on a second-inversion tonic (which features the dominant in the root, telling us there is more to come). Schalk then surprises us with a sudden shift to the third-related key of F major for his second statement of the tune, comprising the hymn's original third and fourth stanzas.

Example 13: All Creatures of Our God and King

This unfolds in the same manner as before. Still in F, Schalk then moves to the minor subdominant region, B-flat minor, for the darkly veiled stanza 6 ("And you, most kind and gentle death"), whose motivic contents strikingly call to mind a similarly dark verse from Schalk's setting of Robert Herrick's "What Sweeter Music" ("Dark and dull night, fly hence away"; see measures 20–22 of that setting).[391] He tellingly moves back toward D major for the last lines of that stanza ("you lead back home the child of God"), climaxing on the most important theological proclamation of the hymn, "for Christ our Lord that way has trod" (measures 46–48). From this confession of truth, the rest of the hymn tumbles forth: "Let all things their creator bless."

One of the virtues of this setting is that it has the capacity to deepen our experience of the hymn in its more familiar realization. When we return to our hymnal to sing these same words to LASST UNS ERFREUEN, we will carry with us our encounter with the text into which Schalk invited us.

Show Me Your Ways, O Lord (SATB, 1995)[392]

Juxtaposed against the intricacy of "All Creatures of Our God and King," this modestly scaled psalm setting demonstrates Schalk's range as a composer and underscores his gift for conceiving a clear structure by which the text can be most effectively articulated. The level of accomplishment in any endeavor, as Schalk's life and work attest, is measured not by fanfare and flourish but by clarity of purpose. Here, the purpose is simply to give voice to a few lines of Scripture in a way that allows them to be clearly heard and received

---

[391] Concordia Publishing House, 98-3993.
[392] Concordia Publishing House, 98-3207.

into the hearts of worshipers through the timeless, boundless means that music affords.

Set in simple Renaissance motet style, this realization of the first few verses of Psalm 25 opens with a simple homophonic prayer: “Show me your ways, O Lord, and teach me your paths,” cadencing on the dominant to set up the middle section. A garland of points of imitation ensue and elegantly come together to prepare the way for the return of the opening section, which this time comes gently to rest on the tonic.

Oremus: Prayers for the Church, Sets 1 and 2 (SATB and Organ, 1986)[393]

These ten choral collects, composed for the 1984–85 season of the Bach Cantata series at Grace Lutheran Church, River Forest, Illinois, exemplify Schalk’s commitment to music that is liturgically useful, accessible to the average choir and parish, and of crystalline conception and enduring musical quality. Particularly noteworthy in the first set is “O Holy Jesus,” with the rising harmonic intensity of its plea to “know thee more clearly, love thee more dearly,” capped by the ardent vow through Schalk’s trademark *échappée* (see measures 15–16) to “follow thee more nearly.”

From the second set, “God Be in My Head” for unison voices and organ achieves a rare yearning quality as the goal of each short phrase falls a note higher than one’s ear expects—from the tonic E up to a B in measure 4 instead of the A one anticipates, and in measure 8 from an F-sharp to a C-sharp instead of the expected B. The broad arch of the larger structure peaks in measures 10–12, “God be in my mouth and in my speaking,” and comes gently to rest on “God be at my end and in my departing” by means of an elegant cadence through the minor subdominant.

As the fourth piece in this second set, “God of Majesty” (SATB and organ) is elegantly governed by the text. In the opening invocation (“whom saints and angels delight to worship in heaven”), the choir sets off into several measures of *a cappella* writing as if the heavenly choir itself were uttering this beloved collect for musicians. Schalk emphasizes the expressivity of each part of the petition so that “music” finds itself at the high point of the first section, followed by a descent through much of the scale as we ponder the joy with which

---

[393] Concordia Publishing House, 97-5906 and 97-5910.

"we on earth may glimpse your beauty." The setting reaches a climax on the dominant as the choir alone extols God's "unveiled glory," whereupon the organ enters beneath with a reprise of the music from the setting's brief introduction. Instead of the expected return to the first section, however, we are greeted with the gentle prayer that closes the collect.

The fifth piece, the Compline collect "O Lord, Support Us All the Day Long," is typical of this set in that the single long line of the opening petition spans thirteen measures in the first section of this richly-hued setting, yet emerges as perfectly intelligible because it reflects the text so clearly. The second section begins as did the first but concludes with a three-part setting of the closing petition, "through Jesus Christ our Lord," notable for the lovely stepwise descent of the alto line from a high E-flat all the way down to the D-flat below before moving up to the tonic E-flat.

A Child Is Born in Bethlehem (SATB, Organ, 2005)[394]

Written at the same time as the carol itself in 2003 for the 100th anniversary of Grace Lutheran Church and commissioned by Grace members Curt and Kathryn Petersen, this choral setting illustrates Schalk's versatility as an arranger and also serves as reminder of his abiding love for the rich harmonic world of thirds and sixths, which unfurls here as a steady stream of tonal splendor. The text is his own, based on a fourteenth-century Latin hymn.

The shape of the tune, whose last part ("Alleluia") rises by step through the D major scale, offers an invitation to rich imitative treatment of which Schalk takes advantage in measures 12–14 and again in measures 50–53. The entire setting, in fact, addresses the question of how many wondrous ways one can sing "Alleluia" using the simple materials of the tonic major scale.

[394] Concordia Publishing House, 98-3813.

Example 14: A Child Is Born in Bethlehem

In a delightfully creative touch at the start of the fourth stanza, Schalk assigns to the sopranos the same syncopated dominant pedal point, two octaves higher, heard in the accompaniment's bass line at the beginning of stanzas 1 and 3.

Out of the Depths (SAB and Organ, 1999)[395]

This realization of Psalm 130 ranks among Schalk's finest works. It is distinguished by its scoring in three voice parts and by its abundance of expert *a cappella* writing, the lack of a tenor part notwithstanding. This is an assignment that only the most facile arrangers would dare to undertake.

Example 15: Out of the Depths

Another quality that commends the piece is the clear musical structure that Schalk devises to support the text. Verse 1a serves as the A section and verses 1b–3 the contrasting B section. This

[395] MorningStar Music Publishers, MSM-50-3410.

structure is repeated using verses 4–6a. The remainder of verse 6 serves an abridged return of the A section. As a complement to the vocal writing, the organ part also contains only three parts (soprano, alto and bass). The transparent scoring lends to the setting an expansiveness that welcomes in the listener.

Sweet Was the Song the Virgin Sang (SATB, Optional String Quartet and Organ, 1993)[396]

Schalk is at his most relaxed and natural when writing carols about the infant Jesus. This luminous work is no exception. Schalk's sweet melodic realization of William Ballet's early seventeenth-century text has all the grace and warmth lacking in the foursquare tune by which this text has previously been known.[397]

One cannot imagine, indeed, a more graceful shape than the lilting tune in triple time that dances gently up and down the E-flat major scale. The organ/string accompaniment features garlands of rich parallel-sixth chords and, alternately for more of an "ancient" feel, parallel fifths in the soprano and alto supported by a sixth below in the tenor.

The quality of rocking addressed in the text ("'Sweet babe, sweet babe, sweet babe,' sang she, And rocked him gently on her knee") is captured by the emphasis on selected offbeats in the organ pedal and the undulating movement above. Overall, the setting provides another example of a modest project that is clearly conceived and realized with the simple elegance of a master craftsman.

Be Known to Us, Lord Jesus (SATB, Children's Choir, Congregation, Organ, and Optional Brass, 1995)[398]

This is a massive undertaking of qualified success at best. Dedicated to the choirs of Trinity Lutheran Church in Sheboygan, Wisconsin, Schalk conceived the setting as an entrance processional for the Easter season. The text he assembled brings together passages from 1 Corinthians 5; Psalms 34 and 118; and Romans 6. (Schalk does not credit Luke 24:30–31, from which the refrain seems to be derived.)

---

[396] MorningStar Music Publishers, MSM-50-1035.

[397] We find it previously in *The Cowley Carol Book for Christmas, Easter, and Ascensiontide* from 1901.

[398] Concordia Publishing House, 98-3202.

With its foursquare pacing and heavy brass/organ accompaniment, the product is leaden and ponderous. Nor are any of the various sections of interest melodically; the music seems designed simply to mark the progression of time. Perhaps in this way, it fulfills its purpose as music to support a worship service's opening procession.

Lift High the Cross (SATB, Congregation, Organ, Brass, and Timpani, 2012)[399]

Richard Hillert hails this setting as "Schalk's most eminent hymn concertato,"[400] and others have echoed the sentiment.

As Paul Westermeyer sagely notes in his *Hymnal Companion to Evangelical Lutheran Worship*, this hymn in the fullness of its history "treads on dangerous waters"[401] in its apparent militancy, particularly concerning what we commonly recognize as stanzas 2 and 3 (respectively, "Led on their way by this triumphant sign, the hosts of God in conqu'ring ranks combine" and "All newborn soldiers of the Crucified"). This makes for interesting comparisons among our hymnals as editors choose, omit, and alter according to their distinct theological and doctrinal convictions.

That saga crops up concerning the two versions Schalk created of this hymn for Concordia Publishing House. George W. Kitchin's original in Michael Newbolt's revision actually contains seven stanzas, including one that remains unknown to Lutherans but has found its way into other Protestant hymnals, "Set up your throne, that earth's despair may cease / beneath the shadow of its healing peace."[402] *Lutheran Book of Worship* and *Lutheran Worship* both contain five stanzas, including "Led on their way" and omitting Kitchin's original stanzas 3 and 5 (respectively, "From north and south, from east and west we raise / in growing unison our song of praise" and "Let every race and every language tell / of him who saves our lives from death and hell"). Sensitive to triumphalists, *Evangelical Lutheran Worship* (2006) follows the lead of *Worship &*

---

399 Concordia Publishing House, 98-4122.

400 Richard Hillert, "Composers for the Church: Carl F. Schalk," 13.

401 Paul Westermeyer, *Hymnal Companion to Evangelical Lutheran Worship* (Minneapolis: Augsburg Fortress, 2010), 511.

402 It is included in the Tabernacle Publishing Company's *Sing Joyfully* (1989) as well as in the *New Century Hymnal* (1995).

Rejoice[403] in omitting "Led on their way" along with Kitchin's two little-known original stanzas and changes "soldiers" in stanza 3 to "servants." *Lutheran Service Book* (2006) opts to retain the original language in stanza 3 and restores Kitchin's original stanza 5, "Let every race."

Schalk's 1980 setting, written for the installation of Rev. James Wind at Grace Lutheran Church, River Forest, is based on the version of the hymn in *Lutheran Book of Worship*. For this recent updating, he restores the original stanza 5 to bring it into line with the hymn as it appears in *Lutheran Service Book*.

One of Schalk's best-selling settings from the time of its initial publication, congregations and choirs alike relish the majesty of the brass textures and the inventiveness of the choral writing—much of it two-part—which never exceeds the technical reach of the average church choir. The soprano descant added to the refrain after stanza 2 and 6 is particularly delightful in its emulation of a trumpet.

Lord, Now You Let Your Servant Go in Peace (Two-Part or Unison Choir, Congregation, Organ, Optional Three-Octave Handbells, 2003)[404]

Written for the Concordia Seminary Chorus on its 100th anniversary, this luminous setting of the Nunc Dimittis (Luke 2:29–32) is a fine example of a work that could easily find its place at the heart of the repertoire of any congregation, large or small. The expressive seven-measure refrain shows Schalk's gift for allowing melodies composed of odd numbers of measures to sound absolutely natural.

---

[403] Carol Stream, Illinois: Hope Publishing Company, 2001.
[404] Concordia Publishing House, 98-3733.

Example 16: Lord, Now You Let Your Servant Go in Peace

The reason for the lengths of Schalk's tunes is always found in the text, and their specific shapes always derive from the composer's desire to call special attention to key words. In this case, the first word, "Lord," receives an entire measure so that we may fully come into the prayerful mindset of supplication. Less sensitive settings might have simply assigned this word to a quarter note.

The verses are taken alternately by men and women and feature expressive dissonances, while the entire assembly is called to sing the Doxology. The transition into each statement of the refrain is typical of Schalk in that it comprises a single measure that succinctly performs its purpose to prepare for the next entrance and expends not a single unnecessary note in the process.

Where Charity and Love Prevail (Two-Part Treble Choir, Oboe, and Organ, 1985)[405]

This lovely setting of the ninth-century text in the translation by Omer Westendorf, known largely through the tunes TWENTY-FOURTH and CHESHIRE, is graced here with a lyrical melodic line whose uncharacteristically wide leaps up and down in the space of just three measures serve to draw out the deep spirituality of the text.

Example 17: Where Charity and Love Prevail

Harmonized with liberal use of warm seventh chords, the tune is further warmed by creative use of the minor subdominant, a highly expressive chord. One hears it twice in measure 10, on beat one as a minor IV in the home key of F and then on beat 3 as a minor IV (first inversion) as interpreted in the fleeting context of C.

Interestingly, Schalk's melody bears a striking resemblance in its first few measures to the verse section of the tune BICENTENNIAL, written by Robert Kreutz in 1976 for Omer Westendorf's "You Satisfy the Hungry Heart" (also known as "Gift of Finest Wheat"). Text and setting were selected as the official hymn for the Forty-First International Eucharistic Congress in Philadelphia in 1976 (thus the tune name), a major event for church musicians across the country since it was only the second time the congress had been held in the United States. But the hymn did not begin appearing in mainstream hymnals until the late 1980s, well after Schalk's setting was composed. Nonetheless, it is distinctive enough that any borrowing, if it occurred, can be heard as a tip of the hat to Kreutz.

[405] Concordia Publishing House, 98-2701. Schalk also used this musical setting for "We Walk by Faith and Not by Sight" in *Alleluia to Jesus: The Choral Music of Carl F. Schalk* (Concordia Publishing House, 2009, 97-7348).

Luther's Morning Prayer; Luther's Evening Prayer (SATB and Keyboard, 2011)[406]

These paraphrases by Schalk of Martin Luther's well-known morning and evening prayers were commissioned by Lutheran Summer Music and have since found a steady place in the worship life of that program. Simple in intent, straightforward in harmonization, and graced by resourceful yet accessible writing for four-part choir, they are stellar examples of the way in which music applied to the liturgy can lead us more deeply into the spirit of what is being sung.

Schalk sets Luther's Morning Prayer as three statements of a graceful eight-measure melody that rises to its peak in the fifth measure before settling back to the dominant on the first and second statements and, on the third, into the tonic, followed by a flowing Amen. In the Evening Prayer, the lovely melodic line has an extra measure at its end to provide for a bit of lengthening at the end of the day. Stated four times in contrasting scorings for the choir, it is crowned by an elegant *a cappella* "Amen."

The choral catalog of many prominent composers for the Church consists largely of pieces designed to be enjoyed by the congregation as "additions to the service," in Schalk's own phrase.[407] This is not the case with the vast majority of Schalk's music for choir. Created under the discipline of the liturgy, his music deepens the worshiper's encounter with the living Christ in the order of service that has come down to us through the Church. Schalk provides us with new means of entry into familiar texts and forms in a language that is always intelligible even to nonmusicians but is also never predictable to those with musical experience. For those "with ears to hear," one discovers within these pages a wealth of subtle surprises that breathe life into melodic shapes and musical forms. And always, at every turn, the story of salvation by grace through faith in Jesus Christ is being told.

---

[406] MorningStar Music Publishers, MSM-50-8610.

[407] "Congregations that have come to view music as 'additions to the service,' however beautiful, must be carefully, gradually, and winsomely led to see the organic relation between liturgy and the church's song," Schalk writes. *Luther on Music: Paradigms of Praise*, 53.

CHAPTER NINE

Choral Music (Collections): Critical Analysis of Selected Works

Music in the church is both proclamation and ministry.[408]

Carl Schalk has written voluminously over the years on the delights and challenges of music ministry, with a special interest in congregations that have limited resources. If his thoughts on the subject could be distilled into one sentence, it might go something like this: Concentrate on the wealth of hymnody that is already in our midst, and use it creatively with whatever forces you have on hand. This is the premise on which his books of choral collections are based. However, he remains sympathetic to the tendencies of many directors to program big anthems that do not attend to the liturgy.

The Crown Choir Book: Easy Anthems for the Small Parish (1964)[409]

The Crown Choir Books encapsulate these beliefs about what good liturgical choral music should be and what directors should be concentrating on. Nearly fifty years after publication, this volume—like its companions that came later—remains a staple in the library of many smaller parishes. Spanning the liturgical year, the first Crown Choir Book provides an indispensable tool to address this purpose. The fourteen hymn arrangements in this volume, written in the later years of Schalk's time in St. Louis, fall into four categories: unison chorale melody with organ accompaniment, *a cappella* settings in two parts, canonic settings in two parts with independent organ

[408] *Luther on Music: Paradigms of Praise*, 51.
[409] Concordia Publishing House, 97-7618.

accompaniment, and unison chorale melody with descant and organ accompaniment.

Together, they provide a paradigm of arrangements that are faithful, accessible, and yet which sport delightful creative touches. For example, Schalk allows himself to briefly depart from the melody in stanza 2 of "Savior of the Nations, Come" (page 4) when the women and men successively enter with the melody but then gracefully depart in order to form pleasing harmonies as they move toward the end of the stanza. The same is true of stanza 2 of "All My Heart This Night Rejoices" (page 7), in which a few subtle adjustments permit it to work in perfect canon at the distance of two measures.

In similar fashion, stanza 2 (page 10) of "How Lovely Shines the Morning Star" features a fanciful embellishment of the tune for unison women, and in stanza 3 (page 13), a few melodic tweaks permit a delightful imitative structure between men and women at the unusual distance of three measures,[410] a device that is replicated in stanza 2 of "Soul, Adorn Thyself with Gladness" (pages 34–35). And the Nunc Dimittis (page 37), in Schalk's own original setting, unfolds as a crystalline canon between upper and lower parts. Remarkably, it is never mechanical and always musical. The harmonies throughout are conservatively triadic, but one encounters a wealth of thirds and sixths in the organ accompaniments along with many gracious harmonic touches, such as the major seventh chords located at strategic positions in "All My Heart This Night Rejoices."

A Second Crown Choir Book (1969)[411]

In these eleven settings, Schalk adds the occasional use of four-part choir to the four categories of the first book, along with settings that use guitar (a tip of the cap to worship trends of that time) or another descanting instrument. This approach is exemplified in "The

---

[410] Unfortunately, this setting will rarely find itself called upon these days since it uses the now archaic-sounding Catherine Winkworth–based translation from *The Lutheran Hymnal* (343). Both *Lutheran Service Book* and *Evangelical Lutheran Worship* employ the gracious translation developed by the Inter-Lutheran Commission on Worship for the *Lutheran Book of Worship*. For that reason, one welcomes the alternate text Schalk provides for this setting, "O Holy Spirit, Enter In," although Schalk's delightful stanza 2 works better with the text of the former hymn.

[411] Concordia Publishing House, 97-4882.

King Shall Come When Morning Dawns" (pages 6–7), which lacks a keyboard accompaniment altogether and provides only for vocal line and instrumental descant with guitar chords. In terms of the chords, only the tonic, the minor subdominant, and the minor dominant are represented; without a little more resourcefulness on the guitarist's part, this makes for a setting of limited scope.

A nice feature of this book is Martin Luther's "In Peace and Joy I Now Depart." Although a core hymn of the Lutheran tradition, it is one that congregations may find difficult to navigate, especially at a tempo fast enough to make it intelligible. Choirs may therefore become well acquainted with the hymn through this nicely varied setting so that when the congregation is asked to sing it, the choir may lead effectively.

A Third Crown Choir Book (1988)[412]

In these ten arrangements, Schalk features some three-part writing along with that for two parts and more varied forms of accompaniment—light percussion and handbells, instruments likely to be readily available in smaller parishes. Simple bell parts (block chords and some random ringing) adorn "We Praise, O Christ, Your Holy Name," while finger cymbals and tambourine enliven "Brightest and Best of the Stars of the Morning" using Schalk's own tune DAWN. This setting was later adapted for *Thine the Praise: The Hymntunes and Carols of Carl Schalk*, in which triangle, tambourine, and hand drum were the featured instruments.[413] Also welcome is an arrangement of Schalk's own "Sing, My Tongue," featuring two well-crafted *a cappella* stanzas for three-part choir, a stanza that is set for two treble instruments only (or the right hand only for the organist) to accompany the voices, and a powerful descant for the last stanza.

Alleluia to Jesus: The Choral Music of Carl F. Schalk (Two- to Four-Part Mixed Choir with Organ and Instrumental Accompaniments, 2009)[414]

This compilation of previously published settings, most long out of print, and two newly created pieces for the volume serves the needs of choir directors with limited resources who are seeking to introduce

---

[412] Concordia Publishing House, 97-5969.

[413] Chicago: GIA Publications, Inc., 1996, 154–155.

[414] Concordia Publishing House, 97-7348.

variety and character into the choir's weekly tasks. All pages are reproducible. Modest in scope, the volume includes the following.

- A lively two-voice canon on the rhythmic version of "A Mighty Fortress" (first published in 1965), which works perfectly with just a few melodic tweaks. Stanza 2 of this setting is actually stanza 3 in the hymnal version, and its use for choir during the singing of the hymn would call attention powerfully to stanza 3, "Though devils all the world should fill," although today's directors will need to correct the underlying text to reflect the wording of hymnals currently in use.
- "As Jacob with Travel Was Weary One Day" (to the tune JACOB'S LADDER), a vigorous unaccompanied four-part setting of the hymn best known in the Anglican tradition, whose refrain contains the text that is the title of this collection ("Alleluia to Jesus, who died on the tree, And hath raised up a ladder of mercy for me").
- Three little-known nativity carols, also in four parts: "Heaven's Dawn Is Breaking Brightly" and "Shepherds of Bethlehem" from Slovakia and the Appalachian carol "Jesus, Jesus, Rest Your Head," first published by Concordia in the late 1970s.
- A lean, wiry setting of "O Love, How Deep, How Broad, How High," featuring trumpeting reeds on the organ (or trumpets, if available). It offers the choir director an ideal package that is easy to assemble and large in impact.
- Two modestly scaled new works, the collect "Remember, O God" and a setting of "Strengthen for Service, Lord," whose disjointed melodic line and wandering modulations (moving from G major to B-flat and briefly to D-flat before suddenly returning to G) obscure the simple clarity of this text from the Syriac Liturgy of Malabar.

Four Psalm Motets (SATB, Unaccompanied, 2010)[415]

In this collection, Schalk exercises his command of polyphonic choral style of the high Renaissance. One hears this in the long,

[415] MorningStar Music Publishers, MSM-50-2520.

arching phrases, the clarity and balance of structure, the ample use of rich consonances, the equal participation of all voice parts, the finely intertwined imitative sequences, and the composer's acute responsiveness to the text.

In the first motet, a paraphrase of Psalm 128, it is only the warm lyricism of the opening line, which floats upward through an arpeggiated octave in the first four beats, and a few subtle harmonic touches that tell us this is a product of our age. The latter include the incorporation of a shimmering sixth into the first-inversion subdominant approaching the cadence at measure 12 and a delightfully surprising seventh chord built on the minor second degree, suspended romantically over the dominant in the bass and setting up the half cadence in measure 18 that leads to the return of the first large section.

The third motet, "For the Lord God Is Sun and Shield" (Psalm 18:11–12) expertly emulates a different aspect of Renaissance motet style. Using verses of Psalm 84 that affirm simple truths ("he bestows favor and honor. No good thing does the Lord withhold"), the setting is primarily proclamatory as one voice part takes the lead and others follow together. Yet if one listens closely, unmistakable Schalkian traits may be detected. Foremost among these is the *échappée* just after the high point of the middle section ("No good thing does the Lord withhold"), by which the melodic line, on its descent from the upper octave in measure 28, takes an expressive turn from the sixth degree up to the seventh and then down to the fifth.

Gospel Motets for the Church Year (SATB, Unpublished, Completed in January, 2012)

In an extraordinary effort, Schalk amassed this collection of thirty-five original polyphonic settings of verses from the assigned Gospel readings spanning the liturgical year as a component of his offering to commemorate the 100th anniversary of Grace Lutheran Church in River Forest, Illinois.[416]

In his preface to the collection, Schalk offers three possibilities for how the motets may be used.

[416] The set originally comprised fifty settings, but Schalk whittled it down to thirty-five for his formal presentation of the set to Grace Church. Other components of his offering for the centennial included a history of music at Grace and a series of adult education classes.

- They can be sung at the point where they occur in the reading so that the choir literally "sings the Gospel" in the course of the reading. If more text in the assigned lesson remains, the pastor then continues to the end of the reading.
- They can be sung at the conclusion of the Gospel reading, as a recapitulation of an important thought or phrase from the lesson just heard. In this case, there should be a brief moment of reflection before and after the singing of the motet.
- The motet could be sung during the distribution of Holy Communion as a reminder of an important phrase or sentence from the Gospel reading.

Astute observers will note that Schalk does not suggest that they can be sung at the offering or elsewhere in the service where they do not perform a liturgical function.

Schalk also notes in his preface that the motets "are intended to present the Gospel in a simple and straightforward manner. They are not concert pieces nor are they given to overly dramatic musical devices."

Stylistically, the pieces in the collection are grounded in the Renaissance motet style with its propensity for imitative sequences between the four voices. While similar in approach, each has a distinctive character derived from the reading at hand. To offer just a few examples, in "And the Shepherds Returned," a realization of Luke 2:20, one hears through delightful points of imitation during the first fifteen measures the shepherds returning joyfully to their flocks, one following closely on the heels of the other. In a sequence of rising and falling melismas, we then encounter them "glorifying and praising God for all they had heard and seen" and finally reflecting in quiet, awestruck joy on the miracle itself "as it had been told them."

For "And the Word Became Flesh" (John 1:14), the first part of the verse is declaimed soberly through careful imitative treatment. The heavens then open for "and we have seen his glory," after which the landscape is flooded with cascading scales that give voice to this proclamation.

In Schalk's setting of "And They Worshiped Him" (Luke 24:52–53), the composer paints a vivid picture of the concluding verses of Luke's Gospel, which allows us to more fully experience them:

And they worshiped him, and returned to Jerusalem with
great joy;
and they were continually in the temple blessing God.

The voices combine, two at a time, to repeat the word "worshiped" in swooping melismas that suggest the very actions of the disciples' praise—hands raised aloft, sweeping the air, striving to express as deeply as they can their profound joy.

Launched by an urgent series of rising fourths, "Arise, Shine, for Your Light Has Come" (Isaiah 60:1) articulates this text for the Day of Epiphany more effectively and profoundly than does Schalk's earlier treatment in his "Songs from Isaiah."[417] After the initial proclamation of the first half of the verse, Schalk reduces the dynamic level so that the next section, "and the glory of the Lord has risen upon you," is able to unfold gradually in great magnificence. This culminates in a series of undulating parallel fifths in the soprano and alto, supported in the tenor by the sixth below the alto, a stirring sequence that calls us back to another era of human history. When the baritone finally re-enters in its low register twelve measures later for the chordal affirmation, *pianissimo*, of "of your people Israel," (RSV), the effect is breathtaking.

Arguably the most winning setting in the entire collection brings to life one of the most modest and yet delightful texts in all the lectionary. It features excerpts from John 2:10, for the second Sunday of Epiphany in Year C, in which the amazed chief steward proclaims, "Everyone serves the good wine first. . . . But you have kept the good wine until now." (Schalk shrewdly omits the middle section, "and then the inferior wine after the guests have become drunk"; NRSV.) A series of beautifully crafted imitative entries create a richly textured undulating tapestry by which we experience the simple truth that "everyone, everyone, everyone" serves the good wine first. "But you," the tenors begin and the other voices then affirm, "you, you have kept the good wine (*forte*, whole notes, top of the scale) until now" (slowing motion, diminishing intensity, finally coming quietly to rest) as the entire worshiping assembly, with the chief steward himself, marvels at this miracle.

---

[417] The second half of this verse as Schalk has presented it is actually a conflation of Isaiah 60:1 and Luke 2:32. Isaiah reads, "and the glory of the LORD has risen upon you," while Schalk has "and the glory of your people Israel." The setting could work just as well with the full Isaiah text with only minor adjustments.

While not technically demanding and certainly within the reach of average church choirs, the success of Schalk's Gospel Motets in worship will hinge on the skill of the director to allow the uncluttered eloquence of these settings to emerge clearly. It will also depend on a well-conceived plan by the parish's leadership team that integrates the music smoothly into the reading of the Gospel. For example, there should be as little silence as possible at the points where the motet connects to the reading of the lesson. And there should definitely be no announcement on the order of "Now the choir will sing the next portion of the Gospel reading."

On first encounter from the pew, the experience of these motets will turn heads or at least raise eyebrows. Those who listen carefully will be rewarded not only with insight into the readings but also by a first-hand experience of these texts through the lens of the worshiper's own imagination in a way that music alone makes possible.

Scenes from the New Testament (SATB and Lector, 2009)[418]

The concept behind these twelve Gospel motets is compelling. For each of six sets of Gospel readings, Schalk has provided two settings—one of key verses from the Gospel reading, in the traditional manner of a Gospel motet, and the other a realization of a poem by Jill Peláez Baumgaertner inspired by that reading. Schalk suggests that the first "should be sung as part of the reading or chanting of the Gospel in the service of Holy Communion (or in other services where these stories are appointed)." The setting of the poetic meditation, then, "could be sung as a reflection on the Gospel text, either immediately following the reading of the Gospel (in services of Holy Communion) or in noncommunion services where these lessons are read, or as a motet during the distribution of Holy Communion."

The most arresting feature of the collection is not so much the traditional motets Schalk has written, which display his usual control of craft and carefully considered responsiveness to the text, but the subtle flights of musical imagination that are sparked by Baumgaertner's verses.

For example, in the setting of Luke 2:14, "Glory to God in the Highest Heaven," praises ascend in the four voice parts to form a rising swell of rich triadic harmonies that tumble over one another

[418] Augsburg Fortress, ED004368.

joyously as they reach a climax in an open fifth sustained *forte* in midair on "heaven" before descending again in gentle prayer for the last phrase of the verse. But Baumgaertner's "Let the Tender Girl Hold the Wonder," which focuses our imaginative lens on the young mother and the infant, who slumbers "in cosmic peace" through the angelic song, draws from Schalk a captivating rocking lullaby with a graceful flute part couched in the minor mode. Its gentle harmonies are tinged with an ageless quality; were they written two millennia ago, or just yesterday? At the end, the ear delights in the subtle alternation of minor and major modes as Baumgaertner invites us to ponder, questioning, "this world, this infant, God's gift."

A similar effort by Schalk and Baumgaertner was published by Augsburg Fortress in 2011 as *Simeon's Song: The Nunc Dimittis*, comprising six motets, three on verses drawn from the Nunc Dimittis from Luke's Gospel and three companion meditations.

Four Choruses from the Song of Solomon (SATB, scheduled for publication by CPH, 2014)

These four choruses, three from chapter 2 and the fourth being the familiar text "Set Me As a Seal" from chapter 8, are written in much the same style as the Gospel motets but are broader in scope and more broadly expressive in intent.

Paradoxically, the most powerful of the four is the text that has the least dramatic impact on its own terms, "I sat down under his shadow with great delight, and his fruit was sweet to my taste" (2:3, KJV). Set in C major, it is as if nature holds her breath in the opening eight measures. The first three words, "I sat down," are intoned softly again and again in half-note alternation between a second-inversion tonic (the most proleptic of all chord constructions since its very quality resides in the expectation of that which has not yet come) and a second-inversion minor seventh chord built on the second degree. It is a stirringly original construction that invites the listener into the singer's rapt apprehension of her lover, her breath held in the highest anticipation, as she positions herself in his shadow.

A dancelike section in 6/8 proclaims that "he brought me to the banqueting house, and his banner over me was love," reaching a climax on that last word in an ecstatic minor seventh again built on the second scale degree. Then, in an inspired move, Schalk brings back the rapt chordal alternation of the opening for the repetition of the last two words of that line as if the entire world was holding its breath. Over this, the first soprano (the parts have divided here) intones the first three words of the setting, "I sat down," hovering in midair before the lower voices enter again to conclude on the same hushed second-inversion tonic with which the piece began.

Even more than in Schalk's separately published choral works, here in his choral collections, one finds a thoroughgoing commitment to liturgical intent. These carefully crafted resources contribute greatly to the "fullness and richness" of the liturgy in which "God's people can best express their *common* worship and praise."[419] It is good news as well that these collections are easily within reach of congregations of modest means. All that they require is four voice parts (often fewer), keyboard support, and a director who possesses theological sensibility and the willingness to allocate adequate rehearsal time. Offered in worship with the care and consideration that is their due, these modestly scaled pieces will be welcomed into the faith life of worshiping communities as cherished traditions through which the living Word makes all things new.

---

[419] *Luther on Music: Paradigms of Praise*, 52.

CHAPTER TEN

Is It Too Late?
Where Do We Go from Here?

For more than a half century, Carl Schalk has written of, spoken about, and advocated for the highest standards of practice in the music and worship of the Lutheran Church. In his books and articles, in his workshops and lectures, in his playing and composing, Schalk has been uncompromising in his insistence that, in its liturgy and hymnody, church music must always be telling some aspect of the story of salvation and that the story must be told with all the craft and expertise at the musician's disposal.

Because his message always emanates from the heart of a faithful servant, because it is delivered in humility without any attempt to earn him prestige or power, and because his lively good humor has gained him no enemies, Schalk has long stood as church music's most ardent champion. His profound witness to the Gospel of Christ across the breadth of his contributions to the Church has shaped the worship life of countless Lutherans in ways that many do not even begin to recognize.

But what of the future? Has the rip tide of pop culture pulled the Church irreparably off course?

Reality Check

It is a reality that many Lutheran congregations today have moved to embrace a nonliturgical praise format in at least some of their worship services. The resulting polarity between "traditional" and "contemporary" worship styles ("blended" usually comprises far more of the latter than the former) tends to divide those parishes into opposing camps. It also creates opposition within the staff. Typically, the musician becomes the defender of established liturgy and hymnody, and the pastor or pastors carry the banner for more contemporary styles under the assumption that this is what their members want.

It is also a reality that in those parishes whose worship life is grounded in historical Lutheran practices, undertaken faithfully, and informed by conviction and creativity, participants through Word and Sacrament are invited into an encounter with the living Christ *in the continuum of time*.[420] This encounter does not address who we are at this moment. Instead, it places us as forgiven sinners at the intersection of who we have been as the Body of Christ and where we are headed. In what ways, over the ages, has God formed us through the Church? How does He continually forgive us? Who is the Spirit calling us through the Church to become? Salt, light, and leaven! It is imperative that church musicians remain attentive, informed—and optimistic.

As music's visionary witness to the Gospel, Schalk frequently gets asked what he thinks the future holds for the music of the Church. "People want to know, are you optimistic? Where is church music going?" He always gives the same level answer. "I tell them, I am neither optimistic nor pessimistic. Like everything else in the Christian life, we live in hope. We stand in hope. Even though our best efforts don't result in what we would like, we remain people of hope."[421]

Schalk is quick to emphasize that in saying so he is not ducking the question.

"To me, there are three scriptural images which address how Christians are to live in the world," he explains. "They are salt, light, and leaven. You only need a little bit of salt to bring out the flavor. You need just a little bit of light to illuminate the darkness. You need just a little bit of yeast to leaven the bread. *We* are the light in the dark

---

[420] It is encouraging to read that an increasing number of youth and young adults are seeking this experience. Writes one Christian blogger, "Young Christians are going over to Catholicism and high Anglicanism/Lutheranism in droves, despite growing up in low Protestant churches that told them about Jesus. It's a trend that is growing, and it looks like it might go that way for a while: people who grew up in stereotypical, casual evangelicalism are running back past their parents' church to something that looks like it was dug out of Europe a couple hundred years ago at least." thechristianpundit.org/2013/07/17/young-evangelicals-are-getting-high. See also faithandleadership.com/node/3653 for a similar appeal by another young writer for the restoration of historical worship practices.

[421] Conversation with the author, July 26, 2012.

place, we are the salt, we are the leaven. So I am optimistic, because we live in the hope that the salt will bring out the flavor, that the yeast will leaven the bread, that the light will shine in the darkness."[422]

Opportunities in the Small Parish

It is especially important that musicians serving in smaller parishes not become discouraged, for—as Schalk is fond of saying—this is one of the most inviting contexts the vocation affords.

The key, he points out, is that smaller congregations accept what they are instead of trying to become what they are not. "Perhaps we need to recognize that when the smaller parish does not seek to imitate the larger church down the block," he writes, "but rather builds on its own strengths, fashioning a worship style and church music program suited to its resources, we will be on the road to a more meaningful, realistic and effective church music style geared to the situations in which most parishes find themselves."[423]

Develop Objective Standards

Many liturgically trained Lutheran musicians find they must contend regularly with pressure to substitute contemporary Christian songs that are theologically questionable for material from the pew hymnal. For them, Schalk has compelling words of hope.

"It is too easy to quote Ephesians 5:19[424] and then assume that all is well in the world of Church music," Schalk told *CrossAccent* assistant editor Victor Gebauer in a recent interview.[425] "It is too simplistic to tolerate or even encourage the view that the maudlin and the mundane are readily acceptable as long as one's intent is missional or evangelistic." Often, this kind of music is never even

---

[422] Conversation with the author, July 26, 2012.

[423] "Thoughts on Smashing Idols: Church Music in the '80s," *The Christian Century* (September 30, 1981): 963.

[424] ". . . be filled with the Spirit, as you sing psalms and hymns and spiritual songs among yourselves, singing and making melody to the Lord in your hearts . . . ."

[425] Victor Gebauer, "An Interview with Carl Schalk," *CrossAccent* 17, no. 3 (2009): 7. Here, Schalk echoes Erik Routley, who a half century earlier wrote, "I expect to find in Christian belief, derived from Scripture, clues to the right behavior of musicians in church, but I do not think that we need to be content either to quote Eph. 5:19 and to say on the basis of that text that all is well with church music, or to quote Amos 5:23 and say that the whole practice of church music is irrelevant to the true and sincere Christian life." Erik Routley, *Church Music and Theology* (London: SCM Press Ltd., 1959), 13.

questioned. "To apply a theological critique to the maudlin and the mundane," he continued, "seems irrelevant to many. To those who view such questions as beside the point, Church music is simply a tool, a means to ends other than the proclamation of the Gospel and the praise of God."[426]

What, then, are musicians to do?

"At some point, musicians in the church need to say clearly and forthrightly that A is better than B," Schalk advised. "That there are objective standards by which music in the church can be and needs to be judged. To do so, however, will be to fly in the face of a culture, also in the church which says otherwise."[427]

Everything Schalk has written contributes to the clarification of those standards. His lifelong study of church music has been undertaken not in a theoretical sense but in the realm of actual practice, Paul Westermeyer told the assembly gathered at Concordia University Chicago's Lectures in Church Music to celebrate Schalk's eightieth birthday in 2009.

"It has not been an archaeological dig for him, one that dredges up interesting artifacts to bury in a treasure tube or to place in a museum. Carl has analyzed, pondered, made judgments, and as a functioning church musician has brought practical wisdom to bear on what he has studied. He has learned from the Church's mistakes, figured out what has been faithful and worthy, and has applied his insights to the Church and its music in our time and place. We have learned from him not only about the past, but how the past can inform the present, how we in our time and place can sing and play in the most faithful ways, and how church musicians can live out their vocations with integrity and not get trapped in momentary fads or ingrown fancies."[428]

A Road Map for New Life

Whether in a small or large parish, the willing musician may discern among Schalk's writings a simple road map for faithful proclamation that will lead to a vibrant worship life.

---

[426] Victor Gebauer, "An Interview with Carl Schalk," 7.

[427] Ibid.

[428] Paul Westermeyer, "Celebrating Carl Schalk's Eighty Years: Scholarly Care, Practical Wisdom, Musical Integrity" (banquet address, Concordia University, River Forest, Illinois, October 18, 2009).

- Use the hymnal. "The hymnal is more than a simple collection of hymns. In its liturgies and hymns it is a confessional statement of the faith of the worshiping community, and as such the basic resource for congregational worship, teaching, and renewal. But it will not be so unless it is intentionally used. It is of no use to have a hymnal in the pews and never pick it up to open it except for the hymns. In worship we demonstrate who and what we are as a Christian community. The hymnal helps us articulate what we believe, who we are, and our mission in the world."[429]
- Use the hymnal creatively. "The congregational hymnal is the first place to begin in shaping a more effective program of church music in the smaller parish," Schalk urges. "To overlook this collection of music is not only to begin at the wrong place; it is to disregard what may well be the richest resource available to everyone in the parish."[430] This applies to choral as well as congregational singing, as his early *Crown Choir Books* demonstrate.
- Help foster a body of new hymnody that will be "closely united with the needs and practices of the parish." These hymns can be welcomed into the community's repertoire and appreciated as a product of the people's creative expression. Avoid sponsoring hymn competitions as some congregations do, because "much of this type of promotion seems strangely remote from the 'growing edge' of the Church—the local parish." Instead, the responsibility for any growth in the local context "falls upon the leaders of worship and the hymn-writers of the parish. Here is where such development must begin and where it must ultimately flourish."[431]
- Drawing on the example of Martin Luther's hymns, all hymnody should demonstrate *liturgical intent* and *liturgical orientation*.[432] In this way, the hymn becomes not "a vehicle for some kind of vague 'participation' in worship" but a

---

[429] Victor Gebauer, "An Interview with Carl Schalk," 9.
[430] "Getting More for Less," 21.
[431] *Lutheran Hour Music News* 1, no. 5 (May 12, 1960).
[432] "The Hymn in the Liturgy," *Currents in Theology and Mission* 16, no. 3 (June, 1989): 214.

means by which the people "might possess and embrace a vehicle for participation *in the liturgy*."[433]

- Resist the view that sees the hymn "as a general Christian song loosely attached to worship," for this "too easily leads to the use of hymnody for a variety of social, psychological and manipulative purposes."[434]
- Advocate for resonant acoustics that enhance the voice of God's people in prayer. "A renewed understanding of the church as the people of God and liturgy as their work," Schalk wrote thirty years ago, "suggests that not only is the arrangement of the worship space important but an acoustical environment which enables the people to do their work is crucial."[435] Schalk devoted one of the issues in his Church Music Pamphlet Series to the topic, Scott Riedel's exposition on *Acoustics in the Worship Space*.[436]
- Ascertain that all proclamation is also teaching. "When we proclaim the Good News, we are teaching," Schalk asserts. "The content of our teaching should be the Good News of the Gospel. As described in the New Testament, the content is *kerygma*, the proclamation. I do not see *kerygma* and creedal content as disjunctive at all. Much of contemporary religiosity seems to avoid kerygmatic content at any cost. Much of contemporary 'spirituality,' including many new hymn texts and the texts of choral music heard in the Church, consists of a foggy haze of vaguely religious verbiage . . . offending no one."[437]
- Teach good hymnody to our children, recognizing that what is "old" to us can be experienced as "new" to them in an exciting way. "Children can learn most any hymn if taught with interest and enthusiasm," Schalk insists. "Too often the problem is not the children but the teacher who either does

---

433 "The Hymn in the Liturgy," 213.
434 Ibid.
435 "A Lament for Resounding Praise," *The Christian Century* 100, no. 9 (March 23–30, 1983): 270.
436 St. Louis: Concordia Publishing House, 1986.
437 Victor Gebauer, "An Interview with Carl Schalk," 7.

not know or is not prepared to teach the hymns of the church."

Schalk says, "Sometimes we hear the question, 'Why do we always sing so many new hymns?' or 'Why don't we sing more new hymns?' The terms are essentially meaningless, for what is new to me may be quite old to another and what is old to me may be new to another. To sing Luther's 'We All Believe in One True God' may be an eye-opening new experience for many though it is quite an 'old' (traditional) hymn for many others. The 'old' hymns are very learnable." It's not that people can't learn good hymns, he explains. "Too often Church musicians or pastors don't give congregations credit for what they could do. Then we decide not to use this or that hymn because 'the people don't know it.' Of course! We haven't taken the time to teach them."[438]

Living in Hope

The antithesis of hope is despair. Whenever musicians of the Church find themselves tempted to fall into despair, they may look to the words of Carl Schalk to recover their calling as the salt, light, and leaven through which the Church may "pray to the God who . . . ," "praise the God who . . . ," "adore the God who . . . ," and "give thanks to the God who . . . ."[439] Schalk reminds us that "the ultimate predicate of 'the God who . . . ' is finally '. . . *raised Jesus Christ from the dead.*' Christ's death and resurrection is at the heart of what is proclaimed in worship. We dare never let it go unsaid. It is not something to be tacked on as an afterthought, but something that is part of the very fabric, the very warp and woof, of the tapestry we call the Church's song."[440]

Ever and always, church musicians seek to mediate the heart of God to the hearts of God's people. That which "truly touches the heart and reaches to the depths of our human condition, offering the word of hope and comfort, is always the song that speaks the Gospel clearly and directly," Schalk writes. "It is the song that rehearses the story of what God has done, not what we have done, and that rejoices in who we are in Christ as a redeemed community."[441]

---

[438] Victor Gebauer, "An Interview with Carl Schalk," 9.
[439] "The Church's Song."
[440] Ibid.
[441] "The Church's Song."

Carl Schalk is the very embodiment of hopeful living. His enthusiasm never flags. He will answer a question for the tenth or the one-hundredth time with equal spirit and patience. He never tires of the subject of church music. He acknowledges that he essentially just says the same things over and over under a variety of guises, but that doesn't temper his ardor. He is a popular and facile speaker, a ready wit in every circumstance in life, a loyal friend, and a faithful mentor.

At the same time, Master of Sacred Music programs in many Lutheran seminaries are under siege or have suspended operations. Church music jobs that pay a living wage are increasingly scarce. Many Lutheran church musicians are not clear about what it means to be Lutheran and cannot articulate why music is so indispensable to the life of the Church. How many understand what Martin Luther meant when, five hundred years ago, he pronounced music God's greatest gift and praised it as the highest discipline after theology? What becomes of the voice of the prophet if there is no avenue for proclamation and no one even cares to hear the truth proclaimed? Fortunately, we are not yet to that point, but time is growing short. The Church and its people must act if Schalk's clear vision—with Luther, of music as God's creation and gift—is to flourish in the life of the Church.

There are signs of hope. The fifteen-hundred-plus member Association of Lutheran Church Musicians continues to operate under the bold Statement on Worship and Music crafted by Schalk a decade ago and affirmed at its 2003 biennial conference. As well, the Center for Church Music at Concordia University Chicago is being expanded under director Barry Bobb. Those supporting this expansion at the university see it as an opportunity to reclaim Concordia's place as an institution deeply committed to the music of the Church. They plan for the Center to become a place for the training of church musicians and for serious scholarly and practical study of the discipline in its many facets.

In the end, all we can do is continue to extol God's mighty deeds of salvation in Word and song. We affirm with the psalmist that "one generation shall praise Your works to another, and shall declare Your mighty acts" and that "they shall speak of the might of Your awesome deeds. . . . They shall pour forth the fame of Your abundant goodness and shall sing aloud of Your righteousness."[442]

With Schalk's music in our midst and his words ringing in our ears, may God be our strength and our song.

---

[442] Psalm 145:4, 6–7.

INDEX OF TITLES OF HYMNS AND SONGS

INDEX OF HYMN TUNES

GENERAL INDEX